The Noodle Narratives

The Noodle Narratives

The Global Rise of an Industrial Food
into the Twenty-First Century

Frederick Errington,
Tatsuro Fujikura,
and Deborah Gewertz

中

UNIVERSITY OF CALIFORNIA PRESS
Berkeley · Los Angeles · London

University of California Press, one of the most distinguished university presses in the United States, enriches
lives around the world by advancing scholarship in the
humanities, social sciences, and natural sciences. Its
activities are supported by the UC Press Foundation and
by philanthropic contributions from individuals and
institutions. For more information, visit www.ucpress.edu.

University of California Press
Berkeley and Los Angeles, California

University of California Press, Ltd.
London, England

Library of Congress Cataloging-in-Publication Data

Errington, Frederick Karl.
    The noodle narratives : the global rise of an industrial
food into the twenty-first century / Frederick Errington,
Tatsuro Fujikura, and Deborah Gewertz.
        p.   cm.
    Includes bibliographical references and index.
    ISBN 978-0-520-27633-8 (cloth : alk. paper) —
ISBN 978-0-520-27634-5 (pbk. : alk. paper)
        1. Noodles industry—Social aspects—Japan.
2. Noodles industry—Social aspects—United States.
3. Noodles industry—Social aspects—Papua New
Guinea.   4. Noodles—Social aspects—Japan.
5. Noodles—Social aspects—United States.
6. Noodles—Social aspects—Papua New Guinea.
I. Tatsuro, Fuzikura.   II. Gewertz, Deborah B.,
1948– III. Title.
    HD9330.M322E77   2013
    338.4'7664755—dc23

                                            2012046523

Manufactured in the United States of America

22 21 20 19 18 17 16 15 14 13
10 9 8 7 6 5 4 3 2

In keeping with a commitment to support environmentally responsible and sustainable printing practices, UC
Press has printed this book on Rolland Enviro100, a
100% post-consumer fiber paper that is FSC certified,
deinked, processed chlorine-free, and manufactured with
renewable biogas energy. It is acid-free and EcoLogo
certified.

Contents

Illustrations and Table

TABLE

Acknowledgments

We received generous financial support from the Japan Society for the Promotion of Science (grant #21401009), the Japan Foundation, and the Faculty Research Award Program of Amherst College. Colleagues, friends, and interlocutors at our universities and beyond heard or read parts of our manuscript-in-progress. In particular, Akira Adachi, Jean-Paul Baird, Linda Bartoshuk, Niko Besnier, Melissa Caldwell, James Carrier, Fergus Clydesdale, Jan Dizard, Robert Foster, Yasuko Fujikura, Tsuyoshi Kato, William Kelly, Bradley Klein, Luke Lavin, James Leach, Raymond Mahoney, Okamoto Masaaki, Trent Maxey, Deb Orah Maxwell, Edward Melillo, Sidney Mintz, Samuel Morse, Jane Nadel-Klein, Adam Reed, Joe Regenstein, Peter Salmon, Sarah Schear, and Jeremy Whitsitt made important suggestions. Paul Emmanuel, Rebecca Emori, Phillip Klomes, Sophia Kraemer-Dahlin, Livai Roland, Emily Shinay, Valentine Siba, Nancy Sullivan, and Waka Tosa provided valuable research assistance. Finally, special thanks are due to Sae Nakamura, for her insight and engagement, and to Ella Kusnetz, for the best reading of all. We are also indebted to those many in Papua New Guinea, Japan, the United States, and the United Kingdom who helped clarify the complex workings of instant noodles. And we are grateful for our productive collaboration.

Instant Noodles as Quotidian and Ubiquitous

Instant ramen noodles—tasty, convenient, cheap, shelf stable, and industrially produced (unlike "real" ramen noodles)—are consumed by huge numbers of people worldwide. Invented by Momofuku Ando in 1958, apparently to assist his war-torn Japanese compatriots, they have become so pervasive and commonplace that our friends often expressed surprise at our interest in them. "Why study them?" one asked. "My kids grew up on them." Were they, in other words, significant enough to be of any particular interest, to be informative about anything of importance? *The Noodle Narratives,* written by three anthropologists—Deborah and Fred from the United States and Tatsuro from Japan—is our answer to this question and a demonstration that instant noodles are perhaps one of the most remarkable foods ever.

The fact that instant noodles are so quotidian and ubiquitous is noteworthy. Their mass-produced ingredients are inexpensive as well as widely available and, for most of the world's population, broadly acceptable: wheat, vegetable oil, and assorted flavorings, usually including salt, monosodium glutamate (MSG), a meat or chicken essence, sugar, and flavorings readily blended for local preferences. The World Instant Noodles Association (WINA), created to improve the quality of instant noodles and increase their consumption worldwide, estimates that 95.39 billion packages and cups of instant noodles were sold during 2010 across an impressive range of markets.[1] Almost everyone eats or has eaten instant noodles.

Instant noodles are so inexpensive and widespread that they can be used as economic indices. Thus, in 2005, "Mama Noodles," the largest instant noodle producer in Thailand, launched the Mama Noodles economic index to reflect the country's recovery from the 1997 Asian financial crisis; this index was based on the theory that the increase in sales of usually cheap instant noodles occurred because people could not afford more expensive foods.[2] They are so central to the lives of many that their pricing and availability may be a matter of political concern. C. K. Lal, for example, argues that the rise of Maoism in Nepal derived partly from frustration with the market mechanisms that absolved sellers from responsibility for the "quality, quantity, and the price" of products such as instant noodles. (Nepali consumed some 590 million packages of instant noodles during 2009.[3]) Their marketing is so extensive that, as of 2008, instant noodles became a cornerstone of the Nestlé Corporation's strategy of selling a line of "popularly positioned products" to those poor people who live at the "bottom of the pyramid."[4] Moreover, because they are so tasty, convenient, cheap, and shelf stable, as well as so widely familiar and acceptable, instant noodles figure prominently in relief feeding. WINA donated 550,000 packages to quake-hit China on June 23, 2010, and 10,000 packages to flood-stricken Hungary on May 28, 2010. Similarly, during 2011, Nissin Foods donated one million servings to tsunami-ravaged Japan along with seven "kitchen cars," each capable of serving about eighteen hundred cups of noodles daily even where water and power supplies had been interrupted.[5] (On a less grand scale, instant noodles provided the sole sustenance for four Colombian drug smugglers in their small submarine, discovered by the Coast Guard in 2006 to be crammed with "two hundred and ninety-five bales of cocaine, weighing more than seven tons and with a street value of $196 million."[6])

In part because instant noodles are so commonplace, they are frequently the subject of telling elaborations. Here are a few illustrations: During their midday break, Papua New Guinean schoolchildren may purchase cups of instant noodle soup from a mobile cart, drink the liquid, and place the remaining noodles in a scone to make a noodle sandwich. On the other side of the globe, inmates in contemporary American prisons not only snack on instant noodles but also blend them with other commissary-purchased foods into imaginative and often shared "spreads." In fact, numerous websites are devoted to these prison recipes, which make life inside more tolerable, more nearly normal.[7] Bobby B. reports that he was able to make a "version of a peanut butter and grape jelly sandwich" from instant noodles, peanut butter, and grape Kool-Aid.[8] Also in America, although in a very different social context, largely middle-class listeners to National Public Radio responded to a request for noodle-focused personal reminiscences, attesting to the multiple ways instant noodles could articulate with life's circumstances. Sometimes instant noodles figured in happy memories of family conviviality, as with campground meals improvised from whatever was available—meals often commemorated in cherished recipes. Sometimes instant noodles featured in somber recollections of personal endurance, as with recovery from cancer measured by an increasing ability to consume a full bowl.[9]

Other forms of elaboration are prompted by instant noodle producers themselves. The Indonesia-based companies Indomie and Supermie earned places in the *Guinness Book of World Records* during 2005 by creating, respectively, the largest package of instant noodles and the largest serving of instant noodles. Momofuku Ando, who not only invented instant noodles but also founded the instant noodle giant Nissin Foods, achieved his well-publicized dream of sending instant noodles into space when, in 2005, a Japanese astronaut ate Nissin's specially blended (ultra-high-altitude) instant noodles while aloft in the space shuttle Discovery. (Nissin's triumph presumably more than equaled the accomplishment of rival Maruchan, whose instant noodles were consumed in 1987 at the top of Mount Everest.) Through such feats, instant noodle producers tout their capacity for more mundane product development and elaboration. For instance, central to Nissin's strategy of remaining ahead of the field is a commitment to continual innovation, as evidenced in the some three hundred new varieties the company releases annually in Japan—a number equal to those of its competitors combined. This elaboration by Nissin and its myriad competitors is subject to further elaboration, including the commentaries of connoisseurs with highly developed sensibilities who revel in the range of instant noodle offerings. Perhaps the most famous of these is Ton Tan Tin, a Japanese blogger who, as of 2012, has posted reviews of 5,008 varieties of instant noodles he has eaten in diverse parts of the world—reviews commented upon by his many readers, who share his obsession.[10] On occasion, these commentaries veer in a darker direction, as in the tale by videographer and conservation activist Michael Sheridan about environmental degradation—a tale about the transition from an Indonesian rainforest to an oil palm plantation and finally into a palm-oil-prepared package of instant noodles.[11]

So significant are instant noodles that, in a 2000 survey of Japanese opinion, they were voted the most influential invention of Japan in the twentieth century.[12] As a "cultural icon," they ranked ahead of personal stereos, computers, small cameras, and even karaoke.[13] Their significance is additionally reflected by the more than 3.5 million results found in response to an April 2012 Google search. Given their pervasiveness and infiltration into daily life virtually everywhere, we think that their story can provide unusual insights concerning the workings of the industrial food system in the contemporary world economy. In this sense, the study of instant noodles is an anthropology of large-scale capitalist provisioning.

We—Tatsuro, Deborah, and Fred—were all familiar with instant noodles before we began this project. Tatsuro is from the home of instant noodles, where they are not only eaten widely but also commemorated at three museums. Two of these museums, near Osaka and in Yokohama, are dedicated to Ando's achievements. The third, also in Yokohama, focuses on the importance of noodles, both instant ramen and customary ("real") ramen, in Japanese life. Deborah and Fred come from American university settings, where students famously rely on instant noodles and can consult a self-help book about their future lives as grownups called No More Ramen.[14] Yet we had missed the story instant noodles could tell until we encountered them during anthropological fieldwork, in Papua New Guinea (PNG) for Deborah and Fred and in Nepal for Tatsuro. In both places, instant noodles arrived during the mid-1980s and rapidly became a staple for the urban and peri-urban poor, who must purchase much of their food. By 2003, one Nepali journalist opined that, with rapid urbanization, Nepal had become so awash with instant noodles that "if all the packaged noodles sold in Nepal during the past two decades could join hands, they might reach the top of Mount Everest. . . . [Nepali are eating] tons of the stuff."[15] Comparably, by 2006, urban-dwelling Papua New Guineans told Deborah and Fred that instant noodles were among the few foods that they could afford.

This study of capitalist provisioning thus concerns how rich and poor, living in diverse parts of the world, have become caught up in the global phenomenon of instant noodles. In formulating our story we have taken particular notice of Sidney Mintz's classic study of sugar—an industrially produced foodstuff that also, with remarkable speed, became quotidian and ubiquitous. In Sweetness and Power, Mintz documents how slave-produced Caribbean sugar came to connect the world in important relations of inequality.[16] Once an exotic taste and luxury treat for the aristocracy, sugar soon became a commonplace necessity for all, with sweetened tea and treacle-smeared bread the sustaining staple of British factory workers. Eventually, inexpensive sugar pervaded Britain, Europe, and much of the globe, fostering a world food system and transforming contemporary diets—not to mention spreading class-related obesity—with the proliferation of sugar- (and fat-) laden industrial foods.

Other anthropologists have written about globally permeating, industrially produced foods—products somewhat familiar to virtually everyone. Their accounts include consideration of the extent to which these foods both transform people and practices and, as some of our instant noodles examples suggest, are transformed by those who take them into their bodies and lives. For instance, in a masterful analysis of the worldwide spread of Coca-Cola, Robert Foster emphasizes the ways in which local people inflect the product with their own meanings—as when PNG women use Coca-Cola cans to cook rice, or PNG men use Coca-Cola cans as shield motifs. Coca-Cola is distinctively configured in Trinidad as well. According to Daniel Miller, it has become racially inflected as a "black sweet drink," which, when mixed with rum, is the favored local alcoholic beverage. And for those accustomed to eating a burger along with a Coca-Cola in the fourteen minutes typical of a fast-food meal, James Watson's edited collection about the various ways that McDonald's engages East Asians is instructive. Although McDonald's has altered Asian customers' expectations by insisting that they form orderly queues as they approach the counter, customers, in turn, have altered restaurant procedures by lingering as long as they wish at their tables after their (relatively expensive) meals. In Russia, Melissa Caldwell has found that Muscovites have accepted many of McDonald's standards but in addition demand that meat and produce be domestically sourced and that McDonald's meet indigenous assumptions about sociality.[17] (Similar processes of two-way transformation between commodity and consumer also appear in studies of such thoroughly permeating items of capitalist consumption as used clothes and denim—items that, like food, are intimate, although worn on rather than incorporated into the body.[18])

Of these world-pervading industrial foods, instant noodles are distinct. All are seen as modernist, often appealingly so, in the transformations they effect and are affected by. Nevertheless, Coca-Cola and soft drinks more generally refresh people, while instant noodles sustain them. And unlike Coca-Cola and other internationally recognized brands of soft drinks, instant noodles, regardless of brand, are always inexpensive. Burgers and fries—whether sold by McDonald's, other international chains, or local fast-food establishments—also supply nourishment. However, relative to instant noodles, they are expensive—in some cases, extremely so. (The 2009 Big Mac Economic Indicator, as compiled by the UBS Swiss Bank, compared the average working time necessary to buy a Big Mac in seventy-three cities worldwide: workers in Chicago, Tokyo, and Toronto need twelve minutes, whereas those in Mexico City, Jakarta, and Nairobi need well over two hours.[19])

Moreover, though instant noodles occasionally come under fire for their reliance on ingredients with questionable impacts on environmental or personal health (palm oil, salt, MSG, and sugar), they rarely draw much outcry. In this regard they are unlike McDonald's and Coca-Cola, which periodically attract negative attention, if not serious pushback: in the case of the former, for culinary imperialism (in France), religious insensitivity (in India), or supersizing its patrons (in America); in the case of the latter, for environmental depletion (of water in India), labor intimidation (in Colombia), or supersizing its patrons (in America).[20]

Instant noodles, thus, are a uniquely universal, inexpensive, relatively low-profile belly filler—a humble food that permeates all locales, infiltrating everyday life without receiving too much critical attention.[21] As a baseline of the adequate, they become the material means for people to present themselves—to themselves and to others—as acceptably ordinary, and they provide an excellent substrate for various customized appropriations and elaborations.

In fact, instant noodles may well be the most successful industrially produced food, at least in terms of world penetration: they constitute a huge social reality—and one inviting attention. Much like sugar, instant noodles are a capitalist provision that provisions capitalism. In other words, they have an important—and perhaps increasingly important—role in capitalism's reproduction and spread. Because they feed people quickly and cheaply, they appeal to busy and economy-minded people everywhere. This includes students in the United States, Japan, and Papua New Guinea, striving to make ends meet at their time of life. It includes entrepreneurial programmers in the United States and elsewhere, striving to make their start-up companies what the venture capitalist Paul Graham termed "ramen profitable"—that is, accepting modest returns (i.e., sufficient to allow for subsistence on cheap foods such as instant noodles) while waiting for a big buyout in the future.[22] Finally, it includes the chronically cash-constrained urban and peri-urban poor (and not just in developing countries), for whom instant noodles suppress the discomfort as well as the distractions of persistent hunger—helping them hang on either as potential workers or as low-wage workers. To refer to another of Mintz's arguments, instant noodles join sugar (as well as tea and coffee) as a "proletarian hunger killer," albeit of a more contemporary variety.[23] Thus, they partially offset the low wages that might adversely affect the productivity of workers and the survival of their families. In sustaining workers, instant noodles foster a self-perpetuating cycle of production and consumption: workers producing for a market become consumers of what the market offers. Reliably available whenever wanted, instant noodles enable much; whatever the job at hand, they help get it done.

These attributes lead to related and complementary transformations as capitalism extends its reach and penetration into the developing world. Instant noodles not only provision capitalism; they normalize capitalism. They help make routine a world in which commodities, marketed for profit as "goods," circulate, subject to consumer evaluation and choice. Quotidian and ubiquitous—selectable and delectable (enough)—instant noodles may serve as an introductory course in consumption. They shift the daily expectations and activities, the "habitus" (to use the social theorist Pierre Bourdieu's term), of those who acquire and eat them.[24] For instance, in urban and peri-urban Papua New Guinea, this shift in habitus has become pervasive, reaching literally from cradle to grave: babies are often weaned with instant noodles and elders are celebrated in death rituals with instant noodles as elements in ceremonial exchange. Because they are so readily incorporated into daily life, instant noodles ease people worldwide along a path of capitalist acquisition and consumption, shaping who they are and what they do. Instant noodles help produce consumers, "similar kinds of subjects on a global scale" (in the words of the anthropologist Jonathan Friedman), while inflecting, and being inflected by, local realms "of practiced meaning" as they assimilate into familiar engagements, activities, and preferences.[25]

As capitalism extends its influence into the developing world, instant noodles may serve as an antifriction device. We refer here to the anthropologist Anna Tsing's concept of "friction," which exposes "the lie that global power operates as a well-oiled machine."[26] We agree that capitalist penetration is a complex process of conjuncture, filled with the gear-clashing uncertainties and inefficiencies of pause, drag, and redirection (and of "spasms," "seeps," and "spurts," as characterized in the economic analysis of J.K. Gibson-Graham).[27] However, we believe that certain globally flowing, industrially produced commodities grease the skids of capitalism. And when a commodity is as intimate as everyday food—food that is inexpensive, widely available, generally acceptable (or readily modified for local tastes), and relatively easy to convey and prepare—the socioeconomic transformations attendant on globally flowing products may happen with little apparent fuss or muss.

Instant noodles not only reliably sustain and normalize socioeconomic transformations but also contribute to a procapitalist system of value. As unobtrusive and humble fare, they don't call attention to themselves in a manner that would compel many consumers to probe the social processes that brought them into being: to defetishize them.[28] Unlike Coca-Cola and McDonald's, for instance—and certainly unlike sugar—they don't have many potentially disconcerting secrets. Those they do have are largely generic to industrial foods and remain largely overlooked, especially because instant noodles represent, at least in terms of what you get for what you spend, good value. Finally, as instant noodles find their place within various contexts, they lend themselves to the culinary elaborations that add value. In short, they insert themselves deftly into people's lives, nourishing their bodies and often pleasantly rousing their imaginations.

Of course, remarkable as instant noodles are, they didn't get to all corners of the world by themselves. They both required and accumulated an entourage. Inventors, food scientists, producers, marketers, consumers, and bloggers, among others, all contributed in different ways and to different degrees; each brought a different range of competencies, interests, and commitments to the product that links them, directly or indirectly. We spoke to as many of these people as possible, collecting their accounts and perusing their specialized literatures in our multisited ethnographic and historical project. Attempting to understand a permeating product with such a large, diverse, and dispersed entourage required us to be selective: to use a hybrid methodology that traded a measure of depth for breadth, a degree of the intensive for the extensive. We engaged in participant observation and monitored blogs; administered questionnaires and read intensively; conducted interviews and visited trade fairs; sat in food science classes and scrutinized instant noodle packages. Our objective was to describe instant noodles in a way that revealed and contextualized their brilliant career as a globally flowing industrial food under contemporary capitalism. And we sought to do justice to this subject in a manner that made the best use of our anthropological strengths: theoretical, ethnographic, cultural, and linguistic.

We intend our "noodle narratives" to be generous in scope, as they embrace a range of accounts in which instant noodles are central players. We begin with a focus on the human animal to explain the widespread appeal of instant noodles. Noodle manufacturers tap into universal human taste preferences to provide consumers with an inexpensive yet pleasingly filling hunger killer. Then, for insights into the global trajectory of instant noodles, we visit three markets in places broadly familiar to us that are distinctive in instructive ways. These markets reveal a variety of ways in which this humble form of capitalist provisioning enables differently located people to manage their lives.

The first is the Japanese market, where instant noodles were invented and received their greatest embellishment. With both historical and ethnographic data, we show how instant noodles enabled major transformations of post-World War II Japanese society. Eventually, as the Japanese market became saturated, instant noodles were subject to seemingly endless tweaking as variations in flavorings, toppings, and packaging enticed consumers (including the blogger Ton Tan Tin).

We then turn to the U.S. market, where instant noodles first embarked on their worldwide sojourn and have largely remained a relatively basic, price-driven commodity. With data derived from diverse sources—online postings, interviews, surveys, and conversations—we consider particular (and somewhat overlapping) groups for whom instant noodles remain important. We examine two generations of the middle class: those for whom instant noodles provide a nostalgic link to the exigencies and preoccupations of their youthful lives under capitalist provisioning and those—mostly students—for whom instant noodles provide an immediate link to the exigencies and preoccupations of their present lives. We admire the resilience of the incarcerated, who, in the face of institutional fare provided by the likes of Sodexo Marriott and Aramark, transform instant noodles and other ingredients from the prison commissary into a "taste of freedom."[29] And we take note of the "heavy users," the category of the poor targeted by instant noodle purveyors as the most promising.

Finally, we turn to the PNG market, where instant noodles arrived relatively recently and remain basic in form. With data based on long-term fieldwork, contemporary participant observation, interviews, and surveys, we provide examples of the workings of instant noodles in a developing country. Instant noodles, we argue, receive an enthusiastic welcome from Papua New Guineans because they help the chronically cash-short deal with their urban and peri-urban circumstances and transform them into aspiring consumers of industrially produced products.

This three-fold contrast, we must caution, is not meant to suggest that the global trajectory of instant noodles follows a path of specific and inevitable evolutionary stages, as from infancy to maturity. To be sure, markets for instant noodles will change, though these changes may be various. Thus, the U.S. instant noodles market of the future should not be expected to replicate the Japanese market of today, nor should the PNG market be expected to replicate that of the United States. We could have chosen examples of other markets (though it is hard to imagine a book about instant noodles that didn't cover Japan) and would welcome other examples. We hope that this work encourages the contribution of other cases from other places akin to those compiled in Watson's collection describing the penetration of McDonald's throughout East Asia and in Miller and Woodward's volume on the global significance of denim.[30]

Our last data chapter extends our interest in the global success of instant noodles by focusing ethnographically on the contemporary world of industrial food production (whose major players are known collectively as "big food"). To do this, we attended university classes in food science, interviewed food scientists, and visited their laboratories. In addition, we joined the Institute of Food Technologists (IFT), went to IFT annual and regional meetings, pored over the IFT monthly journal, *Food Technology,* spoke with food company officials, and toured factory facilities. As one of the industrial food system's singular achievements, instant noodles are not only the product of this food system as it engages with, and is engaged by, people worldwide; they are, as well, a source of insight into this system in its more general attributes.

In our conclusion, we address the question of what it means to feed the world of the future with industrial food products like instant noodles. What does this mean to those committed to big food–focused capitalist provisioning, those who claim that their industry is both indispensible and virtuous in the contemporary world? What does this mean to the critics of industrial food? And what does this mean not only for who can take or leave these products but for those who might depend on them for cheap calories?

As we shall see, instant noodles have thus far been virtually unstoppable —and, as such, their accomplishments are worthy of serious attention. They are telling in what they facilitate and reveal about global capitalist provisioning: they make a lot happen and show a lot happening.

1

The Taste of Something Good

The circumstances of Ando's invention of instant noodles have circulated widely, with standardized versions of the story appearing in the instant noodle museums as well as in numerous publications, including Ando's autobiography, *The Story of the Invention of Instant Ramen*. Indeed, as featured in our conversations with instant noodle manufacturers, these tales have become a charter myth—a foundational noodle narrative—for a whole industry. Ando, it is said, envisioned a streamlined variant of a food already well known to his postwar countrymen from "real" ramen shops.[1] However, unlike these "real" noodles, which required considerable time and attention to prepare, his instant noodles could provide his hard-pressed and often hungry compatriots with a quick, filling, and relatively inexpensive meal.[2] But success did not come easily, and Ando experimented tirelessly in his backyard shack to make his product commercially viable, suitable for large-scale industrial production. As he states in his autobiography: "I set myself five objectives. First, the noodles should be tasty and palatable. Second, they should keep for a long period of time and be easy to store in the kitchen. Third, they should be easy to prepare. Fourth, the product should be inexpensive. Fifth, the noodles should be safe and sanitary since they were for human consumption."[3] Here we describe how Ando was successful at meeting these objectives. As we shall see, instant noodles are well suited to capitalist provisioning not only because they are inexpensive to produce on an industrial scale but also because their physical properties appeal to a great many hard-wired human gustatory and olfactory pleasures. In this sense, Ando made us all collaborators in the success of his product.

INSTANT NOODLES ON THE PRODUCTION LINE

Like most Japanese noodles, Ando's were made from wheat, an ingredient both familiar and inexpensive, given American food aid at the time. His primary technical challenge was to develop a method of precooking noodles so that they retained their form and were shelf stable, yet readily reconstituted and tasty. The eventual solution was to apply the "principle of tempura": to pass the noodles, already steamed and sprinkled with chicken broth, through a bath of hot oil. In this way, the residual moisture would bubble out, leaving the noodles dehydrated and porous, relatively inert and easily (instantly) rehydrated when immersed in hot water.[4]

At least in its basic form, the technology of instant noodle production has remained relatively the same. And the variations designed to appeal to particular markets—the preferred color, firmness, seasoning, and means of delivering flavor (whether during processing, as with Ando's original method, or, more commonly today, from a flavor sachet)—can be readily incorporated into standard production setups. Instant noodle factories of at least adequate sophistication can be established throughout the developing world in places like PNG (though perhaps with the outsourcing of the flavor sachets).[5]

The wheat flour normally used is made from high-protein (10 to 12 percent) hard wheat to produce a relatively firm noodle.[6] If the noodles are to be enriched (restoring the B vitamins lost during the milling of the wheat) or fortified (with additional nutrients, such as vitamin A, calcium, or iron), appropriate ingredients are included in the flour. The flour is thoroughly mixed with water containing salt (for white coloring, taste, and preservative qualities) and a gum (for texture) to make a dough. This dough is then dropped onto a conveyor belt and caught up in an uninterrupted process. First, it passes through a series of closely paired rollers to form a thin, continuous sheet. (In the two PNG factories Deborah and Fred visited, the rollers and therefore the sheets were about a meter wide.) This procedure manipulates the dough both to facilitate the development of the wheat's gluten (for chewiness) and to bring it to a final noodle thickness of about one millimeter. Next, the sheet passes through a pair of sharply grooved rollers that slice it into noodle-width strands, which are given a slight wiggle to create a wave that allows

FIGURE 1. An instant noodle block. Photograph by Frederick Errington.

quicker and more even circulation of hot water when the noodles are rehydrated prior to consumption.[7] The wavy strands are channeled into lines—each the width of a package of noodles—and conveyed through a steamer to be briefly cooked: this gelatinizes the starch, improving texture, and denatures the proteins, fixing the wave in place. Emerging from the steamer still soft, the noodles can now be cut to their final package length. At this point, the blocks (cakes or pillows) of wavy noodles are ready for the final frying and drying. Still following the principle of tempura, the blocks pass for several minutes through a bath of hot (usually palm) oil. Then they are drained of much of this oil and allowed to cool before moving in regimented rows to a mechanical packager. There, often joined by flavor sachets, they are wrapped in an airtight film. Fried, dried, and sealed, they are now shelf stable.

Ando anticipated that instant noodles would become ubiquitous. As he writes in his autobiography, "I said to myself: 'Food knows no national boundaries.' I suppose that even then I already had a gut feeling that instant ramen would one day become a global food."[8] The fact that Ando was right owes much to the physical properties of instant noodles that he perfected through his experiments—that they would be convenient, cheap, shelf stable, and industrially produced. It also owes much to his insistence that his noodles strike a widely appreciated and basic culinary chord that can be readily elaborated in culturally specific ways.

Yet how to do this? Taste is complex. Scientists writing about gustation, or taste sensations emanating from the tongue to the brain, have long agreed that four tastes—sweet, sour, salty, and bitter—are primary or basic: these are hardwired, in that our responses to them are inborn. In fact, the psychologist Jacob Steiner has demonstrated that, with near universality, newborns exhibit the same facial expressions when presented with each of these four tastes. Some scientists have also come to accept umami (which is a perception of savory) as a fifth primary taste.[9]

Not all substances, though, can be readily classified according to these four or five categories.[10] Indeed, because the receptor cells for different tastes work in complex combinations, what humans experience may be less a set of discrete essences than a gradient of sensations. The sometimes ambiguous line between (for example) salty, sweet, or savory has been fostered in many cuisines. In addition, the tongue and sometimes the mouth more generally perceive other sensations, such as fattiness, dryness, texture, and temperature. To make matters even murkier, the brain registers taste that derives from taste receptor cells found in the gut as well as on the tongue.[11] Moreover, the complexity of taste derives from "olfaction," from the huge range of sensations registered in the nose, some wafting from the upper mouth. And to all of this must be added the effect of cultural, personal, and socioeconomic associations in determining not only if something tastes good, but if it is in good taste to think that something tastes good.

Part of Ando's brilliance, as we shall see, was to choose among the myriad gustatory and olfactory options to create an undemanding, mouth- and nose-friendly product, one so inexpensive in industrial production that it could become commonplace. By combining readily available components that tapped into universal human taste preferences he provided consumers with cheap yet enjoyable calories. Indeed, his hunger killer became quickly accepted even among those lacking a noodle tradition: it was easily affordable, filled you up, and tasted good enough. It had a lot going for it.

THE TASTE OF CHICKEN-FLAVORED INSTANT NOODLES

In his autobiography, Ando explains why he decided that his first commercial venture would be "Chikin Ramen," instant noodles flavored with chicken broth:

> In those days, we raised some chickens beside the research hut in the backyard. Every now and then we had one of these chickens for lunch or dinner.

Once, while a chicken was being dressed, it suddenly jumped violently. This came as a terrible shock to my son, Koki, who was watching the scene. After that he would not eat chicken, not even chicken rice, which had been his favorite dish, until one day when my mother-in-law prepared some ramen in a broth made from chicken bones. Not knowing it was chicken, my son ate it heartily. This gave me the idea of using chicken soup as the flavoring of instant noodles.

Come to think of it, chicken soup has been a basic culinary feature in both East and West for centuries [although likely not in Japan until the nineteenth century[12]]. In retrospect, I think my decision at the time to use chicken broth stands to reason. By using chicken soup, instant ramen managed to circumvent religious taboos when it was introduced in different countries around the world. Hindus may not eat beef and Muslims may not eat pork, but there is not a single culture, religion, or country that forbids the eating of chicken.[13]

To be sure, Ando may have slightly overstated his case, because there are those who eschew eating chicken and other meat for cultural, religious, and personal reasons. A frequently asked Internet search question is from vegetarians wishing to know whether actual meat is used in chicken-flavored instant noodles. The answer is that some brands use the real thing while others, as we shall see below, use artificial facsimiles. However, aside from the instant noodles explicitly manufactured for vegetarians, the usual goal is to make the meat flavors believable, since most humans enjoy the taste of meat and have evidently done so for much of their evolution. And, as Ando aptly realized, chicken is a popular meat flavor.

Chickens have long been widely appreciated (likely spreading in domesticated form from northeast Thailand before 6000 B.C.E.).[14] According to the *Firefly Encyclopedia of Birds*, chickens are among the most prevalent of domestic animals, with an estimated twenty-four billion found worldwide in 2003.[15] They are easy to keep in backyards or villages, stay fairly close to home, and can forage for themselves, without much human assistance. Though sometimes a mild underfoot nuisance, they are not threatening when full grown. Recurrently for their eggs and eventually for their meat, they provide protein in family-useful portions throughout their lives. Readily caught (at least by fleet-footed kids), they can be easily dispatched on occasion to provide meal-sized portions. In addition, they lend themselves to household production as well as to industrial production, where—often under less-than-humane conditions—they efficiently convert grain into protein.[16] They thus provide a familiar and welcome taste to most people worldwide, especially when given local inflections with specialized seasonings. Although there are many other flavorings for instant noodles, chicken remains the most popular.

Moreover, chicken-flavored instant noodles do not only deliver a familiar taste and aroma. They also evoke, especially for many in the developing world, a widespread and fundamentally domestic culinary form: a hot soup as a one-pot meal. Even the meat and bones of aged chickens, when simmered with whatever is at hand, make a thoroughly cooked and flavorful concoction. All ingredients remain within the pot—an enclosed vessel symbolically appropriate for a group of immediate kin. Nothing is fancy, nothing is lost, and nothing is wasted as food is prepared for family commensalism. Convenience merges with frugality and informality.[17] Indeed, in PNG, chicken-flavored instant noodles both suggest the image of such pots and become constituents of such pots as they and their flavorings are cheap extenders of whatever else the pots contain. And even if bowls or cups of instant noodles that are eaten in dorm rooms or at office desks in the United States and Japan do not evoke the chicken soup of one's mother or Koki Ando's grandmother, they may still carry with them some of the comforts of this soup: the ease when convenience, informality, and frugality are all mutually reinforcing.

A package of instant noodles usually reveals whether its flavors come from real chicken or an artificial facsimile. If real, the package's ingredient list will mention, for instance, "chicken powder." If artificial, the ingredient list will make no mention of chicken. To create chicken-flavored broth without chicken requires the specialized skills of food scientists known as "flavorists." They use a palette of various ingredients, including inexpensive vegetable proteins that substitute for more expensive animal ones. Often derived from soy and wheat (which should be mentioned in the ingredient list), these proteins are broken down ("hydrolyzed") on an industrial scale into short chains of amino acids.[18] Blended, mixed, and seasoned according to a usually proprietary formula, these chains come to approximate the animal proteins found in chicken. (A similar alchemy is at work, for instance, in beef-flavored instant noodles.[19])

Since consumers rarely do direct taste tests to compare a bowl of homemade chicken noodle soup (or beef soup) to one of chicken-flavored (or beef-flavored) instant noodles (whether using real chicken or not), the taste and appearance need only be good enough—delivering value proportionate to the inexpensive price. Packages often deliver flavor prompts. For instance, packages of Nestlé-owned, PNG-produced

Maggi instant noodles feature cartoons of cheerful chickens and benign bovines. More generally, the sensation of a chicken (or beef) broth is fostered by the appearance of the noodles: the flavor sachet of beef produces a darker color.

Verisimilitude in taste and appearance varies depending on cost. So, too, does inflection for particular tastes. Accordingly, the website of a Chinese company that creates flavor sachets for instant noodle companies claims competence in research and development and offers "chicken flavor . . . chili chicken flavor, chili beef flavor, tomato flavor, mushroom flavor, onion flavor, shrimp flavor, seafood flavor, etc. (as [per] your requirements)."[20]

Instant noodles (whether chicken, beef, seafood, or vegetarian in flavoring; whether spicy or bland in seasoning; whether firm or soft in texture) can thus be readily tailored for local audiences. These variations, though, depart little from Ando's initial formulation, which was designed for worldwide success. In this regard, the PNG-produced Maggi instant noodles can be regarded as typical in their components. Although the package advises that the soup be divided into two portions, the nutritional information is for the entire 80-gram package: the 520 grams of soup (which include the water) deliver 360 calories; 1,400 milligrams of sodium; 15 grams of fat (including 6.8 grams of saturated fat), primarily from the cooking oil; 45.2 grams of carbohydrates; and 8.4 grams of protein, primarily from the wheat. There is also MSG (listed as "Flavour Enhancer 621" in countries using the "European E" numbering system) and, in most cases (though not in PNG-produced Maggi noodles), sugar, which sometimes rivals salt as the first or second ingredient.[21]

Ando tweaked culinarily acceptable (if bland) and generally inexpensive refined wheat flour to make a tasty, palatable, and moderately filling meal or snack—one that proved appealing to a broad range of people.[22] Without salt, MSG, oil (especially palm oil), and sugar, instant noodles, as we show in some detail, would never have become so universally appealing, so great a moneymaker for instant noodle companies.

SALT

Though sodium is required for cells to function properly, high rates of consumption are linked to high blood pressure and increased risk of heart disease, stroke, and kidney disease.[23] In the United States, the recommended daily allowance (RDA) is no more than 2,300 milligrams of sodium (just about a teaspoon of salt).[24] Americans, though, consume at least 50 percent more than the amount recommended by U.S. authorities, and the Japanese consume almost 22 percent more than the (more lenient) amount recommended by Japanese authorities.[25] A package of chicken-flavored instant noodle soup, for instance, would provide Americans with over 60 percent of their RDA for salt. Certainly part of the appeal (at least to some) of instant noodles is that they are salty. According to the psychologist Linda Bartoshuk, "humans love salt." Indeed, "many (but not all) who become deficient in salt crave it."[26] An extreme case of salt craving concerns a boy who went so far as to consume salt directly from shakers. When hospitalized to discover what was wrong, the boy was unable to augment his diet with extra salt and died. He was eventually found to have an adrenal disease that made it impossible for his kidneys to retain sodium.[27]

We do not know when humans first seasoned their food with salt (or with anything else). Yet despite some perhaps biophysiological differences among human groups in sensitivity to salt, the historical record over at least the past ten thousand years shows that salt has come to be widely valued.[28] The Chinese harvested salt from a salt lake as early as 6000 B.C.E, and by 2000 B.C.E. Egyptians were using salt as a preservative and condiment. As a preservative, salt inhibits the activity of harmful bacteria. In concentrated form, often as a brine used in pickling, salt draws out the water of living cells on which most spoilage bacteria depend. It also kills these bacteria through direct contact. With competition eliminated, harmless, salt-tolerant, and flavor-producing bacteria can flourish. As a condiment, salt enhances taste, strengthens the aromas of food, and suppresses bitterness.[29] An ancient Egyptian papyrus puts it well: "There is no better food than salted vegetables."[30]

Widely traded, taxed, and used as tribute, salt has a historical importance that is suggested by English expressions such as "salt of the earth," as well as by English derivations from the Latin *sal*. These include "salary" (Roman soldiers were paid in salt), "sauce" (the original concentrated flavoring was salt), "salad" (bitter leaves were made palatable when dressed with salt), and "sausage" (chopped meat was preserved with salt).[31]

Increasingly inexpensive due to efficient techniques of extraction, salt has become fundamental to the contemporary industrial food system.[32] Toni Tarver, writing in *Food Technology* (the monthly magazine of the Institute of Food Technologists, the professional organization of food scientists), explains its importance to the modern "food grid": "Although the sodium content of processed foods may be high, food manufacturers would likely make the case that the amount of sodium in processed foods is not arbitrary. . . . Salt . . . plays an integral role in food processing and food safety: It enhances the flavor of foods, unveiling a food's natural flavor, masking bitterness and acidity, and even making sweets taste sweeter. . . . [It works as well to] preserve food and retard microbial growth, thereby extending the shelf life of perishable items." Thus salt appears in significant amounts in "bread, cereal, frozen pizzas and entrees, processed meats, shelf-stable soups and sauces, pasta, and salty snacks [that] comprise the daily dietary intake of most [American] consumers." Moreover, "since the 1970s the sodium content of food at chain restaurants has escalated along with steady increases in portion sizes."[33] And at least "70% . . . of excess sodium intake comes from restaurants and commercially processed foods." According to another article in *Food Technology,* "only 11% of the sodium in Americans' diets comes from their own salt shakers; nearly 80% is added to foods before they are sold."[34]

With concerns, especially in the first world, about the widely publicized relationship between salt consumption and health risks, the food industry would like to respond (while continuing to profit). The problem is that people may want to reduce their sodium consumption, but they do not want to reduce the flavor of what they eat. The Campbell's Soup Company, for instance, has declared that reducing sodium in its soup "is the most challenging [goal] because it has the most complex flavor profile for taste, and salt is an amazing potentiator of taste."[35] Maintaining flavor while reducing salt is especially problematic if the target demographic includes an aging population for whom the increasing risk of high blood pressure is coupled with decreasing taste sensitivity.[36] As the food technologist John Crump told Deborah and Fred:

> For the elderly, taste buds grow less acute; it is harder to get anything to taste good. . . . Elderly people often go protein short because they don't eat as much as they should; because things don't taste good for them. It's been the Holy Grail for some time to reduce sodium in products. The most companies have been able to do is to slowly wean their customers from salt. They take 5 percent out this year and in a couple of years, another 5 percent. If you graph the liking people have for products and the amount of salt in these products, the curves are identical: they group together. There are some technologies to reduce salt; there have been attempts to substitute potassium chloride for sodium chloride, though it has a metallic and bitter taste. Campbell's has begun to use sea salt in its products, which has other minerals in

addition to salt which provide enough flavor so that the total amount can be reduced. And then people have been using umami [MSG] and guanylate [disodium guanylate, an MSG enhancer] which are savory and make you salivate [and, we should note, enhance the saltiness of salty foods]. So food companies have tried complex networks of these ingredients, though they can't take all of the salt out and make the food palatable. It is the case that it takes about three weeks for people to adapt to get used to new diets. There is no quick fix to the salt problem.[37]

Attempts continue to find the Holy Grail of sodium reduction. These include relatively costly efforts to boost flavor by using chili, oregano, and garlic to offset the reduction in salt and to maintain a salty taste by blocking the bitterness of potassium chloride. They also include relatively costly efforts to employ nonsalt preservatives that do not adversely affect taste.

However, it seems unlikely that such efforts at salt reduction will have any immediate effect on the formulation of instant noodles, a product that uses salt liberally as a preservative in the noodles and as a flavor and flavor enhancer (potentiator) in the sachet. Many people worldwide are not concerned about the risks of consuming salt, and for those who are, the instant noodle companies suggest that the sachet be discarded or used sparingly.

MSG

The package of Maggi chicken-flavored noodles sold in Papua New Guinea indicates that the ingredients include two "Flavour Enhancers," 621 and 635. Following the European practice of using E numbers, it does not reveal that "621" is monosodium glutamate and that "635" is disodium 5'-ribonucleotide, which is a mixture of two other enhancers, disodium guanylate and disodium inosinate.

Monosodium glutamate, or MSG, is the best known of these enhancers (and the only one we discuss). This is the amino acid glutamic acid in a stable and easily dissolvable salt form. It was discovered early in the twentieth century by Kikunae Ikeda, a professor of physical chemistry at the University of Tokyo. Ikeda had concluded that certain foods exhibit a distinctive taste that is not sweet, sour, bitter, or salty. This taste is particularly evident in meat and in a fish and kelp-based broth, dashi, that is a central ingredient of Japanese cuisine. Ikeda named this taste "umami" (from the Japanese words umai, meaning "delicious," and mi, meaning "taste"), and it refers to certain savory qualities combined with a pleasing sensation that the mouth is filled with flavor. In 1907 he began experiments to isolate the source of this complex taste from kelp. Success came quickly, and by 1908 he found that MSG (when dissolved) could produce the umami sensation. Marketing of MSG began in 1909 under the brand name of Ajinomoto, which means "essence of taste." Much like Ando, Ikeda hoped that his invention would prove both profitable and beneficial to the public. "Having always regretted the poor diet of our nation," he wrote, "I had long contemplated how it might be remedied, but had found no good idea. . . . It then occurred to me that manufacturing a good, inexpensive seasoning to make bland, nutritious food tasty might be a way to accomplish my objective."[38]

MSG is made today through the fermentation of carbohydrates by select species of bacteria or yeast, and it has been widely employed (for better or worse) by the food industry as an inexpensive seasoning.[39] Nevertheless, it was not until 2000 that umami's status as a fifth primary taste received substantial (though not overwhelming) support. The evidence lay in the discovery of specific receptor cells on the tongue (and, as discovered later, also in the gut) that are attuned to glutamate. Found in many animal and plant foods, glutamate is one of the most common of the amino acids, important to health as a building block for proteins, a major source of energy in the intestine when converted to glucose, a stimulant of gastric secretion, and a neurotransmitter in the central nervous system.[40]

Glutamate appears in two forms. It can be perceived, or "tasted," by the receptor cells only in its "free" form, as the amino acid per se. But it is usually found in its complex "bound" form, joined together with other amino acids to make up a variety of nutritionally vital, body-building proteins. However, because the taste of the free form usually signals the presence of the more common bound form, and thus of proteins more generally, when humans experience the pleasant taste of umami, they are encouraged to continue eating: the detection of the free form conveys that the bound form is nearby. Hence umami detectors may have evolved as a guide to the presence of vital nutrients, since glutamate is the most abundant amino acid and is present in many foods containing protein, including meat, seafood, and aged cheese.[41] Human milk has a high glutamate content.

Yet as Gary Beauchamp, director of the Monell Chemical Senses Center in Philadelphia, notes, many umami sources—like tomatoes, shiitake mushrooms, and kelp—are not rich in protein. For these reasons, he finds this evolutionary hypothesis unpersuasive.[42] Despite his reservation, he looks forward to future research on the adaptive function of umami receptor cells, including the investigation of those taste receptors in the gut: "Umami receptors in the mouth may be just the first step in the path through the alimentary tract along which nutrients such as amino acids are 'recognized.'"[43] Bartoshuk agrees, arguing that the gut receptors may be even more important than those on the tongue because the gut is likely to register free glutamates more strongly as food is digested. She suggests that a process of positive conditioning takes place, with signals from the gut enhancing the pleasure of tasting umami-rich foods on the tongue.[44]

We would like to contribute modestly to this discussion by suggesting that umami responses would still be useful indicators of protein-rich foods, even if these responses were sometimes triggered by non-protein-rich foods. Simply put, the likelihood of a few, relatively nonconsequential false positives (at least, once shiitake have been distinguished from, for example, "destroying angel" mushrooms) would not overwhelm the probable adaptive advantages of many true positives. Moreover, because heat (like digestion) serves to free glutamate from its bound form, the advent of cooking might well change the umami profile of various foods. Meat, for instance, has an immediately scaled-up umami appeal when cooked; especially when browned through roasting, grilling, or frying, it can stimulate umami sensors with mouthwatering intensity. Indeed, humans seeking protein would not go astray if they heeded their umami sensors to pursue a nicely grilled steak—albeit smothered with sautéed shiitake mushrooms and a side of ripe tomatoes (with or without kelp).[45]

The umami-focused pleasures of this sort of meal would be not only gustatory but also olfactory. As we have seen, flavor is the combined result of taste and smell. In fact, glutamate seems to enhance the enjoyment people experience from certain odors, creating a significantly more pleasant overall flavor. As the experimental psychologist Edmund Rolls found, when glutamate is combined with an odor from boiled vegetables, the two stimulate the brain's cortex with "supralinear" effects, stimulating it more than would the sum of their separate activations.[46] This response, according to McCabe and Rolls, is the result of the convergence of taste and olfactory pathways in the human brain.[47] But it is more than taste and smell that are so synergistically united. Rolls found that "some single neurons combine glutamate taste with olfactory, oral texture, oral temperature, and visual stimuli."[48]

More specifically, the addition of MSG (within certain parameters) increases the palatability of hot, aromatic, commercially produced chicken noodle soup made from real chicken. In one study cited by the food writer Thomas Remo, "a group of young Americans said that a chicken soup with a small amount of MSG was richer, more savory and meatier than the same soup without MSG."[49] And MSG increases the palatability of hot and (somewhat) aromatic chicken-flavored instant noodle soup, made with no chicken. In the case of real chicken noodle soup, it works to enhance existing savory qualities; in the case of the chicken-flavored instant noodle soup, it works to create that experience.

An engaging exercise demonstrates how umami increases palatability. We copy this from the blog of Matthew Citriglia, who in turn credits the food writers David and Anna Kaspian.

Prepare the following solutions:

Sweet: 1 cup water with 2 teaspoon sugar
Salty: 1 cup water with 1 teaspoon salt
Sour: 1 cup water with 1/2 teaspoon cream of tartar which is tartaric acid
Bitter: 1/2 teaspoon unsweetened baking chocolate—do not mix with water rather chew and coat the mouth with it
Umami: 1 cup water with 1 tablespoon dried shiitake mushrooms—boil it and then let it cool

By tasting each solution individually you will be able to isolate each individual taste. Make sure you rinse your mouth thoroughly with plain water before tasting each new solution. Taste each solution multiple times to make sure your taste receptors understand their differences. Then taste each solution again but add a small amount of the Umami solution to it. Pay close attention and you will find that the salt and sweet solution become more intense while the sour and bitter sensation are muted or rounded. Remember[,] only add a small amount of the Umami solution, too much will distort the results.[50]

Fred tried this experiment and found that it worked. While he did not do any double-blind tests to rule out the power of suggestion, he did notice that the tastes with umami seemed more familiar. The sweet seemed more like soda pop and the sour tasted more like lemonade.

MSG, of course, has its critics. Some disparage it as an example of food industry bamboozlement. As one food science writer put it, MSG "tricks your tongue into making you think a certain food is high in protein and thus nutritious."[51] Others attack it as the source of Kwok's disease, popularly known as "Chinese restaurant syndrome" (CRS), a cluster of unpleasant sensations including burning, facial pressure, chest pain, and headache that was first described in 1969 in connection with the MSG used in Chinese restaurants.[52]

Some people are undoubtedly sensitive, if not allergic, to MSG, although the general population does not respond with CRS-like symptoms to moderate amounts.[53] Nonetheless, MSG continues to arouse health concerns. Some of these focus on the previously mentioned role of free glutamic acid as a neurotransmitter. One fear is that frequent ingestion of MSG, with its quick release of high levels of free glutamic acid, might overactivate receptors in various parts of the body. For instance, the pancreas might be stimulated to produce excessive amounts of insulin. This would stress the pancreas, contributing to diabetes; it would also result in a sudden drop of blood sugar, encouraging appetite and contributing to obesity.[54] Although none of these particular fears has been confirmed, MSG remains suspect for some, and not only among health-conscious Euro-Americans. According to a brief history of MSG published in *Gastronomica,* "the msg scare had special resonance in Japan" because MSG had been considered a world-class innovation combining Japanese science and traditional knowledge.[55]

The suspicions and alarms have been noted by those in the food industry, creating a demand for products and strategies to make ingredient lists appear less threatening. Thus, Savoury Systems International, the producer of "Savororganic," offers a line of certified organic yeast extracts that can help manufacturers who are having "trouble finding enhancers for [their] natural or organic products, or who just want to clean up [their] labels for the new healthy eating habits."[56] The flavor-enhancing organic yeast extracts would seem to be composed of free glutamates: MSG in another form, though minus the sodium and the possible stigma. (Yeast extracts are a major source of the hydrolyzed vegetable proteins used to approximate chicken and other meat flavors mentioned previously.)

Despite all of the commotion about MSG, Harold McGee, a well-regarded and oft-cited writer about food chemistry and cooking, seems to find the stigma against the substance misplaced. He writes, "Many studies later, toxicologists have concluded that MSG is a harmless ingredient for most people, even in large amounts. The most unfortunate aspect of the MSG saga is how it has been exploited to provide a cheap, one-dimensional substitute for real and remarkable foods."[57] We hasten to add that such a substitution would seem necessary in the formulation of a commodity as ubiquitous and quotidian as instant noodles.

OIL (ESPECIALLY PALM OIL)

Ando's technical breakthrough—of flash frying noodles in a bath of hot vegetable oil—renders them stable yet convenient to prepare; in addition, it gives them a characteristic and generally appreciated flavor.

Their taste and aroma—and the satisfying tactile sensation of the noo-dles in one's mouth—reflect both the frying and the considerable amount of oil that the noodles retain. After wheat (or wheat flour), vegetable oil is the principal ingredient in instant noodles, delivering calories in a generally appealing form.[58] Almost 20 percent of the weight and 40 percent of the calories in a package of instant noodles come from the oil retained after frying.[59] Indeed, because foods high in oils and fats—together known as lipids—are energy dense as well as meta-bolically essential, human beings are evolutionarily adapted to like them. (Oils and fats are conventionally distinguished by their melting points: oils are liquid and fats are solid at room temperature—usually designated as 20°C or 68°F.)

Energy-dense foods were important to early humans, given our ancestors' relatively large brains. Human brains are two and a half to three times larger relative to body size than those of other primates (who themselves have brains three times larger than other mammals). Maintaining large brains is expensive and places considerable metabolic demands on the body, and humans, therefore, consume diets that are denser in energy and nutrients than those of other primates of similar size.[60] As the physical anthropologist William Leonard put it: "For early *Homo*, acquiring more gray matter meant seeking out more of the energy-dense fare"—namely meat, especially fatty meat.[61] In fact, humans can digest fats and oils more easily than other primates because of their unique gastrointestinal tract.[62] This digestion was additionally facilitated by the discovery of cooking, which helped early humans to extract more nutrients from all of their foods.[63] Fats and oils are also of metabolic significance. Without them, fat-soluble vitamins, specifically A, D, and E, cannot be digested, absorbed, or transported. Nor could cell membranes, the nervous system, and the immune system operate without the fatty acids provided by consuming fats and oils—these are essential fatty acids that humans cannot make themselves. And some argue that specific receptors that register "fatty" (or "oily") exist in the mouth and in the gut.[64] (These mouth and gut receptors would function comparably to those for free glutamates.[65]) Although probably not a primary taste (responses seem too various to indicate hardwiring), fat does seem appealing to most people—especially when combined with other probable inputs, like sugar.

One of the reasons for instant noodles' worldwide appeal, therefore, is that they are fried in oil. Increasingly, the vegetable oil of choice by the food industry for frying is palm oil. Palm oil is relatively inexpensive, and unlike many other vegetable oils, it can be held continuously at a high temperature without deteriorating or igniting. In addition, its residue on fried products resists oxidation and hence contributes to longer shelf life. In short, palm oil is highly "saturated," and that it is naturally so has made it the heir apparent to oils that contain what have become the widely discredited "trans fats." Let us explain in some scientific detail.

Both oils and fats (again, lipids) are "triglycerides": their molecular composition is made up of a frame to which three fatty acids are attached. (One way to visualize this configuration would be to think of the letter *E* with the vertical line representing the backbone and the three horizontal lines representing the fatty acids.) These fatty acids are primarily chains of carbon atoms that vary in length—that is, in the number of linked carbon atoms—in different lipids. Carbon atoms have the capacity to make four bonds to other atoms. Not only is each carbon atom linked with its neighboring carbon atoms to form a chain; each is also linked with one or two hydrogen atoms (with the exception of the final carbon atom in the chain, which is linked with three hydrogen atoms). When each carbon atom is linked with two hydrogen atoms—one on each side of the chain—a fat or oil molecule is described as "saturated," meaning that it is unable to take up any more hydrogen. Moreover, because the carbon atoms are all filled up, the lipid cannot easily take up oxygen, a condition that prevents the rancidity caused by oxidation. In addition, under conditions of saturation, the fatty acid chains stretch out in a relatively straight fashion and therefore can pack tightly together. This process, known as "zippering," means that they may be solid at room temperature and stable when hot.[66] This is especially the case when zippered chains are long. Under these circumstances, considerable heat must be applied to energize the molecules sufficiently so that they can wiggle around freely and "unzip" themselves.

However, when only one hydrogen atom is linked to a particular carbon atom, that carbon atom has (as it were) an unused bond, which then can interact with the next carbon atom in the chain. In other words, what had been a single bond between carbon atoms in a chain becomes a double bond. Under these conditions, with only one hydrogen atom attached to the side, the fat or oil molecule is unsaturated: there is still potential room for another hydrogen atom as well as a point of vulnerability for an oxygen atom to disrupt the chain. With only one hydrogen atom on board, the carbon chain is no longer straight but develops a "kink" at the unsaturated carbon atoms. A monounsaturated fat or oil molecule has only one unsaturated carbon and only one

TABLE 1   LIPID COMPARISON

Lipid	Saturated fatty acids (%)	Monounsaturated fatty acids (%)	Polyunsaturated fatty acids (%)	Solidity at room temperature
Pork fat (lard)	40	45	11	solid
Soybean oil	14	23	58	liquid
Manufactured vegetable shortening	31	51	14	solid
Palm oil	49	37	9	semi-solid

kink; a polyunsaturated fat or oil molecule has more than one unsaturated carbon and more than one kink. The more kinks, the less zippering, resulting in more fluidity at room temperature and less stability at high temperature. That is, very little energy is necessary for the molecules to move freely—indeed, to vaporize.

Generally speaking, fats are derived from animal sources and oils from plant sources—though all are made up of a combination of saturated and unsaturated (both monounsaturated and polyunsaturated) fatty acids. The ratios of each (and, as mentioned, the length of the chain) affect how solid or how liquid the fat or oil is at room temperature and therefore how stable it is at high temperatures. See table 1 for four examples (with approximate percentages).

Different lipids have had important applications in the food industry, yielding at particular times the optimal combination of low price and heat stability. Lard, a solid and stable animal fat that is useful for frying and as a shortening in baking, was the commercial cooking fat of choice for many during the nineteenth century in Europe and America. Because of the increasing importance of lard and other animal fats in industrial processes including soap making, these came to be in short supply and vegetable-based substitutes were sought—ones that would be, like lard, solid and stable. Hydrogenation provided just these products by converting many of the unsaturated fatty acids in inexpensive vegetable oils into saturated (or more nearly saturated) ones. Adding hydrogen atoms so that increasing numbers of (if not all) carbon atoms in a fatty acid chain had two hydrogen atoms attached reduced (or eliminated) the "kinks" and thus enhanced the zippering. One of the resulting products was margarine. Another was the vegetable shortening Crisco, which is hydrogenated cottonseed oil. (The name "Crisco" is an acronym for "crystallized cottonseed oil.") Initially conceived as a substitute for lard in making soap, it was introduced in 1911 as a food suitable for frying and baking, and sales took off immediately: in 1912, 2.6 million pounds were sold; in 1916, 60 million pounds.[67]

These hydrogenated oils were seen as examples of how science could provide foods that improved everyday lives. They came to be regarded not just as less expensive substitutes for animal fats but as improvements over them. And, as saturated animal fats became implicated during the 1960s in cardiovascular illnesses, hydrogenated oils—which were by then mostly the relatively inexpensive soybean oil—looked even better. The hydrogenation of oils, though, creates molecular configurations rarely seen in nature. Some of the molecules in a fatty chain remain unsaturated (with some carbon atoms still attached to a single hydrogen atom). Moreover, the bond between an unsaturated carbon atom and its neighbor is changed in configuration so that the kink becomes less extreme—the chain becomes flattened. The result of this change in configuration is a nonsaturated fat that behaves (by virtue of its flattening) like a saturated fat. This fat's special bond is in the trans fat configuration. Trans fats do not affect the stability of the hydrogenated oil. (In certain ways they enhance that stability.) Yet, as has become well known in recent years, trans fats and the hydrogenation process that gives rise to them raise serious health issues. Because they, too, are linked to the development of heart disease, food manufactures are increasingly required by many countries to list trans fats on their labels if not to eliminate them from their products.

However, substituting palm oil for hydrogenated oils also raises the question of the healthfulness of palm oil, given that it is more saturated than lard. Opinions differ, and these disagreements have significant economic implications. Many studies, including those supported by largely Malaysian and Indonesian palm oil interests, seek to offset the negative view of palm oil, which they see as a reflection of U.S. soybean interests. (Malaysia and Indonesia provide 85 percent of the world's palm oil supply and the United States provides 21 percent of the world's soybean oil supply.[68]) These studies seek to demonstrate that palm oil has a positive effect on health-relevant cholesterol readings. Studies comparing olive oil, sunflower seed oil, fish oil, and palm oil have found that palm oil may have a neutral or even positive effect on an individual's serum lipid profile (on a par with that of olive oil) because the greater saturation of palm oil is offset by the presence of various antioxidants, including vitamin E.[69] At the very least, there may be a fallback claim that palm oil is more healthful than hydrogenated vegetable oils with their trans fats.[70]

Yet counterclaims abound. Studies suggesting that palm oil is healthful have been challenged because the subject population in many of these studies—young, healthy, thin males—is seen as atypical of a larger population. Claims that palm oil provides a useful boost of antioxidants have in addition been met by arguments that, beyond a certain point, these antioxidants provide few benefits and most ordinary diets do not require any supplementation.[71] A long-term Costa Rica–based epidemiological study of middle-aged men and women concluded that those who habitually consumed palm oil and those who consumed hydrogenated soybean oil (with its high trans fat content) were equally likely to have heart attacks, and that those who consumed palm oil rather than nonhydrogenated soybean oil were significantly *more* likely to have heart attacks.[72] These findings appear consistent with other findings. One U.S.-funded and -based study, for instance, evaluated the health implications of consuming palm oil compared with the effects of consuming partially hydrogenated soybean oil and oils high in monounsaturated fatty acids (canola oil) or polyunsaturated fatty acids (soybean oil). The conclusion was that, relative to canola and soybean oils, palm oil and hydrogenated soybean oil have an equally adverse effect on serum cholesterol measures.[73] Another study considered the effects of an intervention on the island of Mauritius, where the government switched from subsidizing palm oil to subsidizing soybean oil in response to high rates of heart disease. Two evaluations reported similar results: one research group led by K. Srinith Reddy, a physician, and another led by Ulla Uusitalo, a nutritionist, reported significant reductions of 15 percent in serum cholesterol concentrations.[74]

Despite this disagreement, and despite the detrimental social and environmental effects in tropical countries of increasing acreage devoted to oil palm plantations, a topic to which we will return, palm oil has not only become the world's most popular cooking oil but also represents the fastest growing market compared to the various vegetable oils available (including peanut, corn, cottonseed, canola, coconut, olive, and soybean).[75] Since it is naturally saturated, it meets the largely Euro-American concerns about trans fats and holds a clear edge in European markets over its primary rival, soybean oil (including in its nonhydrogenated form). Most soybeans grown in the United States—the world's dominant producer—have been genetically modified, so they and products made from them, including their oil, are subject to significant European Union restrictions.[76] In addition, palm oil is already well accepted by billions of people in most of the world, including in Asia, South Asia, and Southeast Asia. It has become almost as commonplace as the instant noodles to which it contributes taste.[77]

SUGAR

Although sugar is not a listed ingredient in the Maggi chicken-flavored noodles sold in Papua New Guinea, it is a significant ingredient in the flavor packets of many other instant noodles. As Harold McGee suggests, "All human beings share an innate liking for its sweetness, which we first experience in mother's milk (as lactose), and which is the taste of energy that fuels all life."[78] Other scientists have hypothesized that the human capacity to recognize the sweet taste is an evolved trait connected to the body's need for glucose as its main source of energy.[79] Moreover, because sweet things are rarely poisonous, there was no evolutionary need for fine-grained distinctions between types of sweetness. Thus, humans have one "low-affinity" receptor for a large number of different sweet compounds (including many nonsugar substitutes); in contrast, by virtue of many "high-affinity" receptors, humans are able to discriminate among a large number of bitter and possibly dangerous compounds.[80] Simply put, sugars of different kinds (including sucrose, dextrose, fructose, lactose, and galactose) are all indiscriminately appealing. In fact, according to the anthropologist Sidney Mintz, "No society rejects sweetness as unpleasant" and "Sweet tastes have a privileged position in contrast to the more variable attitudes toward sour, salty, and bitter tastes." He continues: "Sweet-tasting substances . . . appear to insinuate themselves much more quickly into the preferences of new consumers. The bitter substances are 'bitter specific'—liking watercress has nothing to do with liking eggplant, for instance. But, in contrast, liking sucrose seems to be 'sweet-general.' Added to bitter substances, sugar makes them all taste alike, at least insofar as it makes them all taste sweet."[81]

It should be noted that sugar is more than good tasting. In its refined form it is remarkably versatile in its culinary applications. No longer the food of kings and aristocrats—spurring breathtaking and novel confections marking the sumptuous excesses of an elite—sugar has become readily and cheaply available for more routine creations of contemporary kitchens and factories. As a substrate for fermentation, a browning agent, a preservative, a texture enhancer, a flavor booster, and an agent that masks other, less pleasant tastes, sugar (including high-fructose corn syrup) is central to our industrially based food system.

One might suggest, however, that sugar—with its obvious link to obesity and diabetes—is too likable, appearing (often in hidden form) in a range of products including cereal, pizza, hot dogs, and peanut butter. The annual per capita consumption in the United States of caloric sweeteners (mainly table sugar from cane and beets and high-fructose corn syrup) increased by forty-three pounds, or 39 percent, between 1950 and 2000. Although there is no RDA for sugar (and some experts believe that we need no refined sugar at all), the U.S. Department of Agriculture (USDA) recommends that the average person on a two-thousand-calorie diet consume no more than forty grams of "added" sugar—about ten teaspoons, or the amount in one twelve-ounce soft drink. However, in 2000 the USDA reported per capita consumption at thirty-two teaspoons of added sugar per day, including the amount taken in from processed foods and drinks.[82]

If the amount of sodium, saturated fats, and—for some—MSG in instant noodles creates unease, if not alarm, the amount of refined sugar appears relatively innocuous. Included in quantities of rarely more than a gram in a flavor packet, sugar might be expected to add a pleasant taste and perhaps mask an unpleasant one. We wonder, though, if sugar's sweet taste might work to enhance other tastes in instant noodles—especially salty or greasy ones. After all, like MSG, sugar seems to pair well with salt, as in many snack foods, and with fats and oils, as with chicken fried in a sugary batter or a burger washed down with a soft drink. When all are combined, such foods are hard to resist.

SOUP AND SATIETY

Finally, we note that instant noodles not only taste (relatively) good going down. They also feel good once they are down—and continue to do so for a substantial time. This satiety factor is a function of their surprisingly low glycemic index. The higher the glycemic index (on a scale of one hundred, with some foods exceeding one hundred), the faster the breakdown of carbohydrates into sugars and the quicker the release of sugars into the bloodstream (and correspondingly, the greater the demands for insulin in metabolizing these sugars). A low glycemic index is less than fifty-five, and that of instant noodles is about fifty.

Although the refined wheat in instant noodles has a relatively high glycemic index of seventy (about that of white rice), this value (as well as any contribution by sugar) is offset by the addition of saturated fat in the form of oil (again, usually palm oil) to the noodles. Large amounts of fat in foods tend to slow the rate at which the stomach empties itself and therefore the rate at which foods are digested.[83] Therefore, the energy provided by instant noodles does not lead to a blood sugar spike and the subsequent crash. After eating them, one feels satisfied.

In addition, the delivery of this energy in the form of a soup seems to contribute to satiation. In an American study of thirty-one men and women in their midtwenties, the nutritionist Richard Mattes compared their responses to the ingestion of chicken breast (among other foods) served either as a solid meal or as blended into a soup. He found that both equally satisfied the hunger of his subjects, though as measured by their subsequent ingestion of calories over the day, the soup led to a longer period of satiety.[84] Mattes attributes this difference to cognitive factors, including the sense of ease that soup (notoriously a comfort food) provides.

In short, Ando's product didn't miss much. Certainly, it seems to have met his original objectives. Hitting basic hardwired gustatory and olfactory spots, his noodles are tasty and palatable. Thanks to the principle of tempura, they are dehydrated and shelf stable while easily prepared through rehydration. Produced through relatively straightforward industrial procedures using readily available and inexpensive ingredients, they are widely affordable. Finally, as we have seen in our discussion of their ingredients, they are (as industrial foods go) safe in reasonable amounts, sanitary, and fit for human consumption. Not subtle, yet effective, they might be regarded as a paradigmatic form of capitalist mass provisioning. They let people get on with whatever jobs they have at hand in a great many different social and cultural contexts.

2

Japanese Instant Noodles in the Market and on the Mind

Nowhere has Ando's invention received more notice than in its country of origin. In Japan, instant noodles have not only been acclaimed in museums and voted the most important Japanese invention of the twentieth century; they have also been most elaborated in product development and merchandising for an ever more competitive market. In addition, they have been explicitly linked, for better or worse, to significant changes in postwar everyday life. We begin the Japanese portion of our noodle narratives by considering their best-known enthusiast, Ton Tan Tin, whose life, times, and engagement with instant noodles exemplify many of the larger social, cultural, and economic processes affecting his countrymen.

Ton Tan Tin (actually Toshio Yamamoto) is a product designer in an unnamed Japanese corporation. At the time of this writing, he has reviewed 5,008 varieties of instant noodles (including packets, cups, and bowls) that he has eaten around the world, rating each from one to five. In his book *Sokusekimensaikuropedia* (Instant noodle encyclopedia), he describes the first 1,046 varieties he considered and provides images of their colorful packaging.[1] Characterizing himself as a "noodle maniac" in his online "ramen noodle diary," he has posted hundreds of video reviews on YouTube.[2] The most popular posting, in the six years it has been available, has been viewed 150,321 times. Following a relatively standard format, these videos feature Ton Tan Tin's hands preparing instant noodles and his voice describing and evaluating the noodles' characteristics. To background music, he first shows the front and back of the package and conveys basic information: review number, manufacturer, product name, country of origin, purchase price, calories, weight, and amount of sodium. Next he opens the package and displays the noodles and the accompanying flavor sachet(s) along with information about the noodles (usually fried) and flavor sachet(s) (generally powdered soup with occasional additions, such as oil and freeze-dried toppings). He cooks the noodles as the package advises while relating cooking time, pours them into a bowl, gives them a stir with chopsticks, and lifts some up for scrutiny. Providing running commentary, he concludes with his evaluation and rating.

Here, in translation from Japanese, with minor changes to punctuation, are three examples:

1) No. 4049. HD Nissin (USA) Choice Ramen, Savory Herb Chicken Flavor from Nissin Foods, USA.

Purchase price: unknown; Energy: 280 kcal; Weight: 80 g; Sodium: 780 mg
Noodle: non-fried; ingredients: powdered soup
Cooking time: 3 minutes

The powdered soup is combined with a non-fried noodle. The noodle is angular and flat, and its texture is sharp, but somewhat too "mechanical." I'd prefer to have some more stickiness in the noodle. The soup is dried and not oily so it's not especially strengthening. The taste is also too simple. However, the black pepper is quite spicy [positive remark]. There's no particular uniqueness in the taste. It would be better to have it as a health food. Rating: 1.5.

2) No. 4402. Nestlé (Malaysia) Maggi 2 Minute Noodle, Assam Laksa Flavor (HALAL).

Purchase price: ¥80; Energy: 349 kcal; Weight: 78 g; Sodium: n/a
Noodle: fried; ingredients: powdered soup
Cooking time: 2 minutes

The powdered soup is combined with a fried noodle. The noodle is thin and its surface is rough, and it smells somewhat cheap. It can be cooked well within two minutes and does not absorb too much of the water [that is, its texture is not completely lost]. The soup has a strong acidity and is spicy, though the umami is not strong enough. Its taste is either like Tom Yum flavor or Tomato flavor (or somewhere in the middle). This is not a taste familiar to Japanese people, and I guess it would be hard for them to accept it. Rating: 1.5.

3) No. 4407. CG Foods (Nepal) Chaudhary's WaiWai, Vegetable Masala Flavor

Purchase price: $3.00; Energy: 375 kcal; Weight: 75 g; Sodium: 950 mg
Noodle: fried; ingredients: powdered soup, oil, chili powder
Cooking time: 3 minutes

The powdered soup, seasoning, and chili powder are combined with a fried noodle. The noodle is sharply edged and its texture is rough, yet it has a presence. The noodle is small in size. A lot of spices used for making curry are used for the soup and it is more appealing than expected. The soup has a moderate hotness and a slight sourness. It's a vegetarian noodle, but we don't feel the usual dissatisfaction [when eating vegetarian instant noodles]. You can enjoy this. We cannot underestimate it. Rating: 2.0.

Tatsuro first alerted Deborah and Fred to this Japanese "noodle maniac." A further introduction emerged from a conversation about our noodle project with the anthropologist Noburo Ishigawa. He subsequently sent Deborah Ton Tan Tin's YouTube web address with this comment: "You would be laughing out loud, if somebody translates what he is commenting on. So serious! Hope you enjoy the Japanese *otaku* fetish culture!"[3]

This *otaku* culture grew up during the 1980s around aficionados of Japanese *manga*—cartoons, comic books, and animated films. The anthropologist Sharon Kinsella explains that "the original meaning of *otaku* is 'your home' and by association, 'you,' 'yours' and 'home.'" It is a "witty reference" to someone who is not accustomed to close friendships, spends most of his or her time alone, and communicates with peers indirectly.[4] An *otaku*, as the anthropologist Ian Condry elaborates, is a loner: an "obsessive, socially inept, technologically fluent nerd."[5] In 1989, the term acquired a dark connotation after a twenty-six-year-old printers' assistant who collected girl-focused *manga* murdered and mutilated four small girls. His trial provoked something of a moral panic as many Japanese feared that unsociable *otaku* youth "were multiplying and threatening to take over the whole of society." At about the same time, however, positive interpretations of the *otaku* generation as "cool" were produced by "sections of the media, by self-appointed representatives of animation and computer subcultures."[6]

The science fiction writer William Gibson, who coined the term "cyberspace," clarifies such cool *otaku* for English speakers as "the passionate obsessive, the information age's embodiment of the connoisseur, more concerned with the accumulation of data than of objects. . . . Understanding otaku-hood . . . is one of the keys to understanding the culture of the web. There is something profoundly post-national about it, extra-geographic. . . . There is a . . . fascination with detail, with cataloguing, with distinguishing one thing from another."[7] Ton Tan Tin's compulsion to sample, celebrate, and catalogue the world's array of instant noodles, using the language of connoisseurship (apparently derived from wine commentary), fits this profile. So does his description of the epiphany leading to his obsession, to his "awakening to instant noodles." In translation from Japanese:

> I was born a few years after Chicken Ramen was first marketed [by the Nissin Corporation], so when I was a child, instant noodles were already common, and I remember seeing many different products as a small child. In about the fifth grade, I could cook packages of instant ramen [by myself]. . . . From the seventh grade, I had Cup Noodles every night as I studied for exams. . . .
>
> When I became a college student and got my driver's license, I began getting away from my hometown, driving my parents' car, and my horizon became much wider. . . . [In] 1982, my friends and I decided to go see the Sea of Japan. . . . We were hungry [when we arrived] . . . and in the corner of a shop I saw varieties of packaged instant noodles that I had never seen before. . . . I was struck as if by lightning, and all my sleepiness vanished. . . . Until then, I firmly believed that instant noodles were the same anywhere in the country. . . . I thought I knew a lot about instant noodles. The world was not that simple, though. . . .
>
> I began to visit as many supermarkets, liquor stores, and convenience stores as I could when traveling to check out if there were strange kinds of instant noodles. It became my habit—or rather, it became the greatest joy and main purpose of my travel. . . . [Once] I hurried into a large supermarket [that] was filled with products . . . that I never heard of. . . . Indeed, it looked like a shining gold mine. Immediately, I rushed toward the gold mine like a hungry beast, and threw them all into my basket. Oh, what a feeling of accomplishment! (To be so fulfilled by shopping for things that cost only about a hundred yen each—I feel I have a very economical hobby.)
>
> For this reason, I have begun to shift my focus overseas. In foreign countries, there are still many chances of surprise and excitement.[8]

That Ton Tan Tin could become a connoisseur of instant noodles invites further discussion. Why are there so many varieties of instant noodles in Japan (and beyond) and why are they of interest to an *otaku?* As we shall see, his noodle-focused autobiographical vignettes—portraying as they do a young man who is just semicompetent in the kitchen, although hard working, bound for college, and eventually granted use of the parental car for trips of pleasure and exploration—mirror broad, interrelated sociohistorical processes in postwar Japan. These include the creation of a middle class with its increasing educational opportunities and expectations, the revision of gender arrangements, the reformulation of domestic spaces, as well as the development of a flourishing consumer culture and sense of general, if short-lived, affluence in the 1980s. In addition, these sociohistorical processes reflect a shift in Japan's position in the world from, as the anthropologist Anne Allison describes it,

"Japan Inc. to J-cool"—from Japan as industrial superpower to Japan as global style setter.[9] To be sure, relatively few Japanese become *otaku* of anything, much less of instant noodles. Yet Ton Tan Tin's obsession can be read as an index of his time, as instant noodles have come to provision Japanese, not only of "Inc." but also of "cool."

INSTANT NOODLES IN SHŌWA JAPAN

Momofuku Ando was born in 1910 and therefore preceded the "single-digit Shōwan" age cohort, which comprises those born between 1926 and 1934, during the first nine years of the reign of the Shōwa emperor, Hirohito (whose era ran from December 25, 1926, to January 7, 1989). Ando's successes, though, depended in many ways on the society that members of this cohort exemplified and promoted. As the anthropologist William Kelly explains, these were people whose childhood and youth spanned the Depression and World War II.

This generation was old enough to have suffered but young enough not to have inflicted suffering. It managed the psychological divide and social chaos in the war's aftermath, becoming the bedrock of postwar recovery and boom. In the early postwar decades, the single-digit Shōwans became, in the popular imagination, "the 'workaholic company men' and the 'education mamas' whose selfless efforts on behalf of corporation and children ensured present and future prosperity."[10]

As adults, they experienced an era of postwar recovery and modernization. With the fading of important prewar socioeconomic distinctions, postwar Shōwa Japan seemed more equitable and homogenous. By the late 1960s, 90 percent of Japanese placed themselves in the middle stratum (whether lower-middle, middle-middle, or upper-middle class) on the government's annual "People's Lifestyle" survey. The popular recognition of this sense of socioeconomic convergence is conveyed by the term *churyu*, which is often translated as "middle class," although Kelly suggests that a more accurate rendering would be "mainstream."[11]

A standard educational curriculum helped equalize social differences, including those between rural and urban dwellers. In addition, farm mechanization—plus an improved rail and road system—allowed many rural Japanese to combine work in the agricultural sector with that in the thriving manufacturing and service sectors. Moreover, many rural people gave up farming entirely, joining both white-collar and blue-collar workers in increasingly available government-subsidized housing surrounding regional centers as well as major cities. Suburban growth was rapid from the 1960s through the 1980s, as "huge apartment blocks . . . sprouted up in what had been rice or vegetable fields."[12] And single-family homes for the more successful spilled out of major cities in all directions.

At the same time, age at marriage was rising and families were becoming smaller. During the 1960s and 1970s, the proportion of extended families in the general population decreased from one-third to one-fifth. By 1975, two-thirds of all families were nuclear. Even in three-generation households, middle-generation members began to demand nuclear family–focused subunits within the home and nuclear family–focused vacations in the nuclear family–owned car.[13] In addition, the number of single-member households, typically of young unmarried workers living in company dormitories or apartments, rose from 3 percent in 1955 to 14 percent by 1975. Reflecting these widespread "modernist" shifts were reconfigurations of suburban and urban domestic space, especially in the newer housing: the dining and kitchen areas were combined and separated from the sleeping area, chairs and tables replaced floor-level seating, and children often had their own bedrooms.[14]

Much else was also happening: companionate "love" marriages were normalized; "workaholic" husbands (the ones often referred to as "salarymen") learned to accept supplemental money from working wives; modern conveniences, including televisions, cars, and labor-saving devices (the first usually a rice cooker) were coveted and acquired; "education mamas" devoted themselves to ensuring that children succeeded in school; national health insurance encouraged citizens to utilize a biomedically based health system, with hospitals becoming almost universal sites for birth and death; and the past was reworked as nostalgic appreciation of regional traditions.[15] To be sure, not all Japanese could fully achieve the material and social lifestyle that defined modernist Shōwa, though many remained mainstream in their aspirations for it.[16] This despite the fact that the rapid industrially based economic growth upon which this lifestyle depended had implications that provoked anxieties about what was gained and what was lost—including what was gained and lost in eating modernist foods like instant noodles.

Tatsuro had arranged for all of us to visit a museum that focused on the emergence of the Japanese mainstream: the "corporate museum" of the Ajinomoto Company.[17] Now specializing in the production of amino acids, Ajinomoto first marketed MSG in 1909 and regards itself as a longtime leader in modernizing important aspects of domestic life.

The museum lies within the headquarters of the Ajinomoto Foundation for Dietary Culture, dedicated (according to the English version of the foundation's guide) to "furthering development in the sphere of public welfare" as it pertains to food. We were met by Yuji Iida, secretary-general of the foundation, and after we exchanged business cards and requisite bows, he took us through the building, emphasizing throughout that the company, although modern and successful, is grounded in traditional Japanese values. The lobby, for instance, displays five large characters (each about six feet high) made by Soun Takeda, one of the most popular calligraphers in contemporary Japan, drawn during Ajinomoto's celebration of its hundredth anniversary. The first two characters stand for "health"; the third, for "food"; and the last two, for "gratefulness."

Just outside and visible through large windows are an impressive waterfall, carp-filled pools, a teahouse (named "one flower" after the last poem of the monk Dharma, who lived twenty-eight generations after Buddha), and three millstones used in the original production of MSG.

After visiting a display of woodblock prints from the Edo period (1603–1868) concerning Japanese foodways, we watched a six-minute introductory video in English about the discovery of umami and the founding of the company. Next was the museum proper, where much of the information was presented in both Japanese and English. The pamphlet explained that the museum is divided into "four eras spanning the period from 1900 to the present." It also explained that "exhibits evoke the spirit that has guided the Ajinomoto Group as it has developed, constantly in pursuit of better meals and lifestyles, hand in hand with people and their daily lives." The first set of displays concerns changing patterns of domestic life. We saw an old-fashioned dining area (circa 1925) arranged around a small, low table. Iida encouraged us to sit at the table to make the point that it was small because Japanese were small at that time. We eventually saw four different kitchens and, along the way, learned of corresponding developments within the company.[18]

The most interesting kitchen for our purposes, focusing as we are on the Shōwa period and the emergence in Japan of nuclear families, is from the early 1960s. Tatsuro recognized this kitchen from his childhood, when he lived with his "single-digit Shōwa" parents in their government-subsidized apartment.

This kitchen is displayed under the heading of "The Dining Kitchen and the Popularization of Western Food" and the subheading of "The

FIGURE 2. *(top)* Health, food, gratefulness: calligraphy in the Ajinomoto Foundation lobby. Photograph by Tatsuro Fujikura.

FIGURE 3. *(bottom)* The Ajinomoto garden. Photograph by Tatsuro Fujikura.

Rationalization of Food and Lifestyles." The English caption reads: "In 1966, housing developments constructed by the Japanese Housing Corporation achieved the division of dining and sleeping spaces by incorporating dining-kitchen areas. Evoking images of an abundant American lifestyle, the dining-kitchen was rapidly embraced and meals were moved from the tea table to the dining table. Kitchens featured electric rice cookers, refrigerators, and other electric appliances,

FIGURE 4. A Shōwa kitchen from the 1960s, part of a display at the Ajinomoto Museum. Photograph by Tatsuro Fujikura.

enabling housewives to save a great deal of time.[19] Instant, frozen, and retort-packed [pre-cooked, sealed, and shelf-stable] foods appeared in rapid succession, greatly simplifying the task of preparing meals."

Many of these new instant, frozen, and retort-packed foods used MSG as a flavoring—including instant noodles. Iida clarified that these new products were not valued simply because they were convenient and tasty; they were appreciated because they were modern.[20] This was also the emphatic opinion of Professor Akira Adachi, an anthropologist at Kyoto University, with whom we had earlier discussed instant noodles. He stressed that for many in Japan, instant noodles were part of the "developing process." Here is a close-to-verbatim excerpt from Deborah's notes:

For Japanese in the [late] 1950s they were a symbol of modernity. When packets of instant ramen first became available, they were amazing. You would put the ramen in a Chinese [ceramic] bowl, just add hot water, cover the bowl with a plate, and wait three minutes. You couldn't even wait that long so you picked it up after two. And there was noodle soup. Wow! We were in a bad way then but instant noodles made us feel we were technologically progressing. It had everything we were familiar with: MSG, salt, spices. Japan was in a bad situation and ramen made us feel we were taking off. There were lots of instant things coming on to the market—instant cameras for example, and instant juice [powdered juice] which you put in water and it bubbles. I felt excitement that Japan was on the way up because it had instant things.[21]

Small wonder, then, that the Ajinomoto Company recognized a good thing in Ando's MSG-enhanced instant noodles. Indeed, Ajinomoto acted as their initial distributor in the United States. Ando, in turn, had high praise for his counterpart at Ajinomoto: "In the summer of 1960, Mr. Saburosuke Suzuki, Chairman of Ajinomoto, showed up one day at [Ando's new plant] . . . . He looked curiously at the production equipment and said, 'I'm sure there will be a huge market for this product.' He was friendly and passionate about business. Wanting to know more about instant noodles, he visited the plant many times. I think Mr. Suzuki was the first person in the food industry to recognize the future potential of instant noodles. He is one of the entrepreneurs that I greatly respect."[22] Characterizing the importance of such food-focused entrepreneurship, the historian George Solt argues that "particularly in Japan, instant ramen, curry cubes, instant coffee, and frozen foods fundamentally altered eating habits," leading to an obsolescence of inherited cooking knowledge that further opened the door to the food industry.[23]

As Ando states about the instant noodle company he founded, "Nissin was a child of the times."[24] It was both product and producer of the era. His invention both articulated with and contributed to the emergence of mainstream consciousness—a modernist point of view fostered by relatively full employment, rising income, and uniformity in consumption patterns. His invention also addressed—shaped, gratified, and assuaged—the specific and shifting forms that modernist needs and aspirations, as well as modernist anxieties and regrets, were to take. Thus, Nissin, and instant noodles more broadly, fit with and could move adroitly with the times.

Ando's decision to make his instant noodles with wheat flour proved strategic. Japanese were already acquainted with wheat noodles, and after World War II Japan was flooded with inexpensive wheat imported from the United States.[25] Moreover, not only could his noodles be presented as reasonably familiar yet wonderfully modernist, they additionally could be promoted as especially wholesome—as the kind of food that should feature more centrally in the Japanese diet. Nissin's advertising sought to exploit postwar anxieties that the traditional Japanese diet was less healthful than the American one by featuring images of American-like children. One early advertisement described by Solt depicted "Chibbiko," a "healthy, happy, and mischievous child," who was "the image of health itself" and looked conspicuously like an American kid with "blonde hair, freckles and a baseball cap." These anxieties were fostered in articulation with U.S. postwar interests in finding a market for surplus commodities while transforming a defeated and impoverished enemy into an ally with a strong workforce.[26] In fact, both the U.S. and the Japanese government began to advocate the consumption of wheat over rice—as well as meat over fish, and dairy over soy—all to grow bigger Japanese citizens (who presumably could no longer sit comfortably around a small tea table).[27]

As Ando's invention caught on, Nissin faced growing competition from other Japanese firms. Nissin had patented instant noodles, and for a time it defended its patent through litigation and licensing fees. However, these efforts had limited success and were abandoned in 1964, with Nissin maintaining its domination in an open market. Sales of all brands of packaged instant noodles for the domestic market soon rose dramatically, from 13 million in 1969 to 2.35 billion at the end of the Shōwa period in 1989. Beginning with Nissin's introduction of its Cup Noodle in 1972, sales of cup noodles for the domestic market rose from 4 million to 2.20 billion in 1989. Hence, by the end of the Shōwa period, 4.55 billion servings of instant noodles—package and cup—were being sold in Japan each year. Correspondingly, per capita consumption climbed from negligible to about 37 packages and cups annually.[28]

In driving up its sales, Nissin especially targeted unmarried men, young housewives, children, and students. These constituted the market segments most affected by the shift in postwar ways of life: for instance, by the nuclearization of formerly three-generation families, the alteration of domestic spaces with more convenient kitchens, and the educational reforms. Simply put, people in these segments were likely to seek out instant noodles to provide, either for themselves or others, quick snacks and light meals. Although Nissin recognized the elderly, especially those forced to provide for themselves, as a significant market segment, it decided not to target them directly, to avoid suggesting that they lacked family support.

Not surprisingly, the growth in the consumption of instant noodles, attendant as it was on broad social transformations, was not without controversy. While many undoubtedly agreed with Adachi concerning the "wow" that instant noodles (and other modernist products) conveyed, others were more ambivalent about rapidly shifting lifeways, including shifting foodways. For these people, the very attributes that led to the success of instant noodles—that they were tasty, convenient, cheap, and industrially produced—made them suspect. Indeed, instant noodles became, on occasion, a contentious typification of an era, and the "wow" was periodically offset by "woe" or "whoa."

Of those targeted by Nissin, unmarried men were the least controversial market for easy-to-prepare foods. Many of them lived in single-member households where it was assumed that they would not cook much. These arrangements were to be temporary, and these men could look forward to more varied and elaborate provisions once they were married.[29] Matters were less straightforward for young housewives, in part because they were implicated in the feeding of others—including their children, as prospective "Chibbikos" and as older students, and their own and their husband's parents, as elderly dependents. Though living with modern "dining kitchens" and increasingly entering the labor force to earn important supplemental incomes, these women were still influenced by the traditional injunction that they be good wives and wise mothers.[30] Such an injunction charged them with multiple and sometimes conflicting obligations. They were expected to earn money and, at the end of day, to provide "mother's cooking" (perhaps augmented by dashes of MSG) for their tired "salarymen" husbands. In addition, they had to provide a real meal for their academically serious schoolchildren—regardless of whatever earlier snack those children might have had. Furthermore, this cooking was to be both Japanese—providing "the taste of mother's miso soup," as a "tearjerker" popular song described by the anthropologist Merry White put it—and Japanese-modern, as augmented by wheat, meat, and dairy.[31] To be sure, as suggested by Ton Tan Tin's account, their children, home after school or before an evening of studying, could be satisfied with a serving of instant noodles or manage a snack on their own, and their elderly dependents could get by, at least periodically, on instant noodles. But was this what should be happening?

Modernist lives, especially for young housewives, became even more complicated in the wake of food scandals. Roughly coinciding with the revelation that mercury dumped into Minamata Bay by a petrochemical company had devastated the health of consumers of local seafood, the Morinaga milk incident of 1955 provided a well-publicized threat to public health.[32] As Professors Kichiro Shoji and Masuro Sugai make clear, the incident was particularly disconcerting because milk consumption, especially by children, had been so strongly encouraged.[33] Milk had not been a particular feature of the Japanese diet until the U.S. occupation authority, as part of a dairy-focused initiative to improve children's health, began to deliver canned and powdered milk through the United Nations Children's Fund and to provide powdered milk in school lunches.[34] Then, in 1949, the Japanese Ministry of Health and Welfare and *Yomiuri Shimbun,* a national newspaper, launched a "National Baby Contest" to select the "healthiest" one-year-old boy and girl babies; this had the effect of discouraging nursing, because it was believed that bottle-feeding with infant formula enhanced health— that it reduced infant mortality.[35] The transition from breast-feeding to bottle-feeding was additionally encouraged by the increasing entry of women into the workforce after the war.[36] Eventually, demand became so great that imported milk was replaced by domestically produced milk. The commitment to bottle-feeding continued, further encouraged by the Morinaga Milk Company, a respected purveyor of milk products, including infant formula, which in 1951 sponsored its own contest for the "healthiest" eight-month-old infants.[37]

Yet, beginning in June 1955, infants in western Japan were falling ill with serious gastrointestinal symptoms and a darkening of their skin. Eventually, 12,000 were affected and 138 died. All had been regularly fed with Morinaga milk formula. Investigation revealed that Morinaga had cut its production costs by replacing a pharmaceutical-grade milk stabilizer with an industrial-grade stabilizer that proved to be tainted with arsenic.[38] The shocking violation of public trust triggered a major revision of the Japanese Food Safety Law in 1957 and the development of campaigns calling for the production of "safe" and "no chemical" foods.[39]

Despite the food-focused controversies of their time, instant noodles did, in the end, pass muster. In 1960 Nissin achieved government certification to market its initial product—"Chikin Ramen"—as "a special health food" enriched with B vitamins.[40] One of the first Nissin television advertisements in 1963 depicted a young mother in a high-quality kimono (perhaps an "education mama") giggling with her son and holding up a package of instant noodles while the word *lysine* (an amino acid and protein supplement, likely supplied by the Ajinomoto Company) flashed across the screen.[41]

Instant noodles enjoyed their greatest increase in domestic per capita consumption between 1963 and 1964—from 10.5 to 20.8 servings annually. Coinciding with the staging of the 1964 Tokyo Olympics, this surge may have reflected a form of food nationalism.[42] It also likely reflected the fact that instant noodles were understood as a snack or light meal, as a supplemental rather than fundamental source of sustenance (and certainly not a baby food, at least not in Japan). Few continued to grant instant noodles the status of a health food, largely because of the numerous additives and high levels of sodium they contained; however, they avoided the notoriety of food-focused scandal.[43] Moreover, though created in postwar Shōwa Japan at a period of rapid recovery and economic expansion, they have remained popular provisions during a very different era: that of the Heisei period, which began in 1990 with the "burst" of the economic "bubble" and the precipitous and still-ongoing recession. Sales of instant ramen in Japan did eventually reach a plateau; even so, they were never to fall significantly. Whether in package or cup form, instant noodles seemed to hold their appeal, even when cracks appeared in the mainstream consensus.

BEYOND SHŌWA WITH INSTANT NOODLES

The Momofuku Ando Instant Ramen Museum in the Osaka suburb of Ikeda (where instant noodles were invented) presents Nissin's own noodle narrative about the development of its product and brand over the Shōwa and Heisei periods. Carefully crafted, pleasant, innocuous, and with free admission, the museum provides a palatable account for those favoring a palatable snack with displays celebrating a product that has adapted well across a period of significant change—even in Japan, with its easy availability of "real" ramen. The museum opened in 1999: nine years after the bubble burst; fourteen years after Koki Ando, Momofuku Ando's son, became Nissin's president (in 1985); and eight years before Momofuku Ando died (in 2007, at age ninety-six). Founded with Momofuku Ando's money as part of his contribution to Japanese society and dedicated to Momofuku Ando as "founder," the museum renovated its building and doubled its exhibits during 2004, attracting 540,000 visitors in 2010.[44] Some of the museum's displays are keyed to themes in Ando's autobiography that stress his singular accomplishments. Other displays reflect the corporate challenges that Nissin faced—and faces—under the leadership of Koki Ando in a more contemporary Japan.

Allison helps explain the differences between the Japan of the elder and younger Ando. In the early 1990s, companies responded to the "economic recession brought on by the bursting bubble of the Bubble economy" by downsizing, restructuring, or closing; the result was widespread "precarity."[45] This socioeconomic instability contributed to what Kelly and White describe as a serious fragmentation in the mainstream consciousness of Shōwa Japan. As the confident Japan of the late 1980s faltered, social actors whose experiences ran contrary to middle-class assumptions became increasingly visible and prominent.[46] These included "students," who were unable to enter the best schools; "slackers," who were unable to find full-time employment; "singles," who were unwilling to become good wives and wise mothers; "seniors," who were unable to count on family support; and "strangers," who were unable to pass as native-born Japanese. All of them have become "marginal categories to the ideological mainstream, though less marginal in economic or political terms."[47] And all have become likely buyers of instant noodles, especially at the twenty-four-hour convenience stores—*kombini*—which, as White suggests concerning the late 1990s, have become "so much part of people's lives that people wonder how they ever lived without them."[48]

Momofuku Ando did not have to worry much about selling to these marginalized people. Koki Ando must worry about them, and about the more mainstream as well. His strategies for doing so are reflected in the title of his autobiography, which he offers explicitly as a contrast to his father's. Calling it *Mission: Destroy Cup Noodle! How a Second-Generation President Maddens the Founder with His Marketing Style*, he insists that to maintain market share in a more fragmented Japan, Nissin must innovate continually.[49]

The Japanese market in instant noodles has long been highly competitive, with many companies vying for market share.[50] By 1987, the domestic market in instant noodles was slowing down, and by 1996 it was fully saturated, leveling off to an annual per capita consumption of about forty-one packages and cups. In such a market, genuine differences among brands, including price, had become minimal, and shelf space in convenience stores and supermarkets was at a premium. As the title of Koki Ando's autobiography suggests, the company could not afford to rest on the laurels of Cup Noodle. Currently, Nissin introduces about three hundred new instant noodle varieties yearly into Japan, each claiming at least marginal distinction. This is half of the some six hundred introduced annually into Japan by all instant noodle producers.[51]

FIGURE 5. Schoolchildren at the Momofuku Ando Instant Ramen Museum. Photograph by Tatsuro Fujikura.

We visited the Momofuku Ando Instant Ramen Museum on a weekday during school holidays (on September 2, 2010), and then Tatsuro returned alone to interview museum officials (on October 3, 2011). On both occasions, the clean, modern, and spacious museum was filled with mothers and children apparently enjoying themselves, as well as with young couples on dates. On Tatsuro's second visit there were also many schoolchildren on class outings. As Shin'ichi Taniguchi, vice-chief of the secretariat of the Ando Foundation, told Tatsuro:

> We get quite a few couples on dates. Frankly, this is a very cheap place to visit. . . . It is also a very good place for a family outing. I have children, too, and if you take your whole family to an amusement park or a theme park, you easily end up spending 10,000 yen [about US$130]. Compared to that, visiting this museum makes a lot of economic sense. In the information magazine *Family Walker—Kansai Area* (during May 2010), the museum was listed as Number 1 on the "Top 5 Popular Spots which Mothers Visited and Liked." . . . The main target of the museum is elementary school and junior high school and the museum encourages schools to visit as a field trip as part of *shoku-iku* [food education, promoted in Japan since the end of the nineteenth century].[52]

FIGURE 6. A statue of Momofuku Ando, holding a package of Chikin Ramen and standing on a Cup Noodle–shaped pedestal. Photograph by Tatsuro Fujikura.

The displays seem to be of three types: instructive displays, which show how remarkable the founder was and what inspiration should be taken from his life and accomplishments; participatory displays, which encourage identification with and enjoyment of Nissin's brand and its products; and informational displays, which dazzle with the range of Nissin's instant noodle innovations.

The instructive displays begin before visitors enter the building. Just outside the entrance is a statue of Momofuku Ando holding a package of his original Chikin Ramen and standing on a pedestal in the shape of Cup Noodle.

Inside the museum, the first exhibit is a reproduction of the backyard shack where Ando invented instant noodles. Just beyond that, the Cup

FIGURE 7. A reconstruction of the backyard shack where Ando invented instant noodles. Photograph by Tatsuro Fujikura.

Noodle Drama Theater (an enclosure shaped as a Cup Noodle) focuses on Ando's other major invention. Headphones are available to provide translations in Chinese and English of the Japanese commentary about each display. The commentary about Ando's accomplishments stresses a mainstream Shōwa perspective: insight, hard work, insistent problem solving, and dedication to innovation within a company that is committed to high standards lead to rapid economic growth, commercial success, and general public benefit.

Thus, the narrative in the shack provides the largely standardized story of Ando's special abilities. It conveys how, after noting the long queues of hungry people after the war waiting wearily for (real) ramen to be prepared, he was able to see a need and, through focused work, to imaginatively adapt existing technology to develop good tasting, easy-to-prepare, affordable noodles that could be stored without refrigeration.

Much the same message is conveyed in the Cup Noodle Drama Theater, where Ando's entrepreneurial problem solving is depicted in a charming animated cartoon. In the course of promoting his packaged instant noodles abroad, he met with a potential client in the United States who chose to eat his instant noodles in a cup. This led Ando to consider whether instant noodles could be made more convenient if purchased, prepared, and consumed in a cup. But what kind of a cup? Styrofoam was used in the United States to make tapered (stackable) cups; in Japan, however, Styrofoam was used only to make cartons for packing fresh fish. So the first thing was to bring this cup technology to Japan. But how to seal the cup? This problem was solved when Ando noted the peel-back foil top of a package of nuts that he was served on an international flight.

Further product development was necessary. To fill the tapered cup, the noodles had to be molded in the shape of a truncated cone, sprayed with broth, and then cooked in oil. Inserted into the center section of the cup, they would provide lateral support at the side of the cup, space for hot water to circulate at the bottom, and a platform for various dried or freeze-dried ingredients at the top. Yet a technical problem persisted. If these noodle cones were dropped into the cups, they would end up stuck at all sorts of odd angles. If the noodles were to rehydrate evenly, this would not do. The cartoon showed Ando struggling day and night with this problem. Tossing and turning on his mat, he dreamt he was swirling in the air, upside down. Upon awakening, he was inspired to think about the problem in new way. What if the position of the noodles and the cup were reversed? The solution became obvious: to have the noodles come out on a belt with the narrow end of the cone on top and have the open ends of the cups descend to fit down around them. The lesson of this, according to the cartoon Ando, is never to let difficulties stop us. Rather, we should keep looking at problems from different angles until we solve them.[53]

Other exhibits about Ando's life offer more of what the museum's brochure terms "traces of Momofuku Ando": displays of his various awards, including honorary degrees; pictures of him meeting famous people and playing golf; exhibits of his personal possessions, including an iPod with a caption stating that he remained interested in new technology until an advanced age. In addition, a special section is devoted to what may have been Ando's last great accomplishment: the launching into outer space of specially formulated instant noodles—"Space Ram"—with a Japanese astronaut on a 2005 voyage of the space shuttle Discovery. (Since water in space boils at 70°C or 158°F, these noodles had to cook at a lower-than-usual temperature. Moreover, they had to be especially viscous to prevent them from drifting out of their cup at zero gravity.)

FIGURE 8. Cup Noodle revealed: an exhibit near the Cup Noodle Drama Theater. Photograph by Tatsuro Fujikura.

If Momofuku Ando is the star of the instructive displays, the Nissin "chick"—known as "Hiyoko-chan" (*hiyoko* means "chick" and *chan* is a tag of affection)—is the star of the participatory displays. Referencing the company's signature chicken instant noodles, this chick became the primary visual representation of the company in advertisements in 1989, replacing "Chibbiko," the healthy Americanized boy.

With the notable exception of the displays focusing on Momofuku Ando, Hiyoko-chan is the predominant figure in the museum, appearing in large, freestanding form and on signs, decorations, garments, and products sold at the museum shop. As many Japanese know—certainly many coming to the museum—Hiyoko-chan has lived since 2001 in "Chicken Town" on "Chikirar Island" with twelve chicken friends.[54]

FIGURE 9. Hiyoko-chan, the Nissin chick. Photograph by Tatsuro Fujikura.

Games featuring these thirteen characters, known collectively as "Chikirars," can be downloaded as iPhone applications, and Chikirar storybooks are available online. All of this seems designed to make Nissin's instant noodles into a "lovemark." As the international advertising firm Saatchi and Saatchi explains:

> Lovemarks transcend brands. They deliver beyond your expectations of great performance. Like great brands, they sit on top of high levels of respect—but there the similarities end.
>
> Lovemarks reach your heart as well as your mind, creating an intimate, emotional connection that you just can't live without. Ever.
>
> Take a brand away and people will find a replacement. Take a Lovemark away and people will protest its absence. Lovemarks are a relationship, not a mere transaction. You don't just buy Lovemarks, you embrace them passionately. That's why you never want to let go.[55]

Thus, when we look at Hiyoko-chan and learn about the other Chikirars through iPhone games or online, we are not supposed to think of the giant food conglomerate Nissin, or about its present CEO, Koki Ando, or even about its founder, Momofuku Ando. Rather, we are to embrace the endearing and the cute and make them our own. As the anthropologist Christine Yano suggests in her analysis of "Japanese cute" (focusing on Hello Kitty, "that ultimate symbol of cute

FIGURE 10. Personalizing Cup Noodle, one of the Momofuku Ando Instant Ramen Museum's participatory displays. Photograph by Tatsuro Fujikura.

femininity"), "cute" charms and woos consumers on a global scale.[56] Certainly this is the case in Japan's highly competitive instant noodle market.

Indeed, the participatory displays seem designed to charm and to woo. The first, "My Cup Noodle Factory," engaged the three of us in a personal and pleasurable relationship with our instant noodles. It was fun. We each paid ¥300 (about US$3.30) for our own empty Cup Noodle cup. Then we were instructed in hygienic guidelines: we were to clean our hands, leave protective lids on our cups, date them, and consume their contents within a month (though not in the museum). Next, bringing our cups to a table where there were different colored Magic Markers, we were encouraged to be creative while limiting our decoration to a designated section of the cup.

Once finished, we moved to the processing stage. There, an attendant removed the protective cap and placed each inverted cup into a device so that it was filled with a cone of prefried noodles delivered by the "noodle shooter." Instructed to turn a crank, we rotated the now-filled "cup noodle" into an upright position. We were then able to customize

FIGURE 11. Mana Fujikura chooses toppings for her personalized Cup Noodle.
Photograph by Tatsuro Fujikura.

the contents of our personalized cups. We could choose from four soup flavors (chicken, seafood, curry, or corn) and from eleven dried toppings (including asparagus, onion, shrimp, and egg).

After the attendant applied the foil top, heat-sealed it, and shrink-wrapped the cup, one additional option remained. We could place our cup in a plastic bag and, with a hand pump, inflate the bag to form a protective pillow to which a red cord could be attached. Designed to be worn decoratively around our necks, these pillow-encased cups became a take-home memento of our experience. (However, we were cautioned by a sign in Japanese and English that, if we were to travel on a plane, we should not inflate the plastic bag.) As the museum's brochure promised, for ¥300, we could do quite a lot: "Freely design the cup, choose the soup flavor, and add the ingredients you prefer. Visitors can take home their original, one and only 'Cup Noodle' in the world. Sense the importance of 'thinking upside down' [as Ando claims to have done] through this fun experience."

The second participatory display, "Handmade Chicken Ramen Hands-On Workshop," also looked like fun as we observed it through

FIGURE 12. Making Chicken Ramen in one of the museum's participatory workshops. Photograph by Tatsuro Fujikura.

glass walls. Attendance at this workshop requires that participants understand Japanese (or be accompanied by a Japanese speaker) and bookings take place weeks, if not months, in advance. (Our visit was in early September and the first openings were in November.) What we saw, in a well-lit, cheerful, and immaculate room, were groups of adults (mostly women), many with children. Dressed in red aprons and headscarves printed with images of Hiyoko-chan, the groups clustered around white tables to see an introductory video. Moving to food-preparation islands with stainless steel counters and equipment, they apparently enjoyed the hands-on experience of mixing flour, stretching dough, and cutting, steaming, and flavoring noodles. As the brochure explains, this is "the world's one and only workshop where you can reproduce the world's first instant noodle product, 'Chicken Ramen,' yourself . . . up to the process of drying the noodles by 'The Flash-Frying Method.'" That the hands-on nature of this display was intended to foster identification with the product became additionally clear to us when Tatsuro overheard a museum guide telling a man on a private tour that if people worked the dough and made the noodles themselves, they would be convinced that the ingredients used in instant noodles were pure.

There is no single star of the informational displays; instead, there is a whole galaxy composed of an impressive array of Nissin products. One display, "Instant Noodles of the World," documents (according to the brochure) "the spread of instant noodles throughout the world which changed the food culture of the world" with about 91.6 billion packages sold worldwide (at the time the display was constructed). It additionally indicates Nissin's worldwide reach by showing packages of Nissin products from the United States, Brazil, Mexico, Europe, India, Thailand, Indonesia, the Philippines, Shanghai, Beijing, Hong Kong, and Guangdong, each one "specially made to suit the taste of each country."

Roughly consistent with the documentation of Nissin's worldwide reach is a display calling attention to Nissin's quick response as a donor of instant noodles for international disaster relief. There is also a repeating video about Nissin's humanitarian outreach, specifically to Kenya. Local Kenyans, mostly schoolchildren, are shown eating instant noodles as the result of a Nissin nonprofit initiative involving collaboration between Nissin representatives and Kenyan university professors to create instant noodles appropriate to Kenyan technology, cultural tastes, and nutritional needs. (Executives at Nissin's Tokyo headquarters later told us that the company is planning to open a simple instant noodle plant and train Kenyans to operate it. This will accomplish three things in a country—and continent—relatively "untouched" by instant noodles: it will feed people, provide employment, and develop a taste for noodles to open the market.)

The most visually dramatic of the informational displays is the "Instant Noodles Tunnel," which provides a timeline of many of the Nissin products introduced after the launching of instant noodles in 1958. The acceleration in product development is obvious. One fairly recent product, for instance, represents a tweaking of the original "Chikin Ramen": in this variant, a block of instant noodles contains a shallow depression into which a raw egg can be broken before the hot water is added.[57] In addition, there are numerous "bowls" of instant noodles, all eye-catchingly packaged, including ones that mimic the tastes of real ramen available at famous shops (complete with the endorsement of celebrity chefs) and others that purport to capture flavors of real ramen from particular regions of Japan, such as Kyoto or Okinawa.[58] Koki Ando explains this acceleration:

FIGURE 13. The Instant Noodle Tunnel, which provides a timeline of Nissin products. Photograph by Tatsuro Fujikura.

The new product race is a war of attrition. To win a victory, you have no choice but to keep fighting. . . . The food preferences of consumers are diverse, and they change from day to day. . . . Despite some degree of risk, we aim to be the first product brought to market and keep on firing until we're out of ammo. Consequently, the BM system [the brand management system, designed to create internal competition among Nissin's product designers] has turned into a kind of multi-product development system, under which 300 items are annually produced and put on the market almost automatically.

Needless to say, the POS system [the point of sale system, which keeps track of what is selling and, therefore, what should be stocked] has accelerated the new-product race.[59]

The anthropologist Marilyn Ivy echoes Koki Ando in her description of the challenges of the contemporary style-conscious Japanese market (now that Japan Inc. has given way to J- cool): "Producers have been compelled to appeal to (and create) highly targeted, diversified, and nuanced types of consumer desire."[60] And, we should add, unlike the choice of, say, an expensive camera or stylish pocketbook, the consequences of choosing among the many new and eye-catching variants of instant noodles appearing and disappearing almost daily are not that great. Under these circumstances, loyalties cannot be assumed. The Heisei market in instant noodles is, to repeat, one of small and (producers hope) moderately engaging differences.

The Momofuku Ando Instant Ramen Museum is designed to be interesting in its instructive displays, engaging in its participatory displays, and impressive in its informational displays. It is fun—because, as Koki Ando understands advertising, "it's not a commercial unless it's entertaining."[61] People are expected to come away disposed to like Nissin and its product line. Indeed, so popular is this museum that in 2011 a much larger rendition and even more participatory Yokohama-based "Cup Noodle Museum" was opened, in which visitors themselves become noodles and move through a giant Cup Noodle production line. Although free for students up through high school, adults are charged ¥500 admission (about US$6.50 when the museum opened). Taniguchi told Tatsuro: "Apparently people feel it is worth paying the money; it was a good thing we decided to charge an entrance fee. If it were completely free for adults, we would have attracted far more people than we could easily handle." The experiences at both museums, it seems, are much like Koki Ando's understanding of the instant noodle–eating experience: pleasant, and good enough. As he writes in his autobiography: "There aren't too many people who say *Cup Noodle* is really delicious; most say it tastes okay. If they get a little hungry, they'll often feel like having another one. I think *Cup Noodle* is a food that superbly balances taste satisfaction with a feeling of fullness. That's why it never gets in the way of the three main meals. As a snack, it has kept its position as the best brand of instant noodles for almost forty years."[62]

EATING INSTANT NOODLES IN CONTEMPORARY JAPAN

We also collected information that illustrates contemporary Japanese practices of instant noodle consumption. Our conversations, interviews, and surveys were mostly with those likely to be of the mainstream: graduate students (at Kyoto University), undergraduate students (at Kyoto University of Foreign Studies), and faculty and staff members (at Kyoto University).[63] Many with whom we spoke directly found our academic engagement with instant noodles surprising. When talking with Deborah and Fred, they were more interested in discussing Japanese culinary traditions—an amalgamation, it seems, of the numerous local foodways that developed in what once were semi-independent polities. Or in explaining that Japanese like their food raw and so are sensitive to the taste differences between vegetables grown in different localities. Instant noodles, for the most part, did not strike anyone as noteworthy—just a snack of somewhat uncertain nutritional value, eaten alone or at an office desk. Thus, one twenty-six-year-old male graduate student reported: "I eat them while studying, rarely at other times." A thirty-two-year-old female university researcher wrote: "At lunchtime, on holidays, I do my housework and meantime I can have a quick, cheap bite."

However, one of our survey questions asked if respondents had any instant noodle stories to share, and this question sometimes elicited stories in which instant noodles were described as noteworthy—for example, in association with a (moderately) abnormal event. A twenty-eight-year-old female accountant said, "I remember eating them while chatting with friends in front of convenience stores, especially when drinking, when we all missed the last train." A twenty-five-year-old male graduate student related that "I once participated in a boy scout camp with my brother. As we were told, each of the participants brought two packets of instant noodles, and we cooked our meal putting all the packets into a single huge pot. I don't remember the taste, but it was fun. I'd like to try that again." A twenty-seven-year-old female office worker remembered, "I went to climb a mountain with my father in winter. We went to a place near a lake on top of the mountain, and we stopped at a point where it was beautifully covered with snow. There we set a fire and cooked instant noodles in a pot. We put snow in the pot to cook them. We sharpened a wood stick and made chopsticks. I had a great time."

Instant noodles may also be considered noteworthy when they substitute for a typical domestic meal cooked by a mother for her husband and children. A fifty-year-old female said, "When I was in the third grade of elementary school, my mother was admitted to a hospital and I was living with my father. I have a memory of having eaten instant packet noodles several times when my mother was away. In my childhood my mother always prepared meals. Instant noodles were more like emergency food then." A fifty-seven-year-old female university employee noted that "instant noodles are one of the very few dishes that my husband can prepare by himself. It's good to keep some around because he can have them whenever I'm out."[64] She also recalled: "When I was in elementary school, three of my sisters had fun cooking instant noodles for Saturday lunch when our mother was away for work." A twenty-two-year-old male graduate student said that "instant noodles were something to be prepared by my father, especially on weekends, not by my mother." And, as a departure from normal domestic circumstances, one eighteen-year-old male undergraduate student reported that "when my father gets drunk, he suddenly starts cooking instant noodles and invites the family to eat."

Finally, a twenty-seven-year-old female graduate student recalled an instant noodle–focused transgression that seemed liberating: "Instant cup noodles never appeared on our dining scene [because they were thought unhealthy]. So it was shocking when our family went to a nearby swimming pool (we were both still in elementary school), and my sister and I saw our father secretly eating Cup Noodle at the corner of the poolside (there was this Cup Noodle vending machine at the poolside). We ran up to him and begged him for a bite." She, her sister, and her father joined in a joyful antidomestic conspiracy that gave her a taste of independence. In fact, she had earlier told us in conversation that instant noodles have a special meaning to her age group, whose members have "embraced the freedom to eat anything they wanted. After all, we aren't living at home."

Though largely from the mainstream (or, in the case of the undergraduate students, still aspirants to it), those we spoke to may have included alienated students and freedom-loving singles. We were not able to interview the slackers, strangers, or seniors of the posteconomic bubble generation concerning their consumption of instant noodles, although we know that Nissin has a marketing plan to accommodate those whose lives have departed from the mainstream track. As Koki Ando describes this plan: "*Cup Noodle* may bring back the pathetic memory of the lifestyle one had when one didn't have much money, lived in a tiny apartment and had to eat *Cup Noodle*. We don't want our products to have this kind of image so we've produced commercials that emphasize the joy of youth in order to wipe out any such dark associations."[65] These commercials have won awards. Perhaps the most famous is the series involving cavemen trying to run down giant prehistoric animals. Following each humorous misadventure, an alternative and more convenient food source is suggested to them with the "Hungry? Cup Noodle" tagline.[66] Thus, Nissin tries to keep everyone entertained and mildly intrigued with its rollout of well-packaged products and its flow of engaging advertisements.

TAKING INSTANT NOODLES SERIOUSLY?

Nissin and its competitors, of course, do take instant noodles seriously. Nissin's mastery of the commonly recognized four *P*'s of marketing (price, product, promotion, and place) is impressive. However, the company's serious agenda to augment its bottom line depends, at least to some degree, on customers not taking instant noodles that seriously—as long as they keep buying them.

To be sure, at least one customer—Ton Tan Tin—is serious in an ironic way about instant noodles. As he tells us, with a perhaps self-deprecating chuckle, "To be so fulfilled by shopping for things that cost only about a hundred yen each . . . [is] a very economical hobby."[67] The purpose of an *otaku* is to take seriously that which others do not: to become an aesthete of the trivial—of the accessible and everyday. It is precisely because instant noodles are so ordinary that Ton Tan Tin follows their worldwide existence; it is because they are so ordinary that he becomes a connoisseur, a "curator" (to use Gibson's word), of their small differences.[68] Correspondingly, he has a following because the product in which he is an expert is so accessible and everyday.[69] People are curious and amused by his YouTube videos, and since the instant noodles he reviews are just a cheap snack, they can try them out and perhaps post their reactions on his blog.

As we have suggested, Ton Tan Tin's engagement with instant noodles mirrors broad sociohistorical processes in postwar Japan. As a child of the Shōwa era, born in 1960 (as he says, "a few years after Chicken Ramen was first introduced"), we know that his family owned a car during the early 1980s and therefore seemed to be doing well in Japan's general period of prosperity. He most likely grew up with a dining kitchen (and all that it meant about the reformulation of domestic space), and instant noodles became part of his snacking experience at home: he cooked packages of them himself as early as the fifth grade and stocked up on cup noodles for his nightly studies in the seventh grade. He undoubtedly did well on the national educational exams; after all, he is not a slacker but has a job as a corporate product designer, a job that allows him to travel rather extensively. As a young college student in 1982, he became dazzled in his travels by the variety of instant noodles available in Japan. Their availability signaled the increasing competition among instant noodle producers for the attention of fickle consumers—a competition that prompted Nissin's all-out push for product development. This push, as mentioned, has led to some six hundred new varieties of instant noodles introduced in Japan alone each year—all of which Ton Tan Tin would presumably like to sample, celebrate, and catalogue. And, as Nissin and other instant noodle producers continue to compete for profits with their mix of products for the worldwide market, Ton Tan Tin—and the three of us—will be right there with them. Our approach differs from his, of course. Yet Ton Tan Tin and we agree that the success of this fundamentally ordinary capitalist provision, voted Japan's most important invention of the twentieth century, is remarkable, and well worth thinking seriously about.

3

What Instant Noodles Reflect and Affect in America

We learned much about the instant noodle market worldwide when we visited the Tokyo headquarters of Nissin Food Holdings. There, after bows and an exchange of business cards, we met with four dark-suited executives (all, apparently, authentic "salarymen"): an executive adviser, an executive officer of corporate communications, a manager of corporate communications, and a specialist in product development. Tatsuro translated, although we all knew that some of them spoke serviceable English.

They told us about the importance for Nissin in maintaining its dominant share in the saturated market of Japan, as well as in increasing its share in markets elsewhere. The most promising are the large and rapidly growing markets of Brazil, Russia, India, and China—and, as mentioned in the previous chapter, perhaps of Africa. Nissin is also quite active in smaller markets, such as those of Korea and Thailand. In addition, it is working hard to increase its sales in the United States.

The strategies Nissin pursues to further its international interests are various. In some cases, it extends its own initiatives; in others, it works with companies already in place that it has either acquired or become allied with. Regardless of how access is fostered, ultimate success in many markets may require that, once cooked into a soup, Nissin's noodles have "the taste that mothers in various places would make."[1] This tailoring of taste to place, we were told, has little to do with the noodles themselves. Rather, the flavorings and toppings make the soup fit with particular food traditions. In Thailand, for instance, Nissin's "Tom Yum Goong" uses locally popular peppers, fish sauce, lemongrass, and cilantro in its spicy shrimp-based noodle soup. In Korea, Nissin's "Kimchi" uses a locally popular spicy fermented cabbage condiment in its soup. To mesh with existing culinary traditions, Nissin typically contracts with local firms to develop recipes. Once these recipes are approved back in Japan, they are implemented with the assistance of Japanese technical experts. As the specialist in product development told us, "The goal is to accomplish product differentiation from competitors without sacrificing product excellence. The challenge is to reduce the costs." To be sure, the need for localization varies according to market. So, too, does the need, as in Japan, for an extensive product range as well as for ongoing innovation. The American market doesn't require much of either. It is the "complete opposite," according to the executive adviser, of the Japanese market.

When Deborah and Fred previously visited Nissin's U.S. headquarters in Gardena, California, they heard the Japanese and American markets described in similar terms by a public relations official. Because Japan has a long history with noodles, the official said, "instant noodles have a different feel in Japan; they are not just a 'commodity.'" Instead (in apparent reference to upmarket bowls of instant noodles), they are a "quality product that can cost between [US]$2.00 and $2.50, and therefore are made of excellent ingredients and condiments. But in the United States, depending on the manufacturer, noodles cost between [US]$0.20 and 0.50. This should give some idea of how different the markets are." It was a pity that Nissin was not the leader in the United States. After all, Nissin was the first to enter the American market, with its instant noodle packages in 1970 and with its Cup Noodle in 1973.

> These are Nissin's core products—its workhorses. Other items come and go. Many do not stick because they are degraded into a commodity item given the price wars here, many of which are driven by Maruchan [the major company supplying instant noodles in the United States].[2] The strategy of this company is not innovation; it watches what someone else does and then does a "me too," but cheaper.[3] In Japan, there can be lots of advertising and brand equity but here we find that the instant noodle world is a matter of pure price. . . . Americans see instant noodles as a standard product.[4]

Though at the time of this interview, Deborah and Fred had not heard of Ton Tan Tin and so could not mention him, this official likely would have agreed that no one could have been dazzled into (something like) *otaku*-hood by the variety of instant noodles available in the United States.

At our Tokyo meeting, the Nissin representatives were somewhat more appreciative of Maruchan's considerable U.S. accomplishments. (As of 2009, Maruchan controlled about two-thirds and Nissin one-third of the U.S. market.[5]) The executive adviser explained: "Nissin invented instant noodles, so in one sense everyone is copying Nissin. And Nissin was first in the United States and Maruchan came later. However, Maruchan managed to win the competition by reducing price. It won out in terms of price—providing a good product at a fair price by reducing costs. It was innovative in opening up new markets, especially in the prisons and jails."[6] Hence, in Nissin's view, Maruchan's success rested on its recognition that the U.S. market was driven by price and that brand loyalty meant little—no one was likely to accept any brand's instant noodles as a "lovemark." Instant noodles (provided that they were of acceptable quality, even if they did not evoke a "real" ramen shop) were simply a commodity to be sold to as many people as possible.

Certainly, many Americans do buy instant noodles simply as a commodity. As the journalist Christopher Solomon reports:

> Single packages of ramen on the shelves of national grocery chains sell from a dime at Wal-Mart to as much as $2.79 (for the fancy-shmancy stuff) elsewhere. . . .
>
> Usually you can score six for a buck without breaking a sweat, and 20 for a dollar isn't unusual if you don't mind playing dollar-store roulette.[7]

Yet as we began to investigate instant noodles in the United States, we soon concluded that this humble commodity—one without much aspiration to be "real" ramen—provides more significance to many Americans than mere price might suggest. Not surprisingly, this significance varies considerably according to where noodle consumers find themselves in the system of capitalist provisioning. As we shall see, the ways that middle class listeners to National Public Radio, college students, prisoners, and Hispanic Americans considered to be "heavy users" by the Nissin Corporation engage with instant noodles reveal much about how they handle their differently located lives. Instant noodles, thus, become a measure of life's difficulties and a map of how people deal with these difficulties.

INSTANT NOODLES AND THE MIDDLE-CLASS LIFE CYCLE

It is a commonplace observation that college students in the United States (and elsewhere) eat lots of instant noodles. As Solomon put it, "Ramen is as much a part of the college [experience] as the Freshman

1 5 "—the fifteen pounds students are said to gain during their first year at school.[8] It is assumed that those graduating from college will "outgrow" their reliance on instant noodles. In other words, instant noodles are generally understood to mark a phase in a middle-class life cycle trajectory, the movement from a youthful dependence on the cheap, ordinary, and standard toward the adult freedom of increased financial security and choice. That this is a pervasive cultural expectation, especially for those of the middle class, is conveyed, for example, in *No More Ramen*—a book whose cover promises a "20-something's real world survival guide," with "straight talk on jobs, money, balance, life and more."[9]

This same expectation was explored in a 2009 broadcast on National Public Radio (NPR) during its popular news program "All Things Considered" (which airs while many are returning home from work or preparing supper). The audience—including, on this particular evening, Deborah and Fred—was asked to post responses on the NPR website to this question: "Was there a time when ramen noodles were all you ate? Tell us your ramen noodle stories."[10] Eventually, about seventy instant noodle–focused reminiscences were submitted, and some were read on the air. As NPR informed its listeners, "The noodle stories flooded in— those cheap little packages of instant noodles with the silver foil flavor packets served up a big bowl of nostalgia."[11]

What insights, we wondered, might be gleaned from revisiting these reminiscences? The NPR audience consists mostly of adults, men and women listen in (almost) equal numbers, and 86 percent identify themselves as white. In 2009, when the last demographic survey was taken, the median age of the NPR listener was fifty, and most had reached, or were close to reaching, the empty nest stage of life, with relatively few children living at home. Nearly 65 percent of listeners had a bachelor's degree, compared with 25 percent in the U.S. population as a whole, and they were three times more likely than the average American to have completed graduate school. Primarily as a result of educational attainments, NPR households tended to be more affluent than other households; in 2009 the median household income was about $86,000, compared to the national average of $55,000.[12]

NPR listeners, moreover, are not only a relatively homogeneous demographic, but most likely regard one another as living somewhat comparable lives. As NPR listeners, they are bound, or at least influenced, by a loose social contract, insofar as they are encouraged periodically to accept mutual responsibility and exhibit generosity by donating to NPR. NPR, in turn, promises to do its best to present the news and social commentary in an evenhanded way and to entertain in an imaginative yet generally unprovocative manner. In other words, NPR and its listeners are inclined to trust one another—to engage in a relationship of generalized reciprocity, of generalized sharing.

Correspondingly, in their instant noodle reminiscences, NPR listeners often conveyed instant noodle recipes—invitations to join with others in a network of shared sensory appreciation and social connection. After all, recipes are more than a list of ingredients and directions for assembling them; they are offerings making the promise that "I think you will like this." They are small gifts that convey personal endorsement. As the literary critic Susan Leonardi put it: "[A] cookbook that consisted of nothing but rules for various dishes would be an unpopular cookbook, indeed. Even the root of recipe—the Latin *recipere*—implies an exchange, a giver and a receiver. Like a story, a recipe needs a recommendation, a context, a point, a reason to be."[13] The recollections and recipes about instant noodles that were elicited and shared through NPR can thus be seen as a flurry of modest gifts, demonstrating and fostering common ground—all the more so because this ground rests on common consumption of this most common of products.[14]

NPR had set its appeal for noodle stories in the context of two features about Chef David Chang—"Chef Chang's Momofuku: A Romance with Ramen" and "David Chang's Ramen: Not Your Average Noodle."[15] At the time, Chang ran four New York restaurants, ranging from a casual ramen noodle bar to an upscale establishment, all of which were named after Momofuku Ando. Despite his invocation of Ando, Chang described his cooking in the leadoff NPR piece as "American and delicious." He continued: "We don't want to be just a Japanese restaurant. . . . We don't want to be just a Korean restaurant. Why don't we just try to make delicious food? It just shows you how categories and labels fail to actually describe what is happening."[16]

Like most Americans, Chang first ate ramen "in cheap small packets of dried instant noodles." Then he went to Japan and "saw people lining up at ramen houses for homemade noodles tangled with ingredients like dried fish, pork, and chicken." This experience led him to develop his own ramen recipe with a broth that "required pounds of meat and takes hours to prepare"—although the "layers of flavor that result make the prep time pay off."[17] That is, Chang founded his Momofuku restaurants to memorialize the "real" ramen noodles that Momofuku Ando sought to displace. Indeed, Chang's restaurant offerings are the opposite of convenient and cheap (to say nothing of shelf stable and industrially prepared). The second NPR broadcast, for example, included his recipe for "Fuji Apple Salad with Kimchi, Smoked Jowl, and Maple Labne" (a Middle Eastern yogurt). Though undoubtedly delicious, eclectic, and upscale (and lacking noodles!), this dish is neither easy to prepare nor inexpensive—requiring that kimchi be made from scratch and that ingredients be purchased from specialty purveyors. In fact, Chang aspires to something well beyond the attainments of real ramen restaurants in Japan.

The conjunction between NPR's discussion of Chang's effort to reinstate noodles as cosmopolitan and classy and its call for instant noodle stories is worth noting. Those responding to the broadcast about Chang's cooking and restaurants by contributing their remembrances of the time when "ramen noodles were all you ate" seemed to be reflecting upon a life course in which they were—or expected to be—prospering socioeconomically. In other words, NPR invited its listeners to reminisce about a past that they could now look back on nostalgically precisely because its privations were safely in the past—because they were now in a position to either take instant noodles or leave them.

We should stress again that the NPR listeners—especially those contributing their instant noodle stories—were not a random sample. Those who chose to write in did so because they had engaging stories to tell about instant noodles, and NPR selected among them, presumably to provide breadth of coverage and maximal interest. This being said, we found the collection of stories informatively reassuring about the lives of those middle-class NPR listeners; as snapshots of common experiences, the stories were never hard to understand and they readily evoked empathy.[18] A number of contributors spoke of the usefulness of instant noodles on family camping trips. One, for instance, describing instant noodles as "the duct tape of fast foods," combined them with stale beer to create a crispy batter for trout that everyone raved about. Several depicted their moderately successful efforts to recreate noodle tastes experienced in Asia. A fair number provided recipes that either they or their friends had improvised with the addition of easily added ingredients such as Velveeta cheese and Worcestershire sauce. A professor at a culinary institute reported that he was organizing a "Ramen Noodle Cook-off" for his students, "just to see what they can do." Several offered tips to make instant noodles more healthful, generally by eliminating the salty flavor packet and using other spices instead. One woman, by contrast, claimed that the salt in instant noodles had saved her life when she was taking medicine that dangerously depleted her sodium levels. A number of contributors in the military told of preparing a reviving canteen cup of instant noodles when they were cold, tired, and hungry; of making MREs (Meals, Ready-to-Eat) more palatable by adding instant noodles; and of eating instant noodles in the barracks when it was too cold to walk to the mess hall or when it was just too much trouble to put on battle gear to do so. Many wrote about family intimacies surrounding the preparation and consumption of instant noodles: the family who adds them to cans of Dinty Moore beef stew to make "stoodles"; the husband who concocts his own "signature" noodle, egg, cheese, and hot sauce mixture for breakfast, which his wife sees as "one of his oddly lovable quirks"; the daughter who recalls her mother getting up on cold Indiana mornings to fix a breakfast of hot noodles ("not the ten-cent noodles, but those by the case from Chicago's Chinatown that were more flavorable and perfect for those frigid mornings"); the young couple who cooked instant noodles on an illegal dorm room hot plate and consumed them surreptitiously in the "night's dim light"; the newly married college student on a limited budget who used instant noodles in her mother's tuna casserole and ended up preparing a "mushy, gloppy mess" that her husband still teases her about twenty years later; and the parents who became upset when their son, stranded at college for Thanksgiving and failing in his effort to cook himself a nice meal, had to fall back on instant noodles. Finally, a few told stories of instant noodles as marking a return to the ordinary, as with the woman who measured her recovery from cancer by her restored ability to consume a full bowl.

In sum, for these NPR contributors, instant noodles in their various guises were, as many explicitly described them, comfort food. Their noodle stories—snapshots of their lives, often from a comforting distance—were offered as shareable (driveway!) moments, as food for comfortable thought.[19] Even the most dissonant of the stories, offered by a prison teacher whose incarcerated students "massaged" noodles and other ingredients acquired at the commissary to be shared out on bread or tortillas at the beginning of class, was ultimately warm and charming.

But what, we wondered, would the instant noodle stories from those in an early stage of this middle-class trajectory—those college students whose parents most likely belong to the demographic of NPR listeners—sound like? To find this out, we asked Emily Shinay, Deborah's research assistant, to interview students from Amherst College, an affluent liberal arts institution with a meal plan that provides subscribers with plenty to eat and a great variety of foods to choose from.[20] The majority of the fifty-nine (mostly Amherst) students interviewed seemed to regard instant noodles as a "fourth meal" to be consumed late at night while hitting the books.[21] For most of them, price was an important factor. As one put it: "If I'm going to eat food that has next to no nutritional value, I'm not going to pay a lot for it"—especially since, as several students suggested, they purchase noodles with their own spending money. One student said he chose to eat them *because* they were cheap: he had exceeded his budget during his sophomore year. Thirty-one students responded to the interview by offering instant noodle stories of their own. One student mentioned a "record label called 'Fueled by Ramen,'" which he thought was "pretty funny." Another said that she still calls instant noodles "nood-less" because this is how her little brother first pronounced the word. One student described the time that, when drunk, he ate "two packets of ramen and two packets of instant oatmeal" without cooking them. One said he "stumbled upon one of the greatest scientific discoveries of our time" when he "came back from a party late at night" and "decided to eat the pack of ramen noodles raw." Much to his surprise, the following morning he "had no trace of a hangover" and shared his "good news with anyone that would listen." One student told of "one of the top hundred days" of her life, when she had been on the phone for "literally eight hours" with her best friend and they decided to prepare instant noodles while "still talking with each other." Then she saw a plane and "a few minutes later" her friend "saw the same one, which was awesome." Several young women told of visiting their boyfriends and eating instant noodles together. Another said she did not like to do this because she found the sound of slurping instant noodles disgusting. Yet another said that in high school she ate so many instant noodles that she was afraid she would smell of them. One liked them because her "cool" brother and his friends ate them. One recalled that when her mother was dying of cancer she would hide out alone in her dorm room, eat one or two portions a day, and "watch the new *Doctor Who* or *Gilmore Girls*" and thereby "stave off starvation and boredom." She doesn't eat instant noodles anymore because they remind her of "this particularly desperate time." One student who didn't much like instant noodles still felt that the Maggi brand, which her family brought back from visits to relatives in India, was something special. Finally, one student discussed instant noodles as part of a Facebook messaging thread with another student who, unpredictably, became her "current boyfriend" after they had arrived at Amherst. She had told him that she "liked to eat the noodles raw and he said he thought that was weird, at which point [they] stopped talking" because she became embarrassed.

The instant noodle stories Emily collected reflected the age of their tellers as those whose adult lives were just coming into being. The stories did not (usually) concern life's passage, and it remained to be seen whether the tellers would move beyond the instant noodle–eating stage of life. Rather, the experiences these students described were still immediate: they were stories of hangovers averted, friendship verified, self-consciousness aroused, loss foretold, and embarrassment twinged. Nonetheless, there were clear similarities between the responses offered by the NPR audience and by these Amherst College students. Although both groups are relatively well educated and affluent, their instant noodle stories managed to downplay social distinction.[22] Essentially, they were a depiction of the normative—of a middle-of-the-road sensibility. Nothing in them was distasteful or seriously transgressive. Nothing was ethically or morally troubling. Nothing was flaunted or provoked envy. Nothing, even in regard to painful situations that were mentioned, was baffling or bewildering. In consequence, no one appeared unlikable or stuck-up; all were easy to empathize with.

Because instant noodles are so cheap and so ubiquitous and have little inherent significance, the significance they do have, at least for these middle-class Americans, is largely the result of an elaboration, an embellishment, an inflection on a common culinary base; instant noodles, it would seem, may serve as a blank slate for the inscription of small personal stories. Most of the NPR and Amherst College stories are about families being families or students being students. These stories are predicated on, or serve to organize, what Benedict Anderson calls an "imagined community," a homogenous and inclusive grouping of like-minded individuals.[23] The assumption is that anyone with an appropriately elaborated, embellished, and inflected instant noodle story could belong to this community and that each story would be of equal interest and worth.[24]

Thus, recollections of instant noodle experiences in the NPR and Amherst samples lend themselves to easy comparison: the family using Velveeta to render its instant noodles more appealing will recognize the family using canned beef stew to enhance its instant noodles; the man using them successfully to coat his trout will recognize the woman using them disastrously to create her mother's tuna casserole; the woman using them to measure her recovery from disease will recognize the girl using them to avoid sociability during a distressing time in her life. And, we venture, all would recognize one another as members of the same "family of man."[25]

In a number of ways, many of the instant noodle stories told to NPR and to Emily resemble the "home movies" described by the anthropologist Richard Chalfen.[26] Like family photo albums (and now probably home videos), these movies seem designed to select and instantiate, for purposes of reference, particular visions of history. The American middle-class people interviewed by Chalfen about their home movies invariably ignored the advice provided in the instruction booklets accompanying their cameras to plan, plot, and edit their movies with the same care and artistic sensibility that a cinema director brings to his or her creations. Rather, these home movie producers wanted to shoot things as they happened, to capture families and family members as they really were. The goal, they argued, was realism. But, as Chalfen points out, their efforts at realism produced results that were remarkably similar from family to family; with just a few exceptions, the home movies captured the same sort of clichéd vignettes or "moving" snapshots of middle-class family members appreciating one another and having fun together.[27] In addition, we would like to suggest that this realism may well have operated to make things seem real. In order to record a scenario involving families having fun, some editing of history is usually required.[28] In consequence, family history, whether appearing in home movies, family albums, or—we suggest—noodle narratives, is likely to be a relatively benign account.

In our view, therefore, instant noodles lend themselves well to searches for broadly common denominators, even in contexts framed by an article about an upscale New York chef and his complicated recipes, as with the NPR sample, or by college meal plans, as with Emily's sample. In both samples, what resulted was an ostensible democratization, or at least a shift in narrative position, from the culinary sophistication of Chang's restaurant or from the culinary amplitude of an elite college's dining hall. Those in both groups could talk easily about the time that the humble instant noodle figured importantly in their lives because they shared the expectation that this time either was or would soon be over. That is, their stories were premised on normative American biographical assumptions among those relatively well positioned in the system of capitalist provisioning: that their lives would have upward trajectories, or at least achieve a steady state. Correspondingly, there are no downward trajectories suggested in the stories, as in "I used to like eating at Chang's, but now, because I'm fifty-five and unemployed, I must go back to eating instant noodles once more." Eating instant noodles for these middle-class people should become—at least in the course of their own lives—a matter of choice, one of convenience or nostalgia.

INSTANT NOODLES IN PRISON

In crediting Maruchan's accomplishments, the Nissin executives at our Tokyo meeting conveyed that prisons and jails in the United States were a promising market. Not surprisingly, U.S. inmates constitute a demographic strikingly different from that of NPR listeners: in 2009, 34 percent were white, 39 percent were black, 21 percent were Hispanic, and 91 percent were male.[29] And unlike the majority of NPR listeners, needless to say, they are an incarcerated demographic. Rather than listening to "All Things Considered" while traveling home from work, perhaps pondering whether to pick up a rotisserie chicken or to cook, inmates are behind bars in a "total institution" that monitors and controls many aspects of their lives.[30] They are not going anywhere for a while, and though the food served them must meet food safety standards and regulations along with nutritional guidelines, it is not designed to be especially appealing. Prison food is "repetitive despite variation in menus," in large part because of "poor preparation resulting in meals in which soggy vegetables and overcooked meat . . . are indistinguishable one meal to the next." Moreover, prisoners tend to be fed "far earlier than is normal in the free community," and "mealtime is short."[31] Prisoners are frequently hungry, especially late in the day, and those who have money supplement their meals with more desirable food purchased from the prison commissary, including instant noodles.

Provisioning the prison mess halls and often the prison commissaries (as well as campus dining halls and school lunch programs) are corporations such as Sodexo Marriott and Aramark. These food service giants have been criticized for cutting corners on prison food and for profiting from, among other questionable labor, the coerced use of prisoners as a source of cheap labor.[32] (For twenty cents an hour, prisoners may, for example, prepare "the breaded chicken patty your child bites into at school."[33]) These businesses are, without doubt, successful. Concerning its profits from commissary sales, Aramark reports that it "operates over 1,000 successful retail operations that generate

$1 Billion in annual revenue. This enterprise expertise combined with 35 years of Corrections experience has enabled ACS [Aramark Correctional Services] to deliver a commissary alternative." The key to its success is that it operates its commissaries "with the 4 P's in mind—Right Product, Right Price, Right Place, Right Promotion. Like any marketplace, offenders and their families 'vote' with their wallets—if we don't have what they want, when and where they want it at the right price, they will choose not to spend their money."[34]

Frequently hungry, living where they don't want to be, and without control of their routine, prisoners often do "vote" for instant noodles. In fact, they build on them much as NPR listeners do, but in ways that instructively contrast with the behaviors of these middle-class eaters and narrators of instant noodles and tell us much about their different socioeconomic locations. As we have seen, NPR listeners build on instant noodles as a taste of transitory constraint (constraint alleviated by elaboration) against a background of generalized freedom and abundance of choice. Prisoners build on instant noodles as a taste of transitory freedom (freedom enhanced by elaboration) against a background of constraint and restriction of choice.[35]

Our initial glimpse into the prison life of instant noodles came from the "prison teacher" Oscar Bejarano, whose NPR story we referred to above. We quote NPR's transcript in its entirety:

> I teach at the level 4 California State Prison Sacramento and observed that top-ramen is the main staple for my students. They can buy cases of it at the canteen or have it included in their quarterly packages. Ramen is the coin of the realm, used to pay rent, pay off gambling debts or buy protection. Ramen is consumed plain, right out of the bag, like crunchie chips or cooked up with their state meal items. The traditional classroom meal starts with a bang; the ramen package is thrown hard on the table, repeatedly, this tenderizes the ramen. Then the tenderized noodles are placed in a plastic bag, you know, the trash bag size, with hot water and allowed to simmer for a time. As they wait, the mystery meat from the state lunch is diced and added. Other canteen items or procured ingredients from the facility kitchen are often added. Fresh onions or peppers are a bonus. Hot sauce is a must. The concoction is kneaded, almost lovingly massaged. It's ready to be squeezed out in about a half hour. Most squeeze it on to the bread from the lunch, sometimes on tortillas bought at the canteen or sucked out of the bag. The aroma is beyond description.[36]

This story was an eye-opener and caused us to search for more information on the web. We found many instant noodle–based prison recipes with accompanying narrations, all gifts constitutive of an expanding network of shared, albeit constrained, culinary appreciation. A prisoner in California described several creations that he would recommend:

> We are happily surprised to see all the "spread" recipes online![37] We constantly make spreads with whatever is available. Our favorites are hormel chili, noodles, and doritos; Noodles, Tijuana Mama (pickled sausage) with chips; Pickles, Tuna, Noodles, Mayo or Ranch [dressing], pickled sausage or smoked summer sausage and fritos; Sardines, mayo, porkskins, summer sausage, and cheetos. Hot sauce to taste. Mix all the ingredients to taste, and drain most water from noodles, and always add spice packet. We like chili flavored noodles the best with all recipes.
> Enjoy![38]

A mother hoping to provide a gift to her incarcerated son commented about these and other recipes: "I love it. I went here to maybe find something new for my son to try while under federal care, and couldn't believe how great all of you are! You definitely made me smile. Thanks and of course great recipes!"[39]

These recipes rely heavily, if not exclusively, on items available at the prison commissary, where (to repeat) inmates, provided they have money to spend, are allowed periodically to purchase whatever is available up to a specified amount (for example, fifty-five dollars every two weeks, although the amounts vary depending on the correctional institution).[40] According to official statistics presented by the journalist Matt Stiles in a 2010 article in the *Texas Tribune,* instant noodles are easily the most frequently chosen item the commissary has to offer: In 2009 the 160,000 inmates in Texas prisons purchased 33 million packages of instant noodles at US$0.25 per package, spending a total of US$8.3 million.[41] (Commissary prices vary considerably; at some places, instant noodles may cost several times this amount.) Thus, according to our calculations, per capita annual consumption by Texas inmates during 2009 was 206.25 packages with a corresponding expenditure of US$51.56. Extrapolating from this consumption rate, annual consumption by all U.S. inmates during 2009 was about 474 million packages, accounting for slightly more than 1 percent of the U.S. market.

Like the prison recipes, commissary-purchased food may be shared. Sandra Cate, an anthropologist who has written about "spreads" in a California jail, found that "more often than not spreading is a social activity." She quotes an inmate saying, "It's like we bonding in here when we break bread with a spread." Those who break bread together tend to be members of the same racial group, and principles of reciprocity prevail wherein those who "put in" ingredients receive "the even,

FIGURE 14. Prisoners share a "spread" of instant noodles mixed and kneaded with nachos and other commisary items; sharing spreads is a social activity among inmates, akin to breaking bread together. Photography by Robert Gumpert.

same amount." However, some may contribute a bit more so that "brothers who been here, don't have anything to eat . . . can also enjoy my little special meal."[42]

Cate argues that these spreads reflect "personal taste and individual access to resources. As such, it is an inmate's product of choice, not under the control of any authority. And, of course, it is handcrafted, not mass-produced by an institution serving [as with San Francisco County Jail 5] nearly eight hundred men."[43] Nolan Glass, who ran the Texas commissary program for twenty-four years, would agree. In his interview with Stiles, he granted that institutionally prepared food is "probably not going to be as tasty as a bag of chips" and stated his strong belief in the importance of commissary access, because mealtime is "one of the only times in an offender's day that he gets to make his own decisions . . . . It's paramount. It is a privilege that is necessary at this point and could not be done away with."[44] Spreads connote freedom of choice within constrained circumstances and, in turn, evoke a past and a future of more general choice associated with normal life outside of confinement. Cate writes movingly of an inmate named Max Hackett whose planned dish—an Asian stir-fry made with peanut oil extracted from lunchtime peanut butter that is added to instant noodles, leftovers taken from the dining hall, and hot sauce, followed by coffee with melted caramel candies—allows him to say to those sharing with him: "We're going to Tulan tonight [his favorite Vietnamese restaurant, on Sixth Street in San Francisco] and we're going to Starbucks afterwards, have a caramel Frappuccino."[45]

When Hackett gets out, he may well celebrate his freedom with a visit to Tulan—a restaurant purveying what one reviewer described as "basically cheap, hot, Vietnamese food fast food style."[46] But he may also think back to prison life by continuing to make his signature Asian stir-fry, as other former prisoners apparently do with their favorite spreads. Indeed, instant noodle–based spreads have the power to embody experiences and trigger memories of incarceration for people well after the fact. Thus, a blogger named Angie was inspired by a prison recipe she found on the web (essentially instant noodles, American cheese, tuna, and jalapeños) to share her own memories about her time in prison. The recipe was itself a memory, posted by a man who got it from a friend of his dad's, someone "who did a little time in prison." Angie replied:

> Boy o' Boy does this recipe bring back some memories!! Trust me. I had to do a 22 mo. stay in d.o.c. [Department of Corrections] for a D.U.I. [Driving Under the Influence]. I got home in December of 2004. Being I am a woman and of course I went to a woman's prison, ALL the women there were CHEFs!! Let me tell you I have seen Ramen Noodles made in all kinds of ways. I should have known that when I clicked on the "Official Ramen Homepage" the first thing I would see was something about prison recipes. I'm not complaining sometimes it's ok to remember where you been so you don't go back. . . . I am going to print off a couple pages of this site and mail them to a friend (I made during my "lil vacation" as I like to call it) she doesn't get to go home til 2012. I will ask her to mail me a recipe back so I can send it to ya'll. She'll get a kick out of this! Thank you for noticing the less fortunate of us! It's greatly appreciated!!![47]

This sharing is an inclusive invitation to recollect and recognize what life was like when eating life's culinary basics provided a welcome window of normalcy. Like the NPR listeners, former prisoners may look back on their instant noodle consumption as marking a previous stage of their lives. Unlike the NPR listeners, the biographical trajectory from one stage to another is never narratively assumed by the "less fortunate of us" who may view going "back" as a real possibility.

INSTANT NOODLES AND HEAVY USERS

There are many others in the United States who do not look back on instant noodle–eating experiences as marking a particular phase in socioeconomic coping, viewing them instead as central to day-to-day survival. These individuals have become primary targets of both Nissin and Maruchan. Maruchan's dominance, with twice the sales of Nissin, is especially apparent among Hispanics, some of whom first became familiar with the brand in Mexico, where Maruchan, which controls about 85 percent of the market, has become, according to an article in the *Los Angeles Times,* "the generic term for ramen noodles."[48] The U.S.-based journalist Yoko Ito-Petersen reports that, "these days, Hispanics—both here and in Mexico—are Maruchan's fastest-growing market."[49] Maruchan supplies both countries from its facilities in Irvine, California, exporting thirty 53-foot containers to Mexico each weekday.[50] According to a price survey conducted by Goldman Sachs at nine Los Angeles stores during 2010, "Instant noodles are prominent at stores with Hispanics as their core customers. . . . Customers at these stories tend to prefer Maruchan products, which we think may reflect Toyo Suisan's high share in Mexico. With the US Hispanic population growing . . . , we think Toyo Suisan (Maruchan, Inc.) has ample growth potential in North America."[51]

To compete more effectively with Maruchan in the United States, Nissin commissioned an Internet survey in 2011 seeking more accurate information about instant noodle eaters. Although its competition with Maruchan concerns sales of packages as well as cups, Nissin's survey focused on consumers of packages, specifically on "heavy users": those 14 percent of U.S. adults (over eighteen years of age) who eat either Nissin's Top Ramen or Maruchan's Ramen at least once a week, or a combination of both, several times a month.[52] Information was collected in English and in Spanish from a "nationally projectable" sample of 1,229 U.S. adults. These were the findings: compared to nationwide averages, heavy users are poorer and less likely to own their own homes; they are members of larger-than-average households with more children under the age of eighteen; they are less educated; and they are disproportionately male, Afro-American, or Hispanic American. Moreover, this pattern of disproportionate representation among heavy users is much greater for those aged eighteen to thirty-four than for those thirty-five and older. The survey concluded: "The Financial Challenge is Clear— Heavy User Households Have More People Than Average, But Have Lower Total Income Than Average (75% Below $75,000)." Hence, whatever else Nissin might do to increase market share among those exhibiting relatively strong demand, it should not forget that price matters.[53] (That this demographic resembles that of the prisoners and represents a contrast to that of the NPR listeners is not surprising given the well-known associations between race, poverty, and incarceration.)

We then commissioned our own survey. We sought a more vivid sense of how instant noodles might figure—not only literally but also symbolically—in the lives of those whose demand is likely to be ongoing. Again, we wondered, might instant noodles, at least as the subject of inquiry, serve as a register for significant aspects of their experience?

We asked the poet and translator Sophia Kraemer-Dahlin to conduct fifty structured interviews with Spanish-speaking men and women in California. Most of her interviews in San Francisco (Northern California) took place in the Financial District, where many Hispanic Americans are employed, and in the Mission District, where many work, shop, and socialize. All of her interviews in Pomona and Montclair (Southern California) took place at California Polytechnic University and the Montclair Mall, where many Hispanic Americans can also be found.[54] (In addition, several family friends completed interviews online.) She conducted thirty-two interviews with men ranging in age from nineteen to sixty-three and eighteen interviews with women ranging in age from sixteen to forty. Of the respondents, eleven were students, one was unemployed, and one was retired. The rest were working at poorly paying jobs, generally with no job security or health benefits: as nannies, landscapers, fruit sellers, sandwich makers, waitresses, construction laborers, factory workers, and house painters. Twenty met Nissin's definition of "heavy users." Although no interview question inquired directly into patterns of past consumption, seven people revealed that, while they currently ate instant noodles rarely, they had once done so frequently. Some attributed the change to health concerns—as with diabetics who sought to reduce their sodium intake. Some stopped eating them because of personal experiences—such as having already eaten more than their fill due to family poverty or incarceration. Others reported that either they or family members genuinely like them. A nineteen-year-old female student of Mexican heritage reported that she likes eating them at night, when it is "quiet and peaceful," and that when she makes them she often turns around "moments later and finds both my brother and dad chowing down." A thirty-six-year-old male busboy of Honduran heritage said that his son eats them with mayonnaise, which looks horrible to him; nonetheless he humors the boy, who calls them "a special meal." And a thirty-seven-year-old female nanny of Guatemalan heritage said that her seven-year-old niece loves them: "She eats Maruchan with cream all day long."

Most of those interviewed, however, eat instant noodles because they are inexpensive and help them deal with a life that is often hard. Some are students for whom the cost of food really matters—as none (as far as we can tell) was on a college meal plan. An eighteen-year-old male student of Mexican heritage said that he eats them for breakfast, lunch, and dinner because they are cheap. "I get sick of it, but I feel like I don't have a choice." A nineteen-year-old female student of Mexican heritage lived on them during her first semester of college: "I was living by myself, and my food budget was like twenty dollars a month. I'd get the big boxes of them." This young woman also reported that her dad had "been in and out of jail my whole life and he told me about spread. There are tons of recipes. I remember he liked his with Hot Cheetos." And a twenty-four-year-old male student of Mexican heritage, still a heavy user, learned about them "when I was a kid, with my mom. We were poor." Others are employed, yet not making much money. A thirty-two-year-old male cell phone salesman of Mexican heritage said he ate a lot of them when he was in jail and buys them now when money is really low. Even so, he only eats them for breakfast or lunch, "never for dinner because that would be too sad." A twenty-one-year-old male clerk of Salvadoran heritage buys them at Costco, where they "come in big cartons," and eats them "to take the edge off hunger." And a twenty-two-year-old male waiter of Mexican heritage said that when he was young, his mother "would work late sometimes, so my sister would babysit and she didn't cook very well so she would make instant noodles." Though he rarely ate them currently, "the price did matter to me when I ate instant noodles; the price of anything I purchase matters to me because I am not a man of great wealth."

Although a few of those interviewed prefer their noodles "dry and plain" (cooked and drained, either with or without the flavor packet), most adapt them to their tastes. In addition to those previously mentioned with idiosyncratic preferences for noodles with mayonnaise and cream, many elaborate their instant noodles. Some add combinations of chili, lemon, and tomato; several, corn chips and canned vegetables; one, mushrooms, onion, and eggplant; one, seaweed—and we could go on. Kraemer-Dahlin concluded from her interviews that those engaged in "creative additions to plain Ramen" might well have "thwarted desires to cook from scratch." For these, as well as less imaginative noodle eaters, the overall appeal, she said, was pretty basic: "the low price and instantaneity of instant noodles are logically helpful for people who work long hours at low wages."[55] We agree. As such, many of these stories were powerfully affecting snapshots of the role of instant noodles in sustaining those who sustain capitalism.

Thus, while Maruchan and Nissin are, no doubt, happy to sell instant noodle to NPR listeners and college students, they recognize that the prisoners and, especially, the heavy users constitute their primary American market. For those who make up this market, already accustomed as they are to capitalist provisioning, instant noodles help significantly with life's difficulties (albeit, for some, "never for dinner because that would be too sad"). As we shall see in the next chapter, for those less accustomed to this provisioning, instant noodles may play a different role; they may serve as an effective introduction to capitalism as a way of life. Instant noodles provide something for everyone—for better, or for worse.

4

Instant Noodles for the Bottom of the Pyramid in Papua New Guinea

Instant noodles have, indeed, become the global food that Ando antic-ipated. Humble and everyday, they are now readily incorporated into quotidian expectations and activities—into the "habitus" of many peo-ple in many places. In their capacity to mesh with diverse lives, instant noodles both reflect and affect those lives. For example, in Japan, instant noodles may arrive on the market elaborated to the point of saturation, fostering the appreciation of small differences among simi-lar commodities (an appreciation expressed by Ton Tan Tin through his "hobby"). And in the United States, instant noodles may arrive elaborated hardly at all, sometimes fostering the expression of personal experiences centered on common themes, sometimes simply helping people get by.

In the developing world, the capacity of instant noodles to reflect and affect what is happening becomes most evident. There, in a way that speaks tellingly about capitalist provisioning, instant noodles may lend themselves to the creation of the habitus of consumption itself, to the creation of those who understand that the important dimensions of their lives—who they are and what they do—are shaped significantly by the choices they (and others) make as consumers.

The capacity of instant noodles to change habitus in the developing world has been variously documented. In Mexico, for instance, instant noodles have altered daily routines, leading Gloria López Morales, an official with Mexico's National Council for Culture and the Arts, to worry that "Mexican palates have been seduced by this ramen import."[1] As the journalist Marla Dickerson explains:

> Nearly 60 percent of Mexico's work force earns less than $13 a day. Instant ramen is a hot meal that fills stomachs, typically for less than 40 cents a serving. The product doesn't need refrigeration and it's so easy to make that some here call it "sopa para flojos," or lazy people's soup." . . . . [According to the manager of Maruchan's central warehouse near Mexico City:] "Traditions are changing fast, even up in the mountains and in the countryside. . . .You can spend days cooking beans. Maruchan is ready in three minutes. All the mother has to do is boil water and throw in the chilies."[2]

In Brazil there is the clear anticipation by the Nestlé Corporation that selling a product such as instant noodles involves selling a change in expectations and activities—to create, for instance, consumers for whom the Brazilian equivalent of "lazy people's soup" seems a quite reasonable choice. Thus in 2007 Nestlé, the world's largest food company (and the quintessence of "big food"), opened a factory in the rapidly industrializing Bahia region to produce Maggi instant noodles. According to a Nestlé website: "The plant brings direct and indirect employment opportunities to an economically deprived region, while increasing local workforce skills and raising environmental standards. It also helps Nestlé to reach 50 million consumers in this part of the world. Maggi instant noodles are popular in many countries of Latin America, Asia, Oceania and Africa. They belong to Nestlé's family of Popularly Positioned Products (PPP), offering a nutritious food choice for everyone, but particularly for people who have reduced spending power."[3] As Andrew Jack reported in the *Financial Times*, Nestlé is directing its Maggi instant noodles and the rest of its PPP line especially to those "at the 'bottom of the pyramid' whose rising income levels in the past few years have created new sources of growth for the company."[4] Nestlé's strategies of market expansion are instructive. The company has constituted a network of microdistributors comprising local people who use their knowledge and credibility to penetrate poor urban neighborhoods to sell the PPP. In so doing, as Jack says, they are offering "a taste of western consumerism and aspiration to the fast-growing working-class population."[5] In addition, Nestlé has inaugurated a "floating supermarket" to bring its PPP to remote communities located along the Amazon River—to extend its reach to those hitherto less dependent on purchased foods.[6] Suggesting the power of instant noodles to shift the parameters of the everyday, the anthropologist Barbara Piperata reports that women in the Amazon have welcomed instant noodles, finding that they cook quickly with little firewood and that kids like their appealingly different taste.[7] Overall, Nestlé's strategy of down-reach has been paying off. In 2009, sales to the bottom of the pyramid (BOP) accounted for 8 percent of the company's total Brazilian revenue, an increase of 27 percent over the previous year.[8]

Our final and major illustration of the global course of instant noodles comes from another developing country, Papua New Guinea (PNG). The site of Deborah and Fred's long-term ethnographic involvement, Papua New Guinea is also the site of a Nestlé initiative targeting the BOP. As in Brazil, Nestlé has sought in Papua New Guinea to transform the habitus of those purchasing its Maggi instant noodles and the other elements in its Oceania-focused PPP line. And, at least in Papua New Guinea, in order for Nestlé to sell instant noodles to the BOP, it first has had to construct the BOP. In other words, it has had to redefine Papua New Guinea's urban and peri-urban poor. No longer just those who struggle to get by, they have become consumers embarked on an auspicious commodity trajectory that will reward them as well as those who provide them with what they increasingly want. As the PNG example suggests, instant noodles, in their spread throughout the world, have been caught up in a remarkable global project of capitalist refashioning. In fact, instant noodles facilitate this refashioning: the BOP do not just increasingly buy instant noodles; instant noodles increasingly help create the BOP.

By bringing the instant noodle–eating poor into the BOP, Nestlé and its ilk have been promulgating a big-food future of provisioning. This is a future in which supposedly everyone—producer and consumer—will benefit. Once "a taste of western consumerism and aspiration" has taken hold, sales will flourish and prosperity and comfort will become less elusive. Certainly, many in Papua New Guinea, especially peri-urban and urban dwellers, have been convinced by the availability of instant noodles to subscribe, at least provisionally, to this win-win future.

TRANSFORMING THE POOR INTO THE BOTTOM OF THE PYRAMID

The term "bottom of the pyramid" has not always referred to a distinctive and promising market segment. In his famous 1932 radio address, Franklin Roosevelt described it quite somberly: "These unhappy times call for the building of plans that rest upon the forgotten, the unorganized but the indispensable units of economic power . . . [to] build from the bottom up and not from the top down . . . [and to] put their faith once more in the forgotten man at the bottom of the economic pyramid."[9] More recently, within postindustrial consumer capitalism, this Depression-era man has become part of a huge aggregate—whose future, it seems, is far from bleak. Although size estimates vary, C.K. Prahalad (late professor at the University of Michigan's Ross School of Business) saw the BOP as the potential market of "those 4 billion people who live on less than $2/day."[10] Given the size of this market category and its collective purchasing power, many businesses, especially multinational corporations, are following Prahalad's lead. In *The Fortune at the Bottom of the Pyramid,* he argued that not only can money be made from those at the BOP, but good can be done for them at the same time.[11] Thus a report by the Aspen Institute reasons that "if companies are innovative enough to create or tailor their products to the economic realities and life needs of these people, a significant profit can be won. At the same time, this group's entry into the market would hopefully better their quality of life and aid in regional economic development."[12] Elaborating these points, Ted London (also of the University of Michigan's Ross School of Business) states: "Corporate investment at the base of the pyramid could mean lifting billions of people out of poverty and desperation, suggesting that serving these markets will not only generate economic profits [some estimate the BOP to have $14 trillion in collective purchasing power] but also may address the social and environmental challenges associated with a growing gap between the rich and poor."[13]

This is a neoliberal model that promises evolutionary change through market-based mechanisms—a single course of progress linking commercial success with personal and social development. (The distinction between personal and social benefit is largely collapsed in this model.) Prahalad's two subtitles reflect this linkage: "eradicating poverty through profits" and "enabling dignity and choice through markets."[14] Both depend on a critical "take-off"—the creation of "the capacity to consume."[15] And once "the poor are converted into consumers, they get more than access to products and services. They acquire the dignity of attention and choices from the private sector that were previously reserved for the middle-class and rich."[16] Moreover, these newly empowered consumers will constitute a burgeoning market for other goods and services. In the language of the psychologist Abraham Maslow, whose ideas often inform discussions of the BOP's potentialities, once the necessities of survival are met, people will strive for "self-actualization" through their choice of products.[17]

In this marketer's vision, hence, the hierarchy of needs leads people through a hierarchy of products. Multinational corporations are therefore increasingly directing their entrepreneurial lens on the BOP. Forgotten and fragmented no more, the BOP is being constituted by these companies as a socioeconomic category of active market participants. These participants are depicted as eager for products that make their daily lives more secure and comfortable as well as those that open new horizons—products like cheap cell phones that can help them bank, negotiate credit, and otherwise engage in commerce. Such products, it is said, bring them utility, hope, and progress.[18]

Yet many voice concern about this marketing-focused win-win strategy—a strategy, to repeat, that links corporate profit to personal and social benefit.[19] Not surprisingly, those seeking corporate profit ponder whether their products might be linked feasibly to this new category of BOP consumers. Because large volumes must compensate for low unit prices, the challenges in selling to the BOP are considerable. The product must have sufficiently broad appeal to extend beyond any given group or locality. The product must be affordable, a condition often met by selling in small sizes or in single units, provided that costs incurred by inefficiencies in packaging and distribution are controlled. And the product must deliver satisfaction to value-conscious consumers. Finally, even if all of these challenges are overcome, it may be hard to profit in a predictable way from customers who, as the economist Paul Thomas says, may be only "one setback (disease, injury, monsoon, crime, war) away from disaster."[20]

The extent to which consumers find personal and social benefit is related to their satisfaction with the products they buy, including how well these products sustain them under difficult circumstances. Their satisfaction may additionally become qualified if they suspect that the benefits accruing to them as consumers are incommensurate with those accruing to producers and purveyors. With this suspicion, the rhetoric of a win-win deal may fail to convince. Apparently, this was the case in India when, according to the anthropologists Jamie Cross and Alice Street, consumers of Hindustan Unilever Limited's Lifebuoy soap concluded that the balance between corporate profit and the personal and social benefit of enhanced cleanliness was unfairly tilted against them. Their response was political activism expressed in statements like: "Give us drinking water first, instead of [brand name] soap."[21]

Certain food products, however, have the potential for overcoming these challenges in terms of matching product to consumer. The Nestlé

Corporation, as mentioned, has determined that its worldwide line of PPP has the potential for earning it profits through sales to cash-dependent and concentrated urban and peri-urban populations. Nestlé has been particularly successful in Papua New Guinea, as it has in Brazil, with easing its Maggi brand of instant noodles throughout the country.[22]

A BRIEF HISTORY OF INSTANT NOODLES IN PAPUA NEW GUINEA

During June 2009 and for a week during March 2011, Deborah and Fred lived in Lae, Papua New Guinea's second largest city and the head-quarters of Nestlé's Maggi instant noodle operation. There, they interviewed past and present factory executives and sales managers along with supermarket managers and wholesalers who carried Maggi and other brands of noodles. They also interviewed nutritionists and food technologists at Lae's University of Technology who were familiar with Nestlé's PNG operation.

Larry Ori was especially knowledgeable about how Nestlé created and extended the networks necessary to introduce this novel and potentially lucrative product. A Papua New Guinean, he had been involved from the beginning and had recognized a PNG market in the making. Ori told Deborah and Fred that in the early 1980s, Nestlé sold its products into Papua New Guinea through big companies, one of which he worked for. This was a broker business, in which goods were ordered from Australia and bundled into shipments to Papua New Guinea. Then he met a Malaysian Chinese, Erik Gan, who was an export manager for Nestlé. Both agreed that instant noodles were a natural product for the modernizing Papua New Guinea and decided to bring two containers of instant noodles from the Nestlé factory in the Philippines to Papua New Guinea. When Ori took some instant noodles home, his wife wouldn't have anything to do with them because they didn't look like proper food. His kids, though, liked them right away.

In 1985, Nestlé opened an instant noodle factory in Fiji.[23] It was the first Pacific Island instant noodle factory, and it exported noodles to Papua New Guinea. Although there was an immediate interest in instant noodles among Papua New Guineans, Ori knew that "to instill taste and establish the brand" would require work.[24] PNG food was rather bland, yet Papua New Guineans were receptive to more intense flavors. When they poured the flavor sachet onto their instant noodles, they loved the aroma and taste.

Ori and others packed noodles into vans and traveled extensively throughout the "highlands and islands" to "reach the masses with seeing, touching, and tasting" the product. They went into stores, squatter settlements, markets, cultural shows, church fetes, meetings of women's groups, and schools. They offered free samples and asked people whether they liked what they tried. In addition, they used a TV to show videos about cooking instant noodles. Soon, they knew they "were on to something very big." Although some initially balked at the appearance of instant noodles, thinking of them as "little worms," most came around quickly. The chicken flavor won them over, as did the slogan (in translation from PNG's lingua franca, Tok Pisin) "Fast to Cook, Good to Eat." But, says Ori, "we also piggy-backed on rice." In one store demonstration they placed a television and the display of instant noodles right above twenty-kilogram bags of rice stacked on the floor. When people came to buy rice, "we would offer them a taste of noodles, and if they liked them, as they often did, [we would] point to where they could buy them. The rest was word of mouth."

By 1987, Ori explained, sales had picked up sufficiently to justify building a factory in Lae. Permission from the National Investment Authority was granted when Nestlé promised to create jobs. In 2009, as the factory manager told Deborah and Fred, about 190 workers were employed there.

Not entirely by coincidence, Deborah and Fred's first research into urban and peri-urban realities in Papua New Guinea took place during the same year that Nestlé decided to build its PNG factory. They were living in the town of Wewak with Chambri people who were increasingly migrating from their home villages, lured by prospects of urban-based "development." These Chambri had left in search of better educational opportunities and social services as well as modern experiences; they were beginning to feel that spending their whole lives in villages meant missing out. Urban life could be exciting, and Chambri enjoyed wandering around town, often in the company of friends—visiting the crowded shops, markets, bus stops, sports fields, and churches. However, for most of them (and for the migrants from other places) money was short. Thus, according to three months of statistics Deborah and Fred collected during 1987, only 17 percent of Chambri adults living in a Wewak squatter settlement had regular salaries. Most of the other men and women in the settlement were artisans—carvers or basket weavers—and relied on income earned from sales. Yet over the three-month period, many of these artisans made no sales at all. More food-deprived than in their fish-rich home villages, they eked out a living somehow. They subsisted at least partly on smoked fish occasionally sent from home-village kin, green mangoes gathered from trees belonging to others, marsupials killed in the bush, and whatever inexpensive food they could buy with small earnings from street hawking and the like.

A similar picture emerged from more recent statistics Deborah and Fred collected among other Chambri migrants living in a peri-urban settlement near the town of Madang. During 2006, they learned that just 15 percent had regular income, with most of them earning minimal amounts (for example, US$16.80 per fortnight at a tuna cannery).[25] Like the earlier migrants, many of these urban-dwelling Chambri without salaries were dependent on selling artifacts and baskets or on scrounging within a far-from-thriving informal economy. Thirty-four members of six households that included both wage earners and artisans were the subject of more focused research, specifically a survey of what family members ate daily. Virtually all bought the cheapest foods available, which by this time often included instant noodles.

Also in 2006, Deborah and Fred sought an indication of what a somewhat more affluent group of Papua New Guineans ate. They requested that a friend survey the "food baskets" of his colleagues at Ramu Agricultural Industries, the site of an earlier project.[26] This friend asked twenty-two workers (earning between US$41.84 and US$300.00 per fortnight) what they had purchased with their last paycheck. For everyone, the basic items were rice, sugar, cooking oil, canned fish, local vegetables from an open-air market, and instant noodles.

Finally, we should mention that all of this information concurs with the appraisal of Paul Savage, manager of a major food wholesale firm in Lae. On June 29, 2009, he told Deborah and Fred that "noodles began to take off in 1987" and there "has been a dramatic growth" since then that "shows no sign of letting up."

Ori has remained committed to fostering this growth. One of his recent projects followed from his observation that in Asian countries people eat while on the move. This inspired him to create a flourishing "hub" system, a central area where company-approved vendors purchase premeasured ingredients consisting of dry noodles and chopped fresh vegetables (primarily carrots and spring onions). They mix these with hot water and eggs in a standardized ratio to brew up big pots of instant noodle soup for sale from carts—"vending boxes"—owned by the company. These carts (largely in the city of Lae, where there were

FIGURE 15. A hub vending box at the Lae Market sells Maggi instant noodles to Papua New Guineans on the move. Photograph by Deborah Gewertz.

some forty-five during 2009), each sporting a big Maggi-logoed umbrella and brightly painted in the yellow and red Maggi colors, are situated at high-traffic areas like bus stops and entrances to outdoor markets. There, the vendors sell cupfuls of noodle soup for a price of US$0.20 to those many Papua New Guineans milling around in town who are unable to afford more leisurely or expensive fare.[27]

Ori emphasized that the hub system was designed to do more than make sales to mobile consumers, since these sales, though profitable, would never be that large in volume. Of equal if not greater importance to the company is the hub system's promotion of the brand more generally. At the same time, it has won the favor of the government by stimulating an informal sector.[28] Nestlé's decision to try this system in Papua

New Guinea additionally followed from its completion of a "four-tier pyramid study" of the worldwide market and the conclusion that more could be made from the "bottom of the pyramid." Ori elaborated:

> We tested the recipe for one year. We worked out the format with the pre-scribed water level so as to ensure health and hygiene, and the office in Sydney approved.[29] The concept [then] went all the way to Switzerland [Nestlé's corporate headquarters]. Now it is in Africa and the rest of the world. Fijians have come here to look at us, and the income idea for the poor has appealed to them. If people are on the streets selling ice blocks or cigarettes, they get no more than twenty to thirty bucks [US$7 to $10]; while a pot of Maggi noodles gets them fifty [US$17].[30] They buy the ingredients, we prescribe what and how much; we know that if they come back in three days, they are doing it right; if they don't come back then and wait more, they have broken it up [diluted it]. There's a blackboard inside the hub with all the vendors' names and every time one comes in for ingredients, a tick is put next to the name. That's how we keep track and control.

Ori's story is of the creation of a network that introduced a novel commodity. This commodity in turn compelled attention and created desire throughout Papua New Guinea, from "highlands to islands." To be sure, Ori and his associates had to improvise as they went along. They encountered difficulties and obstacles and needed to redirect their efforts as they tried to "instill the brand" and convince Papua New Guineans to "see, touch, and taste" their product. Overall, though, they were able to manage their network and control their brand with skill and imagination, and acceptance came rather quickly; they were "on to something very big." Data from 189 Papua New Guineans interviewed by our research assistants (in two PNG urban centers and in one village near a commercial center) indicate that no one disliked instant noodles and few were indifferent to them. Indeed, they have become the new modernist staple. Although calorie for calorie instant noodles are about two-thirds more expensive than rice, and gram for gram they are about twice as expensive, they are not only reasonably affordable but, for most people and for many reasons (including their gustatory and olfactory appeal), they are distinctively enticing.

Instant noodles have been so well received in Papua New Guinea that the market has recently become flooded with imports, principally from Indonesia, Vietnam, and China. Long-term control over such a permeating product in such an eagerly receptive market would be difficult. To quote Savage once again: "Now, all major wholesalers—every man and his dog—are importing noodles. . . . Everyone wants a bigger cut of the margin . . . [and some of the big stores] have their own brands; there

FIGURE 16. Instant noodles at a roadside stand. Photograph by Waka Tosa.

are brands, brands, and more brands." Yet if Nestlé's careful creation of the PNG market for instant noodles has opened the door for its competitors, Nestlé's senior brand manager in Papua New Guinea, Wanzefri Wanzahari, did not seem unduly worried. In 2009, Maggi still controlled some 80 percent of the market. He told Deborah and Fred that the competition was to be predicted: "There's always competition. It's a free market. So we just have to step up and maintain our share."[31]

Regardless of which brand gets what market share, instant noodle capitalism is thriving in Papua New Guinea. During 2011 an industry insider estimated that in a population of some six million, per capita annual consumption was 20.4 packs. For those urban and peri-urban people dependent on purchased food, the figure would be much higher. Moreover, there seems to be increasing penetration of instant noodles into areas in which they supplement locally grown food. For example, by 2011 they were available at nearly every market and roadside stand located along the 350 kilometers of highway linking the cities of Madang and Lae.

That this thriving and expanding market attracted competitors was not just inevitable under free market conditions. It also could be seen as having created an additional market opportunity. After all, competition creates market choice, and market choice helps transform the merely poor into members of the BOP: those who, as aspiring consumers, may be interested in instant noodles as well as in a range of products. Under these circumstances, Nestlé, with its resources and product line, may continue to do well.

WORKING TOWARD THE BOP IN PAPUA NEW GUINEA

Papua New Guineans have long been promised the benefits of social and economic development. Both the colonial and the postcolonial government invested in roads, schools, clinics, and—especially in remote, "backward" areas—large-scale commercial enterprises, including oil palm and sugar plantations. However, in 1994 there was an important shift in government policy and practice. Faced with increasing budget deficits, the government sought help from the World Bank and International Monetary Fund (IMF). In return, it agreed to make the "structural adjustments" required of indebted countries worldwide. Central to these were "user-pay" policies, which promoted the principle of individual responsibility and substantially reduced government benefits. Despite the unpopularity of these "adjustments," development was still presented as achievable. It would have to be based in the market, though, with consumers increasingly accountable for obtaining and paying for the services and commodities that would improve their lives.

This shift in policy and practice has facilitated the creation of the BOP in Papua New Guinea. The government's retreat from the business of development has enabled companies to move in with their market-based vision linking corporate profit with personal and social benefit.[32] Indeed, Nestlé's application of a BOP template to the specificities of a PNG social field would follow seamlessly from the World Bank and IMF's application of their template of structural adjustments. Nestlé, thus, was allied with other influential players in fostering a social transformation; in the interest of refining and rationalizing its marketing strategies, it worked to change PNG's cash-strapped poor into entry-level consumers.

This transformation can be seen in Nestlé's 2008 "Oceania, Creating Shared Value Report." In title and content, the document is consistent with Prahalad's vision of a corporate as well as personal and social win-win. That is, the products, prices, and promotions seen by Nestlé as

FIGURE 17. Nestlé PNG product line display, featuring Maggi instant noodles, Nescafé powdered coffee, and Milo malted drink. Photograph by Deborah Gewertz.

providing its competitive edge are linked to a BOP vision of Papua New Guinea's promise:

> We want our products to be accessible and affordable for everyone, including the 2.8 billion people around the world who earn less than USD10 per day . . . .

PPPs IN PAPUA NEW GUINEA—MAGGI NOODLES

With around 85% of Papua New Guinea's population sitting at the "bottom of the pyramid"—representing the poorest socio-economic group—affordability and accessibility principles underpin our key products in Papua New Guinea.

The Papua New Guinea Market

- 85% of the population is at the bottom of the pyramid, with a per capita disposal income of under USD 2,700 [about US$7.40/day].
- 820 indigenous languages spoken.
- Large proportion of people living in settlements in rural areas.
- 57% literacy rate.
- People generally consume only one meal per day.

Our Response

Affordability—getting the price and serving size right.

- Small pack sizes have been introduced across our key products in Papua New Guinea, in particular our key PPP in the region: Maggi noodles.

Accessibility—establishment of a comprehensive distribution strategy to insure our products are accessible.

- Increased presence at open food markets through the provision of Maggi noodles and Maggi-branded tables and merchandise for local sellers.
- Provision of Maggi Noodle dishes through food carts.
- Increasing the number of Maggi "Kai" (food) Bars.
- New distribution channels to reach the many villages of PNG.

Health and Nutrition—insuring products are nutritionally sound.

- Awareness and educational activities. Including the promotion of nutritious recipes and nutrition information.
- Maggi noodles contain iodized sodium.[33]

Several observations can be made about how this marketing perspective refuses to get snagged on particularities or hung up on differences (if not disjunctions). Although Papua New Guineans speak numerous languages, a bare majority are literate, and many live in villages, none of these characteristics matters much to Nestlé. Rather, what matters are their BOP characteristics. In essence, Papua New Guinea is a place of interest to Nestlé because its people represent a substantial, relatively uniform, and accessible market: they are poor; they can be reached even if not living in urban areas; and they might be convinced that their main meal of the day should be (at least in part) inexpensive, convenient, filling, and tasty instant noodles. The differences that often engage anthropologists thus prove irrelevant to marketers, at least as their gaze searches for the fortune at the bottom of the pyramid.

Of course, no large company configures products for poverty as well as for extreme cultural particularity—for example, by targeting the 820 different indigenous languages and the concomitantly diverse and varied sets of cultural expectations in Papua New Guinea.[34] The BOP category is premised on a mass market defined by homogeneity—by commonalities among consumers as measured by the widely available products they can consume. In this regard, not only commodities but also potential consumers—the PPP and the BOP, in this case—have been equally "fetishized" (to use Karl Marx's term), perhaps especially so in culturally diverse Papua New Guinea.[35] Both have stripped down biographies that allow their flows through the market to be clean and unencumbered. The throngs of products that arrive at places like Food Mart in Lae are not expected to display the social, temporal, and spatial conditions of their product lives. These factors are deliberately made irrelevant to ensure that their value can be narrowly measured by supply and demand. Similarly, the throngs of potential consumers who arrive at places like Food Mart are not encouraged to speak about the social, temporal, and spatial conditions of their BOP lives. These, too, are deliberately made irrelevant to ensure that their worth and identity can be narrowly measured by what they can afford.[36] In other words, the BOP is understood as an opening to seize an attractive market opportunity, not as an imperative to confront a persistent economic inopportunity: the BOP becomes the diagram of a market, not the diagram of social and economic inequality (with 85 percent in poverty in Papua New Guinea). Market efficiencies require that everything be smoothed out and that dissonance and turbulence be minimized.[37]

DO INSTANT NOODLES MAKE THE CONSUMER?

Instant noodles, we believe, have a role in normalizing and homogenizing the identity of urban and peri-urban Papua New Guineans by "BOP-izing" them into committed consumers. This appears to be Nestlé's intent in sending a Papua New Guinean "Sampling and Events

Manager" and her "road show" throughout the country to instruct and inspire women in villages and towns (often working through women's church groups). She told Deborah and Fred in 2011 that these occasions are received enthusiastically.[38] Called (in translation from Tok Pisin) "Happy Day at Your Place," they are intended to change people's lives. First establishing the nutritional importance of three (not just one, or perhaps two) meals each day, she and her team demonstrate that Nestlé products can be the basis of well-balanced meals, arguing that processed foods are fine if mixed with locally produced ones. Moreover, they suggest that their products can be used to celebrate special occasions like Mother's or Father's Day, as with a breakfast omelet filled with instant noodles and garnished with tomatoes and green onions. They show that Nescafé powdered coffee and Milo malted drink taste better when prepared properly. Finally, they propose that wives, with their new domestic skills and aspirations, deserve to receive good quality cookware from their husbands. All of this is part of Nestlé's "corporate social responsibility" and commitment to "good food, good life." The overall message is that if families eat as she and Nestlé advocate, "the kids will grow up well, will be healthy, have a good education, and get a good job—and the whole community will be happy."

We additionally base our claim that instant noodles help create committed consumers on conversations Deborah and Fred have had with urban and peri-urban Papua New Guineans (Chambri and others) of various ages living in and around the town of Madang and on structured interviews designed to tap consumer preferences in broadly contrasting ethnographic areas.[39] Our evidence is consistent: instant noodles are a multiply palatable commodity, one that, for interrelated reasons, goes down easily. To extend the dictum of the anthropologist Claude Lévi-Strauss, who said that food is not only "good to eat," but also "good to think": it can, as well, be "good to buy" and "good to sell."[40]

First, and most significantly, instant noodles are "good to buy." The 189 Papua New Guineans surveyed by our research assistants in the coastal town of Madang, the highland town of Goroka, and the village of Bumbu (adjacent to Gusap-located Ramu Agricultural Industries) exercise active choice among instant noodle brands. So, too, do most of those with whom Deborah and Fred spoke. When asked whether there was a type they prefer or dislike, 80 percent of those interviewed report having distinct preferences among brands, with many choosing Maggi over imported instant noodles because of taste coupled with in-country manufacture. (One twenty-four-year-old male contrarian, however, said that he enjoys choosing a specific imported brand because it is not popular with his friends.) The choices they make rarely depend on the number of grams a package contains (and most are unaware that packages vary between sixty-five and eighty-five grams). Nor, for 61.4 percent, do these choices depend that much on relative price—since all varieties are inexpensive (costing, in urban contexts, between US$0.26 and US$0.32). Most spoken with and interviewed conveyed the idea that if they like it, they buy it. In addition, instant noodles provide other opportunities for choice. Respondents told Deborah and Fred that they like choosing whether to eat noodles as a snack straight from the package (since instant noodles are precooked) or as an easy-to-cook meal to share with others, often members of an extended family. If the latter, they select whether to incorporate the noodles as a main ingredient or, more frequently, as an extender for rice and root vegetables, sometimes with inexpensive canned fish. They also like choosing how to use the flavor sachet, either as a flavor enhancer with soup or as a condiment with vegetables. One young woman told Deborah that she wouldn't consider wasting the sachet on soup since it is so good as a dip for cucumber.[41] Most reported that instant noodles are variously employed and regarded, either as a carbohydrate when used as the basis of a meal or as a vegetable or a protein when used as a topping. Indeed, instant noodles can be mixed and matched with just about anything.[42] Moreover, people do not report tiring of them. In fact, those interviewed eat instant noodles, either alone as a snack or shared with family members as a meal, on average 6.7 times per week. As one fifty-year-old male enthusiast put it: "If noodles weren't available, there would be no hope because I cannot live without them; they make all meals taste better." A twenty-five-year-old female echoed this sentiment: "Eating instant noodles is something I can't live without."

Second, instant noodles are "good to think." Without doubt, many Papua New Guineans enjoy participating in cosmopolitan networks, such as those connected to evangelical Christianity, in part because such participation suggests that they belong to the modern world.[43] Similarly, because Papua New Guineans know that instant noodles are popular with all sorts of people elsewhere, eating them enables a pleasurable engagement in a wide network of like-minded consumers. In this regard, Papua New Guinea's Paradise Foods recently introduced two varieties of instant noodles called "USA styled" and "England styled." Television ads depicted President Obama and Queen Elizabeth eating them (with the taglines "They are even enjoyed by presidents" and

"They are even enjoyed by the Queen"). Under consideration (during 2011) was another ad showing Prince William and his bride eating instant noodles at their wedding. In this sense, instant noodles are different from, say, "lamb flaps" (another food studied by Deborah and Fred), a local delicacy that repels many outsiders and about which many Papua New Guineans themselves express ambivalence.[44] Instant noodles, by contrast, evoke no such feelings. PNG consumers know that (white) New Zealand and Australian producers and purveyors of lamb flaps generally do not eat them, regarding them as too fatty and mostly suitable for dog food. But if there is a flap about flaps among Papua New Guineans, there's nothing notorious about noodles. Both filling and nonfraught, instant noodles are a double comfort food. Because everyone knows that everyone eats them, they appear to equalize all— even though they are eaten in different amounts and for different reasons by differently located people.

Finally, instant noodles are "good to sell," allowing the companies that produce them to circumvent some of the difficulties of making a profit from the BOP. As mentioned, a major challenge is to provide enough content to be appealing in single-unit sales and in packages small enough to be affordable. However, reducing package size usually means that packaging costs go up relative to content. This is not the case with instant noodles, because the standard size is the small size. Moreover, since one basic product serves all—at least in nonsaturated markets—an instant noodle company need only produce a single product line, tweaked largely with minor changes to the flavor sachet.

For all of these reasons, Nestlé was astute in designating instant noodles the cornerstone of its PPP line for the BOP in Papua New Guinea. They contribute to the sustenance of urban and peri-urban Papua New Guineans while transforming them into aspiring consumers of a modern product that links them to everyone, everywhere. In other words, instant noodles have a daily role in transforming the urban and peri-urban PNG poor into the BOP. And cash-dependent Papua New Guineans are pleased with their access to a world-pervading, competitively priced, convenient, satisfying, daily belly filler—pleased with their access to this particular kind of contemporary hunger killer.

WHAT'S TO COME?

Though helping poor urban and peri-urban Papua New Guineans hang on, instant noodles do not necessarily help them move up. To have been made into the BOP (with or without aspirations for Maslow's self-actualization) may bring its own problems. To be stuck at the bottom of the BOP, we think, may undermine the reciprocity presumed to underwrite the win-win relationship between aspiring-yet-vulnerable consumers and established sellers: this is the expectation that the deal includes both getting value and being of value. Correspondingly, a perceived default on this deal might well elicit strong and insistent demands for the "dignity of attention and choices," as touted by Prahalad.

In this context, the story of Hindustan Unilever Limited's promotion of its Lifebuoy soap to the BOP in India may serve as a cautionary tale about reciprocity neglected. Cross and Street describe a BOP pushback suggesting that in this case a perception of win-win had shifted to one of rip-off. In fact, this BOP response—a politically potent expression of anger that soap was not just soap, but was a self-serving and deceptive substitute for clean water—could be seen as a strategic defetishization of an important and everyday commodity. The response conveyed a salutary warning that social relations, whether of respect or disdain, can well define the deal consumers think they are getting with their respective purchases.

Recent events in Papua New Guinea have also conveyed a forceful warning about who owes what to whom. Shortly before Deborah and Fred's 2009 visits to the Nestlé facility in Lae, cell phones (a product often lauded as beneficially transformative of the lives of the BOP as they move up the pyramid) were used to coordinate the massing of rioters intent on stripping the shelves of certain businesses. These were widespread, loosely organized attacks of negative reciprocity against those whose products and demeanors communicated contempt for the PNG consumers. Instant noodles, thus, may change the poor into nascent consumers; yet unless purveyors of the commodities keep their part of the deal, these nascent consumers may not stay happily in place. Win-win is an ongoing project, a bargain that requires lots of work. Nevertheless, as we shall see in our next chapter, the big food companies are confident that they can fulfill their part of the deal.

5

Making (and Unmaking?) a Big Food World

In developing countries such as Papua New Guinea, the popularity of instant noodles—and of other inexpensive industrially produced foods—has been shifting what the anthropologist Lynne Phillips calls "the markers of food exclusion and inclusion."[1] By bringing the instant noodle-eating poor into the bottom of the pyramid (BOP), companies like Nestlé have been promulgating an inclusive "big-food" future, one in which everyone—producers and consumers everywhere—would seemingly benefit. Thus, as sales of instant noodles flourish (again, 95.39 billion packages and cups globally in 2010), prosperity and comfort become less elusive; slackers, students, prisoners, heavy users, and settlement dwellers (to name some we have discussed) all comprise the reasonably satisfied consumers of what Koki Ando called a reasonably tasty product. In these ways, Nissin, Maruchan, Nestlé, and other big food companies serve not only their own interests, but also, according to their claims, those of the global population. Indeed, because the products of such companies fill so many, allowing them to get on with their lives, Momofuku Ando declared that "the food business is a peace industry."[2] Correspondingly, Koki Ando has outlined a big-food future as essential and virtuous by stating that the "ultimate mission of Nissin is to produce foods that accommodate everyone's desires. This goal ranges from creating foods to enjoy to creating foods that sustain life, eventually supplying enough food [for] a global population that, fifty years from now, is expected to top ten billion," with many living in socioeconomically stratified megacities.[3]

To explore the key aspects of this envisioned big-food world of capitalist provisioning, we now direct our attention to those whose particular skills underlie this world. As with big business more generally, big food must rely on a range of specialists to deal with technical issues in the areas of law, finance, supply-chain management, transportation, distribution, and promotion. However, big food—and the food industry more generally—is especially reliant for commercial success on the food scientists whose techniques and technologies ensure that the industry's products will be edible, if not palatable, when subject to the efficiencies of large-scale manufacture. As we saw in chapter 1, even a relatively simple product such as instant noodles requires the application of appreciable technical skill to be ready for market—to roll reliably off assembly lines as tasty, convenient, cheap, and shelf stable. In fact, it took Momofuku Ando much experimentation until the principle of tempura could be applied with enough efficiency for profits to be made.

In this chapter, we step away for a time from instant noodles per se to focus on those with the expertise necessary to create comparable industrial foods that "accommodate everyone's desires." These are food scientists, latter-day Momofuku Andos, whose work is central to capitalist provisioning. How, we ask, do these scientists formulate and bring (potentially) viable products to market? What are the understandings that underpin their practices? What are their skills? How do they evaluate their accomplishments? And, in considering their critics—those who view their skills and accomplishments with deep skepticism if not outright hostility—how do they justify what they do?

After visiting food scientists in their laboratories, we present two case studies of their work: product biographies of created foods that contrast informatively with instant noodles. The first case is of an industrially produced food supplement that contrasts in multiple ways with instant noodles. Big Shotz is an expensive, nutrient dense, and low-calorie drink designed for discriminating and affluent urban professionals who have lots of choice; a daily portion would cost someone of the BOP a day's wages. The second is of industrially produced military rations that compare complexly with both instant noodles and Big Shotz. Meals, Ready-to-Eat (MREs) are like instant noodles in their convenience, shelf stability, reasonable tastiness, high calorie content, and importance within a context of constrained choice; they are like Big Shotz in that they are moderately expensive and nutritionally balanced. Entirely unlike Big Shotz, they are designed for those living in perilous circumstances with little choice of what to eat. After presenting these biographies, we begin an evaluation of the industrial food system more generally, one we continue in our conclusion, where we consider what Koki Ando might have meant when he said recently that "instant noodles could save the Earth."[4]

FOOD SCIENTISTS AND THEIR LABS

To learn more about the perspectives and activities of food scientists, Fred began auditing food science classes at the University of Massachusetts. One of his teachers was especially helpful in providing an introduction to a food scientist currently active in industry: Peter Salmon, president of International Food Network (IFN), a company with three branches that offers "complete product development services for the food, beverage and nutrition industries."[5] Salmon generously agreed to meet with Deborah and Fred at IFN's facility in Ithaca, New York.

When Deborah and Fred arrived at IFN in July 2008, they discovered that Salmon had been called away because of a family emergency, but John Crump, IFN's managing director, was available to talk with them. Crump, while willing to help, advised that the information he could provide would be only general, because confidentiality agreements bound IFN's food scientists to secrecy. As a result, Crump noted somewhat ruefully, IFN could not even establish its credentials to prospective clients by mentioning other clients, lest surmises be made about the product development plans of rivals.

Crump began his discussion of IFN's role in product development by reviewing recent changes in the food industry:

> During the 1970s and early 1980s, most of the power was in the hands of the manufacturers, who would call up a supermarket chain and say that they wanted to extend three of their lines and dictated the shelf positions they wanted, and the retailers were pushed around. The retailers weren't making much by way of returns and so they consolidated, and the power shifted to the big supermarket chains. It's stores like Wal-Mart now which wield the power. Before, the manufacturers had space for their third and fourth category products. But with the change, the retailers just wanted first and second brand products. They won't take third or fourth.
>
> The manufacturers were forced to respond during the mid-1980s and '90s. There were lots of mergers and acquisitions. . . . As the big companies got bigger, there was considerable cost reduction: mergers are about simplification. They cut staff [including research staff] to get the money to pay for their acquisitions; they paid lots of attention to the costs of materials and in growing their bottom line [net income]. Any top-line growth [an increase in gross sales] was limited by the fact that population was not expanding. A

4 percent expansion in grocery trade is a real reach now because the population is not growing much. . . . They couldn't charge much more either because the consumer begins to see it. So to grow the bottom line, you had to work really hard to grow the top line.

This means that companies have to innovate . . . though they no longer have the people with the expertise to innovate. They can make corn flakes till the cows come home but they don't know much about making a nutrition bar, and that is where we come in. Their expertise is no longer in house, and they need us to do a lot of the work. . . . [When IFN is hired] speed is of the essence. It used to be said that to move from concept to factory door took two years. Now six weeks is usually the maximum, especially if we have something to start with. If a company wants to add to an existing line—a new flavor, from chocolate to strawberry—they want the product out as fast as they can have the package printed. Remember that just the first and second sellers get shelf space. . . . Consumers demand change and variety. . . . Consumers like a product until eighteen months later they are bored. Goji berries are here today, gone tomorrow. So, speed to market is of the essence.[6]

Crump explained that the food scientists involved in product development do not want to go on a "wild goose chase." They try to get as much information as possible about what a client wants. If it's a nutrition bar, how does the client plan to make the product unique? With more fruit? More crunch? Do they want a soft, baked product? A cold product that is extruded, laid out on a slab, and then cut? What vitamins and minerals should it have? How much protein? Do they want to reduce calories from sugar? Do they want to increase fiber? IFN can formulate all reasonable combinations, knowing which ingredients and which combinations will adversely affect taste and stability; it also can line up the appropriate suppliers to provide the nuts, dried fruits, sugars, noncaloric sweeteners, and so on.

In fact, the processes used to develop products are often quite iterative—"almost like turning a handle," another IFN food scientist told us. IFN might be asked to provide six prototypes so that the client can choose the most promising. Yet there is no guarantee that consumers will like the one chosen, or that they will find it unique enough to justify the price the client wishes to charge. Many products get dropped at this point, and only about three in one hundred actually make it to market. Moreover, whatever time IFN devotes to fine-tuning the product gives other companies the opportunity to move into the market; therefore, its efforts may be directed to making the product just good enough.

Crump gave Deborah and Fred a tour of the facility, where they saw some of IFN's twenty-eight Ithaca-based food scientists at work. The labs resemble large kitchens. Men and women in white coats work at stainless steel stations with mixers, gas and electric stoves, and sophisticated equipment including a gas chromatograph used for analyzing compounds. This machine checks, for instance, that all additives are present and still active after processing and that the blending has been consistent—that the various ingredients (for example, in a cake mix) have been mixed thoroughly throughout a particular batch. Another machine, a particle size analyzer, pours ingredients through a small funnel to form a heap; the angle of the heap is measured as relatively flat or relatively steep to indicate the size of the particles and uniformity of the batch. Again, consistency is important: if the batch has particles of various sizes, differential settling of the smaller constituents may occur, reducing uniformity. The heaping test is additionally useful to demonstrate how new products might work when "scaled up" in a factory. It would not be optimal to depend on someone banging periodically on a really big funnel to dislodge sticking ingredients (which is why anticaking and free-flow agents, such as silica products, may be added to a mixture). Finally, there was an artificial stomach in simplified form—a big glass beaker into which various enzymes duplicating those in the stomach could be poured, providing information about how a product would be digested.

Crump also showed Deborah and Fred the production room, where products were adjusted to conform to the demands of large-scale manufacture. Finally, they visited a room filled with "environmental chambers" designed to speed up shelf-life testing. Product developers do not have the luxury of waiting until the expiration of a product's proposed shelf life to determine whether it still meets the specifications on its label or whether it has deteriorated. Therefore, they accelerate conditions by placing products in these special chambers. Crump explained with the example of ice cream, which ideally should be stored at $-10°F$. If it were kept at this temperature, they would need to wait a year to determine whether significant changes had taken place. However, if ice cream is kept at $+5°F$, changes can be seen in five weeks. The lower the temperature, the slower atoms move, so the food scientists speed things up, controlling for temperature, humidity, and light. Crump emphasized that the fate of a product subjected to these accelerated conditions may not be identical to the outcome one would see over a longer time span and more normal conditions. Therefore, IFN always communicates the limits of its testing procedures clearly to clients.

Subsequent to Deborah and Fred's visit to IFN in Ithaca, the three of us (singly or together) interviewed food scientists in the United States,

England, and Japan. Most had personal preferences in regard to the products they made: one admitted that he hated the "ice pop" he was developing because he had consumed more of a comparable product than he cared to while preparing for his colonoscopy; another confessed that he wanted a real cookie during his coffee break, not the low-calorie one with an appetite suppressant he was charged with creating. Still, it was not these food scientists' role to dictate food preferences. Instead, they were to get a job done. They would employ the techniques and technologies of food science to solve food-focused problems (both material, as in preventing rancidity, and legal, as in insuring label accuracy) in a craftsmanlike and cost-effective fashion; the product would then be subject to consumer choice, which would determine market share and profit.

The food scientists we talked with took pride in their competence. They especially enjoyed projects that they could see through from beginning to end, which, as one put it, were "like babies." In addition, many liked projects that presented challenges requiring mastery of "several disciplines." Thus, a food scientist at a lab in Chicago spoke with pleasure about creating a confection that demanded expertise in the properties of starch (which adds body and contributes to a pleasantly full feeling in the mouth), in the techniques of molding (which insures "release" after heating and cooling), and in the principles of coating through "chocolate panning" and "hard panning" (which creates a protective and tasty layer surrounding a filling). Food scientists at a lab in Kyoto were happy to show us a product that they considered a tour de force: vividly colored and perfectly intact freeze-dried flowers. Their assignment to make edible freeze-dried flowers for a flower exhibition had been tricky, requiring them to devise a transparent coating for the flowers that would prevent them from collapsing during processing.

Not surprisingly, the food scientists were gratified when their skills were verified through market acceptance. Many mentioned favorite projects as those actually appearing on grocery shelves (alas, not yet freeze-dried flowers). One described this as "an incredible high." Another spoke of deep pleasure when a gummy candy "opened up an entire category" in the grocery store. However, he recognized, as did everyone else, that market success was hard to predict. Indeed, one food scientist remarked that he never would have imagined that bottled water could become a success—that people would actually pay for water.

Our conversations with food scientists made us interested in gaining more of a step-by-step understanding of their craft. To this end, we

were alert for possible case studies: for instances of product development that were not covered by confidentiality agreements. Two promising candidates for further investigation emerged; in each case, the project required skilled problem solving characteristic of food science
research in general, and in each case, those doing the research were
happy to talk to us in some detail about their project. Moreover, as
mentioned, the attributes of the two products—the expensive, nutritionally dense, low-calorie Big Shotz and the shelf-stable, reasonably
tasty, and high-calorie MREs—provide an instructive contrast with
instant noodles.

MAKING BIG SHOTZ

In May 2009, Deborah and Fred attended a regional (northeastern)
meeting of the Institute of Food Technologists (IFT), the premier professional organization of food scientists employed in academia and the
food industry. There they observed a PowerPoint presentation given by
IFN's Scott Martling featuring Big Shotz, an attractively packaged,
four-ounce (120-millileter), supplement-loaded fruit smoothie. Designed
for daily consumption, one Big Shotz contains eleven vitamins, six minerals, antioxidants, ginseng, prebiotic fiber, and omega-3 fatty acids.
The audience was invited to sample this mango-based blend, and Fred
found it a pleasant drink that went down easily enough, neither medic-
inal tasting nor delicious.

In conversation after the presentation, Martling told Deborah and
Fred that Big Shotz was unusual in that the client with the idea was not
a food company, but an individual: an entrepreneurial British woman
named Deborah Maxwell who believed that her product would both
make money and provide a useful service for consumers. Moreover,
since Maxwell was establishing a brand rather than adding to a brand
line, she did not demand the usual degree of confidentiality. Quite the
contrary, she was happy to publicize the connection between IFN and
Big Shotz, since the respected credentials of IFN added to her product's
credibility.

Hoping that Big Shotz might be an interesting case study, Deborah and
Fred approached Salmon again, asking if they could learn more about
IFN's role in its development. Salmon had no objections, especially since
Maxwell's company by 2010 had gone out of business. He cleared the
way for them to talk with Nick Henson, who had worked directly with
Maxwell to create Big Shotz. In June 2010 they were generously granted

two long interviews at IFN's laboratory in Reading, England, one with Henson alone and one with Henson and Salmon together, and they were able to speak with Maxwell in London.

As both Henson and Salmon explained in the two interviews, many individuals have ideas about potential products, yet few have the resources to bring them to fruition, and IFN, therefore, usually works with big food companies.[7] Maxwell was unusual because she had independent financing. She believed strongly in the benefits of nutrient fortification and wanted to develop a "functional food" in liquid form that could be consumed easily and quickly and that would deliver nutrients with greater bioavailability than tablets. Although a passionate and driven person, she lacked the technical knowledge to convert her vision into a product: a small, fruit-based cocktail containing all the supplements needed for health. IFN's food scientists agreed to formulate a cost-effective product that was stable, fulfilled legal requirements, and made appropriate claims.

One of the first tasks for IFN was to "knock out materials"—that is, to reduce the quantities of various nutrients that the client requested. While many food products are fortified at low levels, acknowledging on the label that they provide, say, 15 percent of the recommended daily allowance (RDA) of this or that, Maxwell wanted to have 100 percent of the RDA of everything important in her product. One significant ingredient was calcium. IFN knew from the start that including 100 percent of the RDA of calcium would produce a big block of chalk. Maxwell had to be shown this before she would agree to have only 15 percent. She also had to be shown how materials interact. Food scientists know, for example, that vitamin C, an antioxidant, is highly unstable when it bonds with oxygen, and that it reacts to heat and light. They know that vitamin A, another antioxidant, reduces the rate at which vitamin C degrades. And they know that thiamine has a very strong taste; many minerals are salty and bitter; and omega-3 fish oils become rancid easily and do not mix well with fruit juice. Fortunately, another company had cracked this latter problem with the technique of microencapsulation, which shields little drops of oil from exposure to oxygen while leaving them dispersible in water and readily digestible. Overall, Henson said, the goal of blending fifteen to twenty materials in a liquid presented considerable and stimulating challenges.

Henson and Maxwell eventually decided to make Big Shotz a refrigerated product with a shelf life of two months. Refrigeration would prevent spoilage and enhance the fruit juice flavor. A relatively short shelf life would decrease the risk that these bioactive ingredients would degrade to the point of causing legal problems. After all, if the label said that Big Shotz contained 40 percent of the RDA for vitamin A (another compromise Maxwell had to accept), then it had to have this 40 percent until the "sell-by" date.[8] IFN ran the standard sensory, physical, and chemical protocols to ensure stability. In this case, the rather short shelf life meant that these tests could be done in "real" time, at a temperature of 8°C (duplicating refrigerator temperature of 46°F); they also ran the tests at "accelerated" time, at a temperatures between 20°C and 30°C (68°F and 86°F) to ensure that the product would not cause illness if left at room temperature.

In addition, suppliers and processors had to be found: fruit from the Philippines, fish oil from Norway, vitamins from China (and bought from a German company), and a manufacturing facility in the Austrian Alps with a specialized homogenizer to blend the ingredients into a consistent liquid. IFN arranged chilled transport from the factory to the distributors. It helped with advertising, including assembling a panel of experts in nutrition (a doctor, two nutritionists, and a professor) who gave it a qualified endorsement. All told, it was an unusually prolonged project that required much trial and error. IFN worked on the food science of it for about 250 days over eighteen months.

Maxwell told Deborah and Fred when they met with her that the project had cost about £1 million.[9] A lawyer by training and an entrepreneur by inclination, Maxwell spent three years on Big Shotz. She talked about the difficulties of being a small player in the food business, of both creating the product and building brand awareness as an individual, without the resources of a large company. Nonetheless, she insisted, developing Big Shotz was a wonderful experience, and she remains convinced that she was ahead of her time in conceiving of an easy-to-consume, nutritionally enhanced drink with active ingredients. Big Shotz failed not because it was inadequate. It failed because the second-level funding fell apart: it was launched on September 17, 2008, two days after the collapse of the Lehman Brothers investment bank. After that, the pledges of support fell away.

Throughout the interview, Maxwell's continuing enthusiasm for her product was evident, even a bit infectious. Here, in somewhat condensed and paraphrased form, is her explanation of why (to cite some of her promotional material) Big Shotz would be "the *real* next big thing": We all know that we have more bad days than good days. We are bombarded with information. We are told that we don't exercise enough—that we are likely to get heart disease, that we are deficient. We worry about marriages, children, jobs. We, the "worried well," belong to three groups. Group One is composed of the young and healthy. They are college graduates, in their twenties, generally fit, employed, on the run, and essentially responsible just for themselves. Such people likely eat a croissant for breakfast, a pizza or kebab for lunch, and then go out with friends for wine and a meal in the evening. They know that they are all failing, that they never or only rarely have an optimal, perfect food day. They can easily afford the daily cost of £1.50 for the convenience of Big Shotz, grabbed on the way to work. They are the major target. Group Two, slightly older, is composed of the "stressed and stretched." They have new families and big mortgages. They are a target, too, although they can less afford to buy. Group Three is composed of the more established though young at heart. They are forty-five and older and want to live life actively. They are also a major target and gave very positive feedback for Big Shotz. The goal was to convince all of these busy people that they didn't have to guess—that they didn't need to worry if they just drank Big Shotz daily. It promised everyday absolution from sin, especially because it contained just sixty-seven calories.

Maxwell had enjoyed working closely with Henson and others at IFN in solving the technical difficulties of developing the product. A final challenge had been to select the right fruit juice base. Initially she favored something like raspberry or blueberry, which would combine a pleasing taste with a pleasing color. But when Henson mixed the ingredients with raspberry, the iron content made the drink look "shit brown"; instead, they sought a final "orangey goldey" color to reference the beta carotene ingredient. They could have used banana for this, which would have been inexpensive, but Maxwell thought the result would not be classy enough. So they decided to go with mango and passion fruit juices.

That Big Shotz failed was, Maxwell said, a "sad story." It was especially sad because, just before the financial crisis hit, Starbucks agreed to give her drink a trial run at a number of U.K. stores, choosing Big Shotz over a large number of competitors for cooler space. She had approached Starbucks both in the United Kingdom and in the United States. She felt they were missing out—their range of food and beverage offerings did not include products that customers actually craved. She told them that their sales in the United Kingdom were declining because they had "great big marshmallowy muffins" made with white flour and loaded with sugar and butter, when people wanted fresh and healthy food. Big Shotz, she told Deborah and Fred in conclusion, was a brilliant idea, certainly better than "a crappy chocolate bar." If her venture had been successful, she would have liked to develop other products with health-focused attributes. Big Shotz was general in its application: one shot fits all. Perhaps there might also be "sport shotz," "bone-health shotz," "sleep shotz," "sex shotz." Why not?

Henson agreed that Maxwell's story was sad: she should have been able to open up a new market category. The two had worked hard to line everything up, and they had skillfully employed the techniques and technologies of food science to create a classy and healthfully fortified product that seemed destined for market acceptance.

We note an irony, however, in that likely market acceptance. While Maxwell would not accept Big Shotz as inhabiting the same culinary universe as marshmallowy muffins or crappy chocolate bars, she recognized that Big Shotz was necessary because of these muffins and bars. That is, muffins, bars, and Big Shotz are mutually enabling: a snack of one can be offset by a swig of the other. Maxwell's product was designed for those who, while not eating right, could nonetheless have the best of both worlds. Choosing Big Shotz would provide them with the high-end win-win of eating their cake (croissant, pizza, kebab, or wine) and not eating it, too.[10] We will return to what the mutuality of such products (and the range of products more generally) suggests about the food industry later. But let us next provide our second case, which differs significantly from that of Big Shotz. MREs are designed for those dependent on military rations who must eat well and stay healthy in the context of constrained circumstances. Having few choices, they may long for their cake (burgers, pizzas, Kentucky Fried Chicken, or beer), yet must make do.

MEALS, READY-TO-EAT

Deborah and Fred visited the Department of Defense (DoD) Combat Feeding Directorate, located in eastern Massachusetts at the Natick Soldier Systems Center. They spoke with Jeremy Whitsitt, the outreach and education officer; Drs. Patrick Dunne and Tom Yang, food scientists; and Alan Wright, a food technician and psychologist.[11] It soon became apparent that the work of those designing military rations is, in substance, like that of food scientists elsewhere. While not directly concerned with opening up a new market category, these designers are interested in innovation and derive obvious satisfaction in employing their array of skills to solve food-focused problems in a cost-effective, craftsmanlike fashion as evaluated by consumer choice.[12]

Designing MREs is a technically demanding and ongoing endeavor, requiring an evolving array of techniques and technologies. "Warfighters" (a term designed to include members of all branches of the U.S. military) are allocated three MREs daily, with each costing the government about US$7.69 (inclusive of transportation). These costs must be contained. For example, Dunne told Deborah and Fred that dental floss might have been included, but the additional five cents per MRE was deemed too expensive, as it would add millions of dollars overall. Despite these cost constraints, much effort goes into pleasing warfighters, even if they have little choice about what to eat while on the battlefield. After all, as posters remind everyone at the center—"it's not nutrition until it's eaten." MREs must be not only reasonably tasty but also nutritionally balanced and calorically appropriate. In addition, they must be able to withstand extreme conditions. They must remain shelf stable and safe to consume without refrigeration for three years at 80°F and for six months at 100°F. They must sustain parachute drops from twenty-five hundred feet and free falls from one hundred feet. And they must be convenient to consume. This means, for instance, that their moisture-proof tan-colored pouches (as well as the packaged food items within those pouches) must be easy to open without implements. As their business cards put it, these food scientists make food that is "technology driven, warfighter focused."

Gerald Darsch, director of the DoD Combat Feeding Directorate, readily admits that MREs were once less than they should be. In a paper he delivered at the 2010 IFT meeting, entitled "Overview of Combat Ration Science" and attended by Fred, Darsch said that during the First Gulf War, General Colin Powell had summoned him to the Pentagon. Powell told him not to bother to take a seat since he had just two words for him: "MRE—fixit." Considerable improvement in menu diversity and palatability followed, and now, Darsch joked, MREs no longer stand for "meals rejected by everyone."[13] Tested on the field (with a nine-point hedonic scale for warfighter responses), they are now available in twenty-four menus, edible either hot or cold, and designed to deliver a culturally acceptable variety of tastes to a moderately diverse population. For example, Menu Eight consists of meatballs with marinara sauce, garlic mashed potatoes, cheddar cheese, tortillas, nuts, a "First Strike" bar (chocolate or apple cinnamon), beverage (fruit punch, grape, lemon-lime,

FIGURE 18. Meals, Ready-to-Eat. Photograph by David Kamm, U.S. Army Photo.

or orange, fortified with a carbohydrate electrolyte), butter granules, and accessory packet C (which contains apple cider, salt, chewing gum, toilet tissue, towelette, spoon, and hot beverage bag).[14] Like all menus, this one (ideally one of three meals a day) delivers about thirteen hundred calories—50 percent from carbohydrates, 35 percent from fat, and 15 percent from protein—to warfighters whose nutritional and energy needs, especially during combat, are likely high.[15] In addition, like all menus, it contains a "Flameless Ration Heater," which produces heat by an exothermic chemical reaction that results from exposing a magnesium-iron compound to water.[16] There are also more specialized MREs, including the lightweight "First Strike Rations." Each of these pouches (costing the government about US$17) contains a day's worth of calories (twenty-nine hundred) in the form of energy-dense, "eat-out-of-hand foods" and is designed to sustain a forward-deployed warfighter during the first seventy-two hours of intense conflict.[17]

A major concern in military feeding is that warfighters often "field strip" their rations: they select items from the MRE pouch that they like and are easy to eat and discard the rest—sometimes by putting the rejected items in a big box from which others can pick and choose. There are several problems with this. First of all, a warfighter who simply eats what he or she likes might develop nutritional deficiencies. Second, it wastes money. Tests have shown that only 70 percent of a pouch's contents are eaten.[18] The way to circumvent field stripping in combat, where warfighters may be far from normal mess facilities for thirty to thirty-five days at a time, is through education by the company commander, who needs to remind the warfighters that staying healthy will help them defeat the enemy and secure their mission. Of course, they're more likely to follow this advice if the food tastes reasonably good.

Rendering foods safe and shelf stable while preserving taste and texture is an especially challenging undertaking. Avoiding food-borne illnesses such as dysentery, to say nothing of food poisoning, is the highest priority. Of these illnesses, the most dangerous threat to human health and the hardest to eliminate is botulism, the result of a toxin produced by the anaerobic bacterium *Clostridium botulinum,* which thrives in nonrefrigerated, sealed containers of moist, low-acid foods. Along with its heat-resistant spores, it must be eliminated from cans or containers such as MRE pouches—not through pasteurization, which kills bacteria but not their spores, but through sterilization, a process using a much higher temperature. Indeed, if *C. botulinum* and its spores are eliminated, all other potentially dangerous microbes will be as well.

The first and most basic technique of sterilization is retorting: subjecting sealed food (such as MRE pouches) within a pressurized container to high-temperature steam (of about 250°F) for a period of fifteen to twenty minutes, depending on the density of the food inside the pouch. Although this classic method is cheap and easy to use, the high temperature and extended heat-up and cool-down periods may adversely affect food taste, texture, and appearance. Some retorted meat items, such as the beef brisket and the pork with barbecue sauce, lend themselves to this variant of "slow cooking" and taste pretty good; others do not. In fact, as Dunne said, in most cases, retorting "cooks the hell out of the food." Freeze-drying and irradiation, on the other hand, render food microbially safe and stable while preserving its appealing properties. However, freeze-drying is usually too expensive, and irradiation is currently prohibited in the United States, except for astronauts' rations. Other techniques, many being developed in conjunction with industry and university departments in food science, show promise.[19]

Microwaving is one such technique. Microwaving sterilizes food in a shorter time and affects food texture and flavor less than retorting does. Chicken breasts, for instance, would taste much better if microwaved. A microwaved salmon filet would be, as Dunne put it, "a real winner": it wouldn't taste like pet food and it would deliver omega-3s naturally. Still, technical problems need to be solved before microwave sterilization is feasible for MREs. A different sort of package without the aluminum foil that blocks the microwaves would have to be developed.[20]

Moreover, large-scale continuous-flow microwave processing, which would reliably sterilize large quantities of food, has yet to be implemented in the United States.

Another promising technique that sterilizes quickly is the major focus of Dunne's own research. "Pressure-assisted thermal sterilization" (PATS) not only sterilizes food but, in many cases, also leaves the food's physical properties relatively intact. In this process, sealed food is immersed in a container of water and microwaved briefly to elevate its temperature quickly. Then, for a period of two to five minutes, the food is subjected to super-high pressure, on the order of one hundred thousand pounds per square inch, during which the water itself is compressed by 10 to 15 percent.[21] The sudden and drastic increase in pressure causes an immediate spike in the temperature of the immersed food, while at the same time (apparently) disrupting the protective coating of any bacterial spores present.[22] Once the pressure is released, cool down is correspondingly rapid. Developed in conjunction with industry, PATS works well for some applications. Hormel uses PATS for its line of cold cuts to eliminate the chemical components necessary to prevent listeria; this enables the company to place a "natural" label on these products. Perdue uses PATS for the chicken strips it adds to Caesar salads. Trader Joe's uses PATS for the avocados in its guacamole, and factories with this technology are being built in Mexico, Chile, and Peru, where the avocados are grown. Pineapples do well sterilized this way, too. The method does have its limitations. It cannot be used on porous foods, such as apples, because browning is triggered as the oxygen is forced out. Green-pigmented foods like beans turn an ugly gray. The high pressure denatures the protein in eggs, leaving a rubbery texture. In addition, starches change under pressure and may have to be modified if they are to be part of a PATS application. Finally, the costs must come down.

There is still another technique under development that makes use of supercritical carbon dioxide ($SCCO_2$) and has been adapted from medical procedures for sterilizing tissue prior to surgical transplantation. When carbon dioxide is heated to the modest temperature of about 88°F while under seventy-three times atmospheric pressure (about 1,099 pounds per square inch), it acts as a permeating wet gas that sterilizes organic material in part by disrupting the protective coating of bacterial spores, in much the same way that PATS does. This method, which sterilizes without cooking, does not significantly alter the structure of food. It would allow the inclusion into MREs of normally refrigerated products like

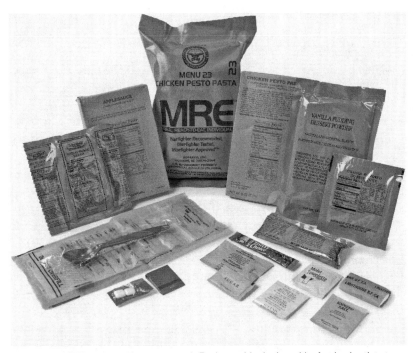

FIGURE 19. MRE package deconstructed. Each meal is designed by food scientists to be reasonably tasty, nutritionally balanced, and calorically appropriate, as well as able to withstand extreme conditions. Photograph by David Kamm, U.S. Army Photo.

cream cheese, which, if cooked, would be rendered unrecognizable, if not inedible.

At lunch at Natick, Deborah and Fred were able to sample items from the First Strike pouches. Fred had a "Bacon Cheddar Pocket Sandwich" (330 calories)—which he said was "fine," with the bacon tasting "pretty good"—and a "Filled French Toast" desert (240 calories), which evoked a somewhat familiar taste. Deborah had the "Nut Fruit Mix" (310 calories), which she found "okay," but not as good as the trail mix she is used to. Dunne had "Honey BBQ Beef Pocket" (290 calories) and one of his favorites, "Lemon Poppyseed Poundcake" (130 calories).

During lunch, the conversation turned to future food innovations. Dunne hoped a decent and stable peanut butter and jelly sandwich could be perfected because the warfighters would like this a lot. Unfortunately, serious technical issues exist, given that moisture migrates from the jelly to the peanut butter and then to the bread, making a real mess. Yang said that he is interested in using the antimicrobial properties of allyl isothiocyanate (AIT), which is found in the leaves, stems, and roots of wasabi plants. The green plastic leaves that often accompany take-out "bento" boxes of sushi (ubiquitous in Japanese train stations and also available in the United States) are not just decorations; they are imbued with AIT and increase the shelf life of sushi from a few hours to about two days. (*C. botulinum* would not be a problem for these boxes, as they contain oxygen.) Perhaps AIT technology could be used to deliver fresh meals to warfighters. Yang had been working on this technology with a Japanese food company through a cooperative research and development agreement, but although the project had promise, the army was putting it on the back burner.

A less exotic project had recently been completed by food scientists at Rutgers University, under contract to the DoD, to infuse raisins with fresh-fruit components through osmotic dehydration. When grapes are placed in a concentrated sugar and fresh-fruit solution, water is drawn out and replaced by the sugar and fruit. This leaves them plump, sweet, rich with vitamins, and apparently tasty.[23] This project grew out of the desire of a dietician at Fort Lee (where army cooks are trained) to see more antioxidants in rations—a preferable alternative to providing warfighters with vitamins A and C in the form of pills.

Ideas for innovations are sometimes generated directly by industry. Food companies frequently come to Natick with ideas. If an idea is accepted—as it was, for instance, with a power bar—then one of Natick's technologists may go into the company's labs to help scale up the product. However, because of the DoD's procurement practices, which demand open competition, the company providing the idea may not ultimately win the contract. Noting that some MRE pouches contain packages of what looked like familiar civilian products, Fred asked whether a company, if successful in winning a contract, would press for its product to appear in branded form. Yes, perhaps, Dunne said. Mars and Nabisco had offered branded packages, though the DoD found it cheaper to get one of its producers to buy the product in bulk and put it into the standard tan MRE wrapper. Wright suggested that providing branded products in their familiar civilian packaging might have positive psychological benefits for the warfighters. He was experimenting to discover if M&M's®, branded as such, would boost morale more than the same product in a generic military wrapper.

No one involved in military rationing to whom Deborah and Fred spoke seemed to doubt that food science and the industrial food system (at least as regulated by DoD procurement procedures) were both necessary and sufficient for the successful provisioning of combat missions. Alternatives, such as foraging in the field, would potentially render warfighters sick, undernourished, distracted, and without the support of local populations.[24] No modern army could reliably operate this way. While MREs—whether retorted, microwaved, or treated with PATS—are not up to mother's best (not even up to usual mess-hall fare), the Natick food scientists think their products are pretty good. Like those who developed gummy candies or Big Shotz, they are skilled at solving an impressive assortment of problems within a set of technical constraints. When it comes to developing food products with the desired array of characteristics for manufacture on an industrial scale, food scientists see their role as indispensible.

Like Koki Ando, with his vision of a big-food future, in other words, they see themselves as indispensable in creating "foods to enjoy" and "foods that sustain life." Their techniques and technologies, as illustrated in our product biographies, yield notable results. Food scientists create many of the fifty thousand or so products that provision our supermarket shelves in an array even more dazzling than that of the instant noodle tunnel at the Momofuku Ando Instant Ramen Museum. Included in this supermarket array, of course, will be instant noodles (whether basic or elaborated). In addition, there will likely be nutritional drinks (not, unfortunately, Big Shotz), infused raisins (in non-MRE form), PATS-prepared cold cuts from Hormel (if not the First Strike bacon and cheddar sandwich), and myriad other products. Who better, then, to sustain the increasing billions expected to inhabit the earth fifty years from now than the problem-solving food scientists who know how to satisfy the desires and meet the needs of multitudes?

THRUST AND COUNTER-THRUST: THE FOOD INDUSTRY AND ITS CRITICS

These skills and achievements, as food scientists recognize, are under attack by those who think their cleverness is misplaced. For example, the food writer and activist Michael Pollan claims that food scientists are members of the "Nutritional Industrial Complex"—a group of "well-meaning, if error-prone, scientists and food marketers only too eager to exploit every shift in the nutritional consensus."[25] While they may be very good at what they're doing, Pollan and others think that what they're doing isn't very good. Perhaps the best-known critic of the food industry, Pollan writes with eloquence, and many find his message compelling. As we shall see, in response to his growing influence (and that of other like-minded critics), those in the food industry have begun to push back.

Pollan became a public figure with the publication in 2006 of *The Omnivore's Dilemma*, in which he castigates the food industry on multiple dimensions. His main criticism is that the industry relies on unsustainable agricultural practices, as in the production of crops such as corn that require massive inputs of oil-derived fertilizers and pesticides, resulting in environmental degradation. The industry then transforms many of these crops into a plethora of often unhealthy products (among them the now notorious high-fructose corn syrup). In his next book, *In Defense of Food: An Eater's Manifesto,* Pollan provides advice about how to avoid these environmentally and personally deleterious products of food science. This advice is directed at his many readers, who, he believes, face an American paradox: they are "a notably unhealthy population preoccupied with nutrition and diet and the idea of eating healthily." This paradox, Pollan argues, is characteristic of what he calls "the Age of Nutritionism," and his solution is not to choose, for instance, Big Shotz over marshmallowy muffins and chocolate bars, but to follow the dictum: "Eat food. Not too much. Mostly plants." And the best way to do this (warfighters perhaps excepted) is to select fresh, locally produced food (avoiding, as a rule of thumb, anything that has unpronounceable ingredients) and, in so doing, "reclaim our health and happiness as eaters."[26]

In a more recent essay (which, when it was published, was the most frequently e-mailed article among *New York Times* readers), Pollan proposes that "the key to improving the American diet" might be the "development of regional food systems, which make fresh produce more available and reduce dependence on heavily processed food from far away"; this, in turn, could help prevent chronic disease, including childhood obesity and adolescent type 2 diabetes.[27] Such a diet, Pollan thinks, would be of personal benefit. It would also represent a move to regional food systems that could encourage more sustainable and less fossil fuel–intensive agricultural practices and thus would be of planetary benefit. In fact, throughout all of his writings, Pollan advocates a vision of sustainability: of sustained personal health, sustained family relationships through a shared commitment to mindful eating, and sustained environmental health. He provides consumer-citizens with a scenario in which they can help themselves and help the planet at the same time—doing well by doing good. Pollan's formulation of sustainability has a powerful aura. It evokes and links a compelling cluster of ideas and practices. It is green, fresh, natural, human, ethical, and responsible, and it is concerned with stewardship, successive generations, the richness of life, and social connectivity.

Not surprisingly, those castigated by Pollan as members of the "Nutritional Industrial Complex" take issue with what he has said about them—including his claim that what they produce isn't really food. Recognizing that he commands a large audience, they have responded in two major ways. First, they have co-opted the message, converting his criticisms of them into marketing opportunities.[28] Thus, in a 2009 issue of *Food Technology*, A. Elizabeth Sloan (president of Sloan Trends) informs readers of "Top 10 Food Trends" and notes under trend four ("The New Pacesetters") that "because Gen Yers [ages 18–32] have the greatest propensity for making healthy snack choices and the most interest in natural, organic, and 'ethical' foods, the demand for healthier kids' snacks will be unprecedented." Under the sixth trend ("Scared Straight") she observes: "With two-thirds (65%) of consumers extremely concerned about the safety of products produced outside the U.S., particularly those from China (73%), Southeast Asia (51%), and Mexico (49%)—and locally grown viewed as the safest food by 51 percent and natural and organic by 44 percent—look for local sourcing to gain more momentum . . . . Country-of-origin labeling will also bolster this trend."[29]

Similar themes appeared at the June 2009 national meetings of the IFT (attended that year by 14,500 academic food technologists and members of the food industry). There, Deborah and Fred went to the fifth annual "Food Technology Trend Panel," where Elizabeth Sloan, Barbara Katz (president of HealthFocus International), and Ron Paul (president and CEO of Technomic, Inc.) were asked to "redefine food value" and explain where "grocery shoppers and foodservice patrons [are] headed." During the presentations, Sloan argued that "addressing consumers' individual passions is another way to add value for some . . . [and that] locally grown, farm-raised, and humanely treated remain among the 'ethical descriptors' most sought after by consumers." Katz coined a new term, "functional fresh," which included "wholesome parameters [such as] fresh, natural, no preservatives, knowledge of the source of origin, and like I'd make at home." Finally, Paul thought that restaurants could gain an edge by adding "premium healthier beverages [and] signature cocktails."[30]

In these food-industry responses, the values Pollan has presented as part of a coherent vision have been disaggregated and extracted, either singly or in a mix-and-match fashion. His critique of the system can be offset and even neutralized by apparently providing consumers with what he advocates: if they want "fresh," they'll get fresh; if they want "natural" in their snacks, they'll get natural.

But are consumers convinced? As Christine Bruhn, an academic food scientist at the University of California, Davis, notes in another article in *Food Technology*, consumers remain confused about what to eat and whether their food does harm to the world. She thinks the confusion might prove productive, as it can impel the development of "a science-based approach to sustainable food production." Hence, she says that in response to the criticisms posed by "some popular writers as well as some widely recognized health professionals," the food industry must act: "We have an opportunity to set the standards for environmental and social responsibility and [to] develop the means to communicate these standards to the public. While an effective program can advance a brand, an industry-wide science-based initiative can advance the entire food industry."[31]

Bruhn's call for a "science-based approach to sustainable food production" moves us directly to the food industry's second response to Pollan's perspective, which comes primarily from academically affiliated food scientists. To be sure, these food scientists work closely with the food companies, in both their selection of research projects and their role in training students for future employment in the food industry. Yet many academic food scientists are less interested in discerning marketing opportunities than in mustering a robust push back to what they consider Pollan's lack of realism, arguing that Pollan's vision is actually unsustainable. Dr. Aaron Brody (of the University of Georgia), for example, argues that "in pragmatic perspective, the fate of the world depends on the meaningful application of food packaging. Local farming being advocated for urban America in contemporary literature is precisely the reason that food shortages exist in most of the world. It is expensive in terms of human resources and food waste and cannot be abided if we hope to rid the world of hunger."[32] And Dr. Fergus Clydesdale (of the University of Massachusetts and a member of the team responsible for the 2005 Dietary Guidelines of the USDA and Health and Human Services) states that "people often do not realize that the food industry feeds the world, and if we are to change how people eat, we must work within the confines of what is possible technically within that industry."[33] Clydesdale elaborates further in "Perspective," a guest column in *Food Technology*:

There is a yearning for the world which author Michael Pollan so eloquently describes in his books. . . . Please understand that no one is going to argue the nutritional virtues of fruits and vegetables picked in your own backyard, rushed to the kitchen and eaten. However, most consumers don't have a garden or year-round growing climate and must depend on the supermarket.

Fresh produce takes about 21 days to travel from the field to the supermarket (one shudders at the carbon footprint) but only hours to get from the field to the processing plant for freezing or canning. As a result, the processed products are often superior in nutrition and flavor to what we call fresh in the supermarket.[34]

With respect to Clydesdale's position, Pollan grants that his "eater's manifesto" is directed largely at the discerning individual eater who can afford the cost of fresh and locally grown foods. Likewise, Alice Waters, whose name is frequently invoked in discussions of sustainability, has been accused of elitism and narcissism because not many can afford to eat at her expensive Berkeley restaurant, Chez Panisse, which is dedicated to serving fresh and local fare.[35] Certainly, unlike California-dwelling Pollan and Waters, most Americans do not live where locally grown products are available year-round for home or restaurant consumption.

Clydesdale, though, does more than charge Pollan with exclusivity. Like Brody, he charges Pollan with promoting an impractical and unsustainable vision. He concludes his essay with this challenge: "The Earth is adding 100 births every 42 minutes and we owe these new global citizens the benefits of technology to provide enough food. Instead of deriding technology, let's take advantage of it so that we can have a modern food supply for a modern world which includes both fresh and processed healthy foods at a price that people can afford and in a form that's appealing, convenient, and safe."[36] Like the food industry executives, Clydesdale is also interested, we believe, in disaggregating Pollan's vision. Yet he is doing this not to market products (as in bringing people "fresh" if they want fresh) but to evaluate whether the parts of the vision actually fit together in a way that is workable in a recognizable world that people can afford to inhabit.

Clydesdale's understanding of what makes a food world feasible generally agrees with a major position paper recently published by the *IFT Scientific Review*, "Feeding the World Today and Tomorrow: The Importance of Food Science and Technology."[37] The paper affirms that "the application of science to agriculture" dramatically increased agricultural productivity at a time when "productivity was not keeping pace with population growth."[38] Through the green revolution of the

1960s and 1970s, which centered on specially bred seeds requiring costly inputs of fertilizer, pesticides, herbicides, and water, serious food shortages were alleviated, particularly in India and China. While granting that "the remarkable advances" and "enormous benefits" of this revolution were not without "substantial cost" (in particular that "larger farmers" were helped "much more than smaller, poorer ones"), the paper is optimistic about the future.[39] The paper continues: "Applications of science and technology within the food system have allowed production of foods in adequate quantities to meet the needs of society, as it has evolved. Today, our production-to-consumption food system is complex, and our food is largely safe, tasty, nutritious, abundant, diverse, convenient, and less costly and more readily accessible than ever before. Scientific and technological advancements must be accelerated and applied in developed and developing nations alike, if we are to feed a growing world population."[40]

In effect, Clydesdale and the IFT position paper argue that Pollan's vision is too utopian in its call for radical change and too discrediting of the food industry's science-based accomplishments.[41] Their vision, in contrast, is presented as based on a sober and realistic understanding of everyday affairs—in the differences between developed and developing nations and in the daily demands for inexpensive and safe food by a growing world population.[42] Furthermore, the food industry possesses built-in mechanisms for self-correction as it responds in a morally neutral manner to consumer demands, including those based on lifestyle preferences. Whether or not consumers want "green" (or, as Maxwell said, "fresh and healthy"), the industry can muster its impressive techniques and technologies to adjust practices accordingly.

Thus, having disaggregated Pollan's perspective in the name of realism and consumer demand, the industry concludes that the present food system is as good as it's likely to get. As for its critics, the position paper's response is characteristic:

> Some books on food in the popular press have implied that the food industry has incorrectly applied the knowledge of food science and technology to develop processed foods that result in poor dietary habits. The premise . . . [is that] knowledge of chemistry and the physical properties of food constituents allow . . . processed foods that result in overeating and cause the general population to abandon whole foods. The argument . . . [is that] the development of processed foods is responsible for promoting bad eating habits and is the cause of chronic disease. Such an argument is specious, because personal preferences, choice, willpower, and lifestyle factor into the decision of what and how much to eat.[43]

Such a response, of course, will not convince the critics. They might note—and we would agree—that it is disingenuous to argue that consumers' poor choices are fundamentally their fault. After all, the position paper grants that much industry effort is made to increase "the availability of indulgent foods," instead of promoting more "nutrient-rich rather than energy-dense foods." It also grants that more responsible marketing is necessary to "assist the consumer in the quest for a healthful diet" and that there must be a greater effort to provide "clear, accurate information" to help consumers make "healthful, economical food choices." This is especially the case given that obesity, which has become a serious problem in the United States and other developed countries, "may be economically driven . . . [since] some of the lowest priced foods are the more calorie-dense and palatable products."[44] In this regard the position paper seems to concede important aspects of the arguments made "in the popular press" by food industry adversaries. Thus, in the revised (2007) edition of her influential 2002 book, *Food Politics,* the nutritionist and food activist Marion Nestle concludes:

> The principal theme of *Food Politics* is that food choices are political as well as personal. That notion, perhaps surprising in 2002, is now well recognized. Then, personal responsibility was assumed to be the primary determinant of food choice. Today, it is widely accepted that food marketing influences food choices and that our "eat more" food environment—one that promotes food that is highly varied, ubiquitous, convenient, close at hand, inexpensive, presented in large portions, and eaten frequently—encourages "mindless" consumption of more calories than are needed or noticed.[45]

Nevertheless, despite its concessions, the position paper concludes that responsibility ultimately remains with the consumer, since "choosing foods wisely is a survival skill" that needs to be taught from an early age.[46]

Clearly, the debate—the wrangling—is not over. And it will continue to heat up as people try to imagine, as Koki Ando has, what the food future will be in 2050. What then will be the evaluation of who is responsible for what? What will constitute a sober and realistic understanding of everyday affairs? And what role will the products of food science—including instant noodles—play in that future?

Big Food for a Huge Population?

At the 2010 summit of the World Instant Noodles Association (WINA), Koki Ando proclaimed that "instant noodles could save the Earth."[1] In this final chapter of our noodle narratives we consider whether instant noodles, conceived broadly as a particular instance of mass capitalist provisioning and as a more general representative of that provisioning, can feed a world of (by most estimates) nine or so billion people in 2050. How, in other words, might instant noodles and similar products feature in the various food futures that are proposed—indeed, promoted and implemented—as feasible for a huge world population that includes those who are habitually overfed as well as those who are chronically underfed?

The food industry sees this future as one of both challenge and opportunity. Thus, since 2009, the Institute of Food Technologists (IFT), together with General Mills, has sponsored an annual student competition, "Developing Solutions for Developing Countries," in which students enrolled in food science programs, whether domestic or international, compete to solve a specified food-related problem. Interestingly, there have been several top-placing submissions concerning instant noodles. For example, in the 2009 competition, with the theme of using "food science and technology to solve health-based issues," the third-place winners, students from Indonesia's Bogor Agricultural University, proposed to create "healthy instant noodle from corn with high protein and rich iron for pregnant women to prevent lost generation in

Southeast Asia."[2] Their goal was to reduce Indonesia's reliance on imported wheat while improving maternal nutrition. They recommended making instant noodles with locally grown, protein-rich corn, which was currently being used inefficiently as animal feed. In addition, the noodles would be enriched with the supplements pregnant women are likely to need; at the same time, those targeted by these reformulated instant noodles would likely accept them as a familiar food.

The 2011 competition had an instant noodle–focused winning proposal as well. The theme was finding a "solution for alleviating iron deficiency in developing countries," and the first-prize winners, also from Indonesia, were from the Faculty of Agricultural Technology at Brawijaya University.[3] Their submission, "fighting iron deficiency through iron-enriched instant noodle production by utilizing local ingredients," involved augmenting wheat flour with Indonesian ingredients, including cassava, sweet potato, and two ingredients that are especially high in iron: tempeh (a fermented soy cake) and eel.

These student competitions represent an effort on the part of the food industry to demonstrate that its techniques and technologies can be used to make money while solving pressing nutritional problems in developing countries. However, although Brawijaya University announced that it would commercialize the iron-enriched instant noodles, it is unclear how lucrative the market for them might be.[4] In fact, one of the judges at the 2009 IFT meetings told Fred that the development of most of the prize-winning products was probably dependent on subsidies that could easily be withdrawn.

More typically, food technologists, including those focusing on instant noodles, are concerned with products for which market demand will be substantial. At the 2011 meeting, thus, Maria Vernaza and Yoon Chang of Caminas State University in Brazil delivered a paper, titled "Effect of the Addition of Three Different Sources of Resistant Starch in Instant Noodles Using Atmospheric and Vacuum Frying." Their research was a direct response to health concerns about the consumption of high-calorie, and especially high-fat, foods. It sought to formulate instant noodles that contain a digestion-resistant starch and to fry these noodles under a vacuum, at a lower-than-usual temperature. This process still drives out moisture (recall Momofuku Ando's reliance on the "principle of tempura"), but the noodles absorb less oil while retaining desirable digestion-resistant properties and a white appearance. At the same time, the process protects the cooking oil from harmful heat-induced degradation.

In addition to the papers, there were poster sessions about how instant noodles might be altered given market demand. At the 2009 meeting, Chuan-Yu Chuang and three colleagues from the Food Industry Research and Development Institute in Taiwan mounted a presentation, "Application of Microwaved Assisted Drying Process on Non-fry Instant Noodles," which described their efforts to eliminate the use of oil in the preparation of instant noodles without unduly extending the processing time and hence the costs. The conventional alternative to frying noodles has been to blast them with hot air: in effect, to bake them for some sixty minutes. In contrast, through microwaving techniques, nonfried instant noodles could be dried in thirty minutes. Although the process still takes longer than the two to three minutes necessary for frying, the resulting instant noodles cost only 20 percent more. Unfortunately, taste tests demonstrated that most consumers still prefer the fried varieties.

Another poster presentation at the 2009 meeting was by Byung-Doo Lee and colleagues from Chonnam National and Chodang Universities in Korea. Entitled "Optimization of Formulation for Soup Base of Instant Noodle (Ramen) Using Natural Ingredients by Central Composite Design," it showed that umami-rich radish powder, shiitake mushroom powder, and a "natural seasoning agent" could be substituted for the salt and MSG usually present in instant noodle flavor sachets. The reformulated contents were said to be suitably soluble in water and tasty.

Such research contributes to ongoing efforts by large food companies to develop instant noodles for every taste (and survival skill level). For instance, at the 2010 WINA summit, Koki Ando also said that the time had come to change "the iconic snack's recipe." One challenge was to reduce the salt content. This would have to be done gradually: "Our longtime customers enjoy the salt in our noodles, so we cannot simply reduce it just like that."[5] Indeed, by 2010 Nissin was already catering to health-conscious consumers with, for instance, its hot air–dried "Lite Cup Noodle" (frequently advertised with a Japanese actress wearing nothing except a very large Lite Cup Noodle container while exercising on a treadmill!). These noodles are "layered with fiber, sprayed with minimal oil instead of being deep-fried and contain nearly one-third fewer calories than regular versions."[6] For its part, Nestlé in Malaysia was promoting a hot air–dried "Tastylite" made from "whole wheat, with every packet providing the same amount of fiber as nearly one-and-a-half slices of whole wheat bread."[7] Correspondingly, the Tastylite label cautions: "Excessive fat intake causes unhealthy weight gain.

Adopt smarter approach, choose baked foods instead of fried foods."[8] It would seem, hence, that anyone can find a variety of instant noodles that suits him or her; no one has a reason not to buy them. For those who insist, there are low-sodium varieties (despite possible taste draw-backs) as well as high-calcium ones; there are organic varieties as well as kosher and halal ones. After all, generating an array of products to engage virtually everyone is central to the operation of the food indus-try. It is, for the industry, business as usual: if you (really) want low salt, we'll give you low salt; if you want high fiber, we'll give you high fiber.

In working hard to give their customers what they apparently want, instant noodle producers claim that they are giving the world what it will increasingly need. Koki Ando, as we saw in the previous chapter, has argued that within the next fifty years much of the world's expand-ing population will live in megacities. Along with this, the number of poor people suffering from hunger is anticipated to grow rapidly. Food security—access by all people at all times to enough nutritional food for an active, healthy life—will be a major challenge, but one that instant noodles will help meet.[9] For instance, WINA views the increasing demand for biofuels as posing a major threat to future food security. This demand, together with the adverse effects of global warming and climate change, have already led to "shortages in wheat, corn, and palm oil," driving up the prices of these commodities, which are basic to the industrial food system.[10] Given the centrality of wheat and palm oil in the production of instant noodles, such shortages are of special concern to WINA. It, therefore, advocates that the "use of raw materials for food should take precedence over the use of raw materials for energy."[11] Further contributing to crucial shortages in basic foodstuffs are funda-mentally wasteful practices of meat production. As WINA argues, instant noodles as a "grain-based food . . . [are] far more calorie-efficient, compared with meat products that need a great volume of feed grains."[12] The future WINA is proposing—one in which "humans became more herbivorous"—is sustainable, it claims, with instant noo-dles contributing to long-term food security and providing environmen-tal benefit through the responsible use of basic food resources.[13]

Through such arguments, which blend self-interest with virtue, WINA (as both an organization and a gloss for instant-noodle interests) attempts to project itself onto a food future that is feasible and desir-able, one in which instant noodles in particular and industrial food in general can prove responsive to important exigencies. In justifying its claim—both literal and metaphorical—that instant noodles can save the world, WINA maneuvers through ongoing food-system controversies. Hence, because instant noodles are grain based, WINA can seek to ally itself with food industry critics who object to current practices of live-stock feeding. Therefore, it can place itself in agreement with Michael Pollan when he was asked to imagine our food system one hundred years hence: "We certainly won't be eating nine ounces of meat per person per day, as Americans do now—there won't be enough feed grain, worldwide, to continue that feast, and presumably we will have faced up to meat-eating's disastrous toll on the environment."[14] And because instant noodles are cheap, WINA can reach agreement with just about everyone that the price of food is and will continue to be a problem for many.

However, what actually constitutes cheapness remains controversial. Critics of the dominant food system argue that cost-effectiveness itself comes at a considerable cost. Thus, Pollan's response to the (loaded) question of how to make "healthful food as affordable as its evil coun-terpart" would likely not be WINA's. "High-quality food," says Pollan, will never be

> as cheap as industrial food, some of which will only get more expensive if we take the steps needed to civilize feedlots, clean up water and protect farm-workers from exploitation. Faux populists in the food industry battle such measures on the grounds they want to keep food prices low for the poor. But the institution of slavery kept crop prices low, too—at a cost we ultimately decided was too great for a democratic society to pay . . . . Cheap food has become a pillar of our low-wage economy, one reason Americans have man-aged to stay afloat as their wages have declined since the 1970s. In the end, if we want healthful and conscientiously produced food for everyone, we're simply going to have to pay people enough so that they can afford to buy it.[15]

Moreover, as Marion Nestle makes clear, cheapness within an industri-alized food system often indexes the plethora of energy-dense, nutri-tionally dubious, highly processed (junk) foods that are associated with high rates of obesity.[16] (Concerning the situation in America, the Cen-ters for Disease Control and Prevention reported in 2010 that "about one-third of U.S. adults [35.7 percent] are obese. Approximately 17 percent [or 12.5 million] of children and adolescents aged 2–19 years are obese."[17]) Correspondingly, the physician Mark Hyman notes: "We have made calories cheap, but real food expensive . . . . You can fill up on 1200 calories of cookies or potato chips for $1, but you'll only get 250 calories from carrots for that same $1. If you were hungry, what would you buy?"[18] And, if you took advantage of a recent Amherst, Massachusetts, supermarket offering to sell sixty packages of Maruchan instant noodles for ten dollars, you could kill your hunger with 380 calories for about seventeen cents.

Proposed remedies to these circumstances might include paying all people a decent wage (a desirable, if politically fraught, undertaking) or, as Pollan recommends, offsetting the price advantage that crop subsidies provide to industrialized food. This might take the form of "subsidizing demand rather than supply: giving vouchers to the poor to buy fresh produce, say, or incentives to retailers to lower prices in the produce section."[19] More conventional remedies might include encouraging consumers to exercise their survival skills—even if it means spending more—to make good food choices. As far as the latter remedies are concerned, instant noodles might still be a viable component in a feasible and desirable food future; given instant noodles' remarkable "tweakability," Nissin and the other developers of reduced-sodium, lower-fat, higher-fiber, better-fortified varieties could be seen as inviting consumers to strike an appropriate balance between their concerns with taste, price, and health.

HOW TO FEED THE WORLD IN 2050

Our task now is to consider in more detail how the push and pull between these usually rival perspectives—that of modestly modified business as usual versus a more radical departure from business as usual—may play out in a considerably more populous future. In so doing, we must appraise the food prospects of both those who can access too many calories and those who can access too few. That the number of overnourished (1.1 billion) in the world recently exceeded the number of undernourished (1 billion) should not distract us from considering the circumstances of those whose survival skills may allow them simply to survive.[20]

In anticipating a future characterized by substantial population growth and increasing urbanization (whether in megacities or in somewhat smaller ones), Koki Ando expressed the conclusions of many scientists and social scientists. Accordingly, the demographer Joel Cohen thinks that most of his colleagues would agree with these four statements:

> First, the population will be bigger than it is now. The world will be bigger by 2 billion to 4 billion people by the middle of the century [with most predicting 9 billion by 2050], and nearly all of that growth will be in poor

countries, not rich.[21] Second, the population will increase less rapidly, absolutely and relatively, than it has recently. Whether population growth ends depends on choices that we make right now about reproductive health, education for women, and many other investments. Third, the population will be more urban than it is now. Practically all of the additional people will be living in cities in poor countries, and that will be an unprecedented epidemiological challenge to infectious disease control. Fourth, the population will be older than it is now. Now is probably the last time in history in which we have more youth than aged, and the last time in which we have more rural than urban population. From here on out it is an urban world.[22]

The problems of feeding so many may be additionally complicated by rising expectations—if present trends in consumption can be projected forward. When modernization increases prosperity, at least for those achieving steady incomes, as in China and (to some extent) India, diets are likely to become more elaborate.[23] According to the Food and Agricultural Organization (FAO) of the United Nations, grains and staple crops will still be important, yet their centrality in the diet will be offset by "vegetables, fruits, meat, dairy, and fish." In addition, there will be a "rising demand for semi-processed or ready-to-eat foods," resulting in a "further concentration of supermarket chains."[24] In sum, the biologist H. Charles Godfray and his colleagues writing about our food future in *Science Magazine* conclude that "there is no simple solution to sustainably feeding 9 billion people, especially as many become increasingly better off and converge on rich-country consumption patterns."[25] That being said, a number of relatively mainstream analysts concerned with food security agree on what might contribute to such a solution.

To begin with, most mainstream analysts, for reasons already mentioned, agree that diversion of food stock into biofuels or into cows is wasteful. They recommend instead the elimination of U.S. subsidies for grain-based ethanol and advocate a shift from feedlot-fed to grass-fed cows and toward other protein sources, noting that chickens, pork, or factory-farmed fish make more efficient use of feed inputs.[26]

Most of these analysts also agree that the current use of nitrogen fertilizer is environmentally destructive, especially given the amount that is leached from fields and the consequent eutrophication of inland and coastal waters, including the Gulf of Mexico. Most think that techniques exist to use this fertilizer more judiciously. These include more "precision agriculture"—for instance, employing GPS technology to apply fertilizer according to specific soil conditions—as well as "reduced tillage" cultivation to preserve root systems that lessen water runoff.[27] Some see promise in plant breeding to convert annuals like wheat into perennials that would remain in the ground for three to five years, developing root systems that would hold water and nutrients.[28] And some believe that crop rotations with "green manure"—nitrogen-fixing legumes—can drastically reduce the amount of fertilizers necessary.[29] Nevertheless, the geographer and environmental ecologist Vaclav Smil says that nitrogen fertilizers are here to stay. Their use will be essential to feed an extra two to four billion people by the year 2050. Supply will be sufficient for the task since the natural gas from which these fertilizers are made is ample. Although Smil claims that "there is no way to eliminate substantial losses accompanying field applications of nitrogen compounds, and hence to avoid all the undesirable environmental consequences of fertilization," he acknowledges that "we can certainly improve the typical efficiencies with which we use nitrogen fertilizers."[30]

Most mainstream analysts agree that huge amounts of food are wasted in the developed world because of the profligacy of some consumers, restaurants, and supermarkets. They suggest that affluent consumers should eat less, throw away less, and learn to accept slightly "bruised" produce. In addition, governments should eliminate unrealistic "sell-by" dates, which mandate that food be discarded rather than sold.[31] In the developing world, considerable losses occur because of the difficulty in transporting produce to consumers.[32] Recommendations include infrastructural improvements, such as improved storage facilities and better roads to improve market access.[33] Indeed, according to the International Food Policy Research Institute's report on climate change, "rural road density has been shown to be among the most important contributors to productivity growth in agriculture" in the developing world.[34]

Most of the analysts agree that water for irrigation will become increasingly scarce. They recommend that drip lines replace above-ground spray systems and that drought tolerance be selected for, either through conventional breeding techniques or through current genetic techniques.[35]

Most of them agree that destroying forests to increase the amount of arable land will not enable much more food production and is environmentally damaging for its elimination of biodiversity and exacerbation of greenhouse gas emissions. Of particular concern to many are current practices associated with clearing land for oil palm plantations.[36] These often involve destruction of rainforests through logging and burning, practices that are financially expedient because the sale of tropical hardwoods can finance the development of the plantation. In fact, the area devoted to oil palm production has been expanding at about 7 percent a year, mostly in environmentally sensitive areas, driven by demand for both biofuels and edible oils (again, of the sort currently favored in the production of instant noodles).[37] Rather than clearing additional land, existing land should be used more efficiently, especially in portions of the developing world such as Africa. There, significant "yield gaps" exist—the differences between what is produced and what could be produced with more effective agricultural techniques including the use of fertilizers. Some believe that smallholders can be encouraged to close these gaps with the promise of land security, which will give them the incentive to make their land more productive, and with the provision of enhanced agricultural techniques.[38] Hence, the FAO argues that "in sub-Saharan Africa, in particular, there are indications of yield gaps that could be exploited with given [seed] varieties and known practices."[39] Comparably, the Bill and Melinda Gates Foundation, which focuses on agricultural development in sub-Saharan Africa and South Asia, advocates helping local farmers, especially women, who are "vital participants on small farms," to increase their productivity through a "comprehensive approach . . . that includes developing heartier seeds, helping them get access to new tools and farm management techniques, [and] opening doors to markets."[40] Falling under the general rubric of a "Second Green Revolution," this initiative promises that small and marginal players will, this time around, be more efficiently integrated into production and that, therefore, many may be encouraged to remain on the land rather than to move to cities. Yet the economist Paul Collier believes that both the scale and techniques of production must be changed in places like Africa. He writes: "Contrary to the romantics, the world needs more commercial agriculture, not less."[41] In addition, he favors more scientific agriculture, suggesting that "to counter the effects of Africa's rising population and deteriorating climate, African agriculture needs a biological revolution. This is what GM [genetically modified] crops offer if only sufficient money is put into research."[42] Thus, his position accords with the general, if highly controversial, endorsement of GM crops by Roger Beachy, director of the USDA's National Institute of Food and Agriculture. Beachy argues: "With new technologies in seeds and in crop production, it will be possible to reduce the use of chemical fertilizers and the amount of irrigation while maintaining high yields. Better seeds will help, as will improvements in agricultural practices."[43]

Most mainstream analysts agree that the earth's rising temperature due to greenhouse gas emissions will increase extreme weather events (what many call "weird weather"), shift seasons, and have generally deleterious effects on agriculture, reducing yields of desirable crops and encouraging weed and pest proliferation. Climate change will especially influence the availability of wheat and other cereal grains, including those used as animal feed. This will require technological and scientific advances that increase agricultural productivity, including the development of GM-derived, drought-resistant seeds.[44]

Most of these analysts agree that many people in developing countries are extremely vulnerable to price fluctuations in basic commodities, including fluctuations caused by "dumping." This may occur when agricultural price supports in developed countries allow their commodities to be sold in developing countries at less than the cost of production. As a result, local producers are driven out of business and their countries are left with food insecurity: with increasing dependence on imports for basic provisions whose prices may skyrocket as a result of speculation, diversion into biofuel, and the like. However (and this is a point to which we will return), many of the proposed remedies seem designed not to roil established first-world food interests. For instance, Godfray and his colleagues write that "food production in developing countries can be severely affected by market interventions in the developed world, such as subsidies or price supports. These need to be carefully designed and implemented so that their effects on global commodity prices do not act as disincentives to production in other countries."[45] Granting comparable wiggle room, the FAO vaguely calls for the creation of "a global trading system that contributes to a dependable market for food, feed and fiber . . . [while] eliminating trade barriers and . . . [ensuring] that safety mechanisms are in place to shield the most vulnerable."[46] It is noteworthy that in neither case are these mechanisms specified.

There is no guarantee, of course, that any of these mainstream recommendations for a more sustainable, food-secure future will be implemented by governments struggling with long-term debt, faced with structural adjustments, and beset by those concerned with maximizing profits. (This is not to mention the irrelevance of such recommendations to extreme situations such as warfare, in which destruction of food crops, looting of storage facilities, and interception of food aid are documented tactics of subjugation through starvation.[47]) Indeed, far from resisting such pressures, many government officials may be willing to benefit from suspect and harmful practices. For instance, according to a study prepared by the Center for Science and the Public Interest in

Washington, DC, "Indonesia's plantation and forestry sectors are infested with corruption, collusion, and nepotism, according to the Indonesian government's own official investigations. Ultimately . . . [these] practices underlie the proliferation of oil palm's destruction of prime rainforest habitat for wildlife."[48] Much the same can be said about the granting of logging concessions through "land grabs" in Papua New Guinea.[49] One example may be the recently announced 140,000-hectare, Malaysian-financed Bewani oil palm plantation in Papua New Guinea, whose prospective estate manager, according to the job description, must have "experience in development of oil palm plantations from primary jungle."[50]

Moreover, even if these recommendations were implemented, the resulting food system would retain strong continuities with the present one. Although one hopes that the new one would be smarter, it would still remain dependent on huge inputs from the developed into the developing world of industrially produced cereal grains (primarily wheat, rice, and corn) which, according to the FAO, are likely to more than double from 135 million metric tons in 2008 and 2009 to 300 million metric tons in 2050.[51] In addition, many of these and other industrially produced inputs may end up in processed foods purveyed by ever more ubiquitous and consolidated supermarket chains.[52]

This, then, is a scenario of capitalist provisioning: one of modestly modified business as usual in which instant noodles are likely to remain important, whether or not, as Koki Ando claims, they will literally save the world.[53] It is a scenario in which the affluent will be presented with too many food choices and called upon to use their survival skills to choose wisely, and in which the poor will have to use their survival skills to get by on cheap food. It is a future that Roger Clemens, president of the IFT, embraces as he takes note of the projections of the 2009 World Summit on Food Security—that by 2050 food production must increase by 70 percent to feed an anticipated world population of nine billion people: "We must move swiftly ahead with scientific and technological advancement in both developed and developing nations to feed the world's population. . . . We've learned that if we are to assure the health and wellness of an ever-growing population, our food system must be consumer driven, flexible, resilient, and sustainable."[54] It is also a scenario that, as may be readily imagined, produces significant levels of distrust, if not outright opposition. Despite the caveats mentioned—such as those about reducing the yield gaps in developing countries in ways that enhance the lives of small-scale farmers (especially women), about erecting safety nets to protect the import-dependent vulnerable, and about making tariffs and subsidies more equitable—the world as projected still seems to favor the already powerful. The consumer-driven food system that Clemens advocates could, in the view of many, be much more democratic if consumers were given real choices and if small-scale producers were given some breathing room.

In their call for a more radical departure from business as usual, most critics of the current regime of capitalist provisioning suggest that reimagining what Clemens calls the "flexible, resilient, and sustainable" requires a shift in scale. They argue that framing the food future in terms of world food security by asking, in effect, "How many million tons of grain will it take to feed how many billions of largely urban mouths?" eliminates a range of feasible, if more local and diverse, alternatives. Whereas food security is determined by whether people have access to enough nutritional food for an active, healthy life, those advocating "food sovereignty" are especially concerned with how, where, and by whom food is produced and distributed.[55] They recognize that increasing the world's production of food doesn't guarantee that people everywhere will gain equitable access to it: the fact that there is enough food to go around does not necessarily mean that it will get around fairly.[56] Relatedly, they are dubious about the effect on farmers in the developing world—especially poor farmers—of a second green revolution, one that focuses on such inputs as genetically engineered seeds. These set up "a highly profitable scenario for seed makers, as farmers would be reliant upon these companies to continue buying their seeds, and would not be able to save the patented, modified seeds" (and, indeed, the Bill and Melinda Gates Foundation is working in conjunction with the Monsanto Corporation, well-known for specializing in patented and modified seeds).[57]

Advocates for food sovereignty stress that agricultural policies should be substantially weighted toward food self-sufficiency—toward local, regional, and national control over food production and importation. They focus on the rights of farmers to produce food appropriate to different food cultures, the rights of citizens to develop agricultural policies, and the rights of nation-states to control their food-relevant trade. In so doing, they strongly object to the policies of the World Trade Organization (WTO): while the WTO claims that liberalized trade is of general benefit, critics see its actions as favoring the already powerful. For example, they see dumping as legitimized by the WTO through tricky deals that define significant agricultural subsidies to first-world crops as not distorting trade.[58] While turning a blind eye to unfair subsidies, the WTO looks closely at efforts by countries in the developing world to regulate food imports, even for health-related reasons.

A recent example of the way the WTO operates in a world of disproportionate power comes from the developing Pacific Island nation of Samoa. Samoa's thirteen-year effort to gain entry to the WTO was successful only when the country lifted its ban on the import, primarily from the United States, of "turkey tails"—a ban intended to reduce the high rates of obesity, diabetes, and heart disease derived from eating fatty foods. (One cooked turkey tail has 196.86 calories, 141.21 of them from fat.[59]) The USA Poultry and Egg Council welcomed the end of the ban, stating that it was "the consumers' right to determine what foods they wish to consume, not the government's." Also welcoming the end of the ban was the director-general of the WTO, who said that entry into the WTO will "enable Samoa to participate more fully in the global economy and will provide the country with a predictable and stable basis for growth and development."[60] Yet a Samoan-based NGO, the O Le Siosiomaga Society (whose name means "What's Around Us"), criticized the accession process as lacking in transparency and as conceding too much, especially on tariffs.[61] Moreover, the anthropologist Penelope Schoeffel, a longtime resident of Samoa, has been unable to determine with any precision how liberalized trade would benefit the country. In an e-mail communication, she wrote: "I still can't find out what the advantages are to Samoa to join. At present Samoa mainly exports labor; among commodities it exports modest amounts of taro, virgin coconut oil, some flowers to Australia and New Zealand and noni juice to China. I asked a politician the other day who replied 'we have to, don't we?'"[62]

Worldwide, objection to the WTO—at least in that it facilitates the trade interests of the internationally powerful—has become central to major political food sovereignty movements. Perhaps the most important of these is La Via Campesina ("The Peasants' Way"), an umbrella organization comprising some 150 local and national organizations, ranging from America's National Family Farm Coalition to Brazil's Landless Workers Movement. La Via Campesina presents itself as committed to defending "small-scale sustainable agriculture as a way to promote social justice and dignity" by opposing "corporate driven agriculture and transnational companies that are destroying people and nature."[63] Thus, according to the geographer Annette Desmarais, the movement provides "an important challenge to the political, economic, and cultural sustainability of a globalized, corporate, market-driven food system."[64]

La Via Campesina's perspective on food sovereignty generally corresponds with the approach to food production taken by agroecology.[65] The food policy specialists Tim Lang and Michael Heasman characterize this approach as such: "There is an increasing emphasis on skills and knowledge management in contrast to the single technician managing thousands of hectares on a 'recipe' basis; it would relink the people with the land, encourage small-scale management units and return alienated farm workers to the land."[66] Lang and Heasman cite Cuba as a case study that demonstrates the potential of producing food in this way. After the collapse of the Soviet Union and in the face of an ongoing U.S.-backed trade embargo, Cuba was unable to import significant amounts of food or fossil fuels and their derived fertilizers. Forced to use agroecological technologies to achieve food sovereignty, Cubans managed to feed themselves. Correspondingly, La Via Campesina has pledged support of Cuba's agrarian reforms and solidarity with its goals of continuing food sovereignty, declaring, "Long live the family farmers of Cuba and the world."[67]

Nonetheless, Lang and Heasman believe that more work must be done to demonstrate that the food sovereignty movement, with its agroecological approach to food production, has widespread applicability to the developing and developed world. Although providing a viable and sustainable livelihood for some local producers, the food sovereignty movement is unlikely to offset urban drift significantly. Furthermore, its capacity to provide sufficient food for an increasing urban population is unclear. As the movement's advocates recognize, it will have to address "the situation of the urban poor and their access to food" more adequately.[68] How, in other words, might such local food movements—even if empowered, for instance, by more secure land titles and better rural road networks—be "scaled up"? Localized production might be encouraged to provide adequate sustenance for a largely rural population, and perhaps for some urban consumers, including "locavores" (those committed to eating food from just their local or regional "foodshed," usually no more than 100 to 250 miles away). But how will food be provided for the urban billions who remain far from the usual centers of agricultural production, either voluntarily (like many in Papua New Guinea) or involuntarily (like many in Nepal)—and may never get to know their farmer?[69] What are the alternatives for them?

Possible answers are provided by a rather extensive worldwide "urban agriculture movement." Some of those growing food in cities make their living from it. They include the members of the Silwood family of Auckland, who hydroponically produce year-round crops of gourmet lettuce for sale to local supermarkets and restaurants.[70] They include hundreds of low-income farmers who, organized into cooperatives, produce one-fifth of Calcutta's fresh vegetables on garbage dumps rented from the city.[71] Other urban farmers grow food largely for their families to supplement food purchases and sell whatever is left for additional income. In fact, urban gardening may constitute a major strategy to cope with real hardship. This might be the case for Argentine pensioners or Tanzanian schoolteachers struggling to make do after structural adjustments, in the name of neoliberal market reforms, left them unable to afford the free market prices of basic food.[72] It might also be the case for the Haitian poor using locally collected garbage to fertilize crops they grow on their rooftops.[73] Overall, the FAO estimates that "130 million urban residents in Africa and 230 million in Latin America engage in agriculture, mainly horticulture, to provide food for their families or to earn income from sales."[74]

In the Pacific Islands, including Papua New Guinea, "urban food gardening," as the human geographer Randolph Thaman writes, "is seen as an important means of overcoming problems caused by unemployment, inequality, poverty, falling real wages, malnutrition and nutrition-related degenerative diseases."[75] Many articles in PNG newspapers support this position. A 2004 article in the *Post Courier,* titled "Making Ends Meet Through Gardening," reported on a couple living in a Port Moresby settlement, at the "bottom of the pyramid," who were exercising their survival skills as they coped with the present and hoped for the future:

> For many, with the current living standards due to skyrocketing of the prices of food items and other necessities, it is a very worrying time.
>
> For the unemployed and low-income earners in many of Port Moresby's squatter settlements, backyard or hillside gardening is their only hope of getting some income. By selling their fresh produce in the city's markets, the people are able to earn money to pay school fees and buy the necessary items for their children.
>
> Otu Amos and her husband, both in their mid-40s, and their children who live at the Erima settlement are one such family . . . . Mrs. Amos said [that] because her husband was unemployed, the family had no means of support and the only solution was to make food gardens to sell the produce. The couple grows kaukau [sweet potato], corn, peanuts and other crops to make ends meet.

"We haven't paid the school fees for our two daughters as yet because we don't have enough money," says Mrs Amos. "We are finding it difficult to save money as we have to buy food to feed ourselves every day. . . .

"We understand that we have to pay the school fees, and we are working hard in our gardens to harvest and sell the produce. We are confident that we will save enough to pay the school fees."[76]

Indeed, in Papua New Guinea and elsewhere, urban gardening may constitute one of the most significant aspects of the informal economy upon which many city dwellers rely.[77]

Not surprisingly, though, given the exigencies of urban life and the reliance on the informal economy, urban gardens may produce food of uneven quality. The gardens may be on industrially polluted soil, irrigated with contaminated wastewater, fertilized with inadequately composted garbage, and perhaps overtreated with pesticides.[78] There are other problems as well, such as erosion of deforested hillsides, evictions and land disputes, and the stench, noise, and depredation of backyard animals—sometimes including aggressive and omnivorous pigs—often fed from such gardens. Despite such problems (which, hopefully, could be minimized), the food produced in these gardens may be especially welcome by urban dwellers. For instance, in Africa and Asia, according to the FAO, "urban households spend up to 50 percent of their food budgets on cheap 'convenience' foods often deficient in the vitamins and minerals essential for health." Correspondingly, "daily fruit and vegetable consumption is just 20–50 percent of FAO/World Health Organization (WHO) recommendations."[79] By providing vitamin- and mineral-rich fruits and vegetables, urban gardens may offer a vital contemporary service by helping urban dwellers—particularly the urban poor—compensate for their need to purchase industrially produced food.

However, in our view, urban agriculture and other relatively localized sources of food can provide only partial answers to how to feed urban billions. Without doubt, local growers should be encouraged (not only for the nutrients they provide, but because growers—especially urban growers—seem to gain considerable satisfaction in producing food[80]). The fact remains, though, that much of this production is concentrated on fruits and vegetables, which may be seasonal in their availability. Moreover, urban agriculture cannot address the likely ongoing need by urban billions for large amounts of edible oils and cereal grains (rice, wheat, and corn, among others). These provisions, it seems to us, will still have to be produced by some variant of (perhaps smarter) industrial, fertilizer-augmented mono-cropping and would be subject to some variant of industrial processing and mass distribution. It is likely, as well, that many of these products will end up in supermarkets that provide the convenience and the sorts of food that urban people seem to want. To be sure, these imported and processed foods could still be supplemented by regionally grown produce. Such a combination might meet Sidney Mintz's objective of "food at moderate speeds": neither too conveniently fast nor too impractically slow.[81] Nevertheless, in the urban world we imagine, filling bellies with securely available foods is going to be necessary. (Although some of these bellies may well be over-nourished.) That is, unless there are major game changers—such as the collapse of the ecosystem accompanied by a major decline in the population or the demise of capitalism accompanied by a major decrease in the production of food for profit—some currently recognizable form of large-scale capitalist provisioning will remain in place.

Our hope is that the future will provide at least a modest mosaic of choices—a mosaic in which competing orientations toward food, with an emphasis either on security or sovereignty, will continue to challenge one another in a socially and environmentally productive way. Lang and Heasman, in their account of the contemporary "food wars," come to a similar conclusion. While arguing (among other things) that "there will be a 'green shift,' away from the intensification of food supply to extensification schemes such as the promotion of organic and natural products," they also find that "there will be continued consolidation of agriculture and agribusiness, a continued decline in the numbers of small farmers, and widespread but contested use of GM technology."[82] Thus, we hope that critics like Michael Pollan and Marion Nestle will continue to challenge and provoke people like IFT's Roger Clemens. At the very least, we hope that companies like Nissin, Maruchan, and Nestlé might be provoked into better fortifying their instant noodles for their "heavy users" worldwide. And we hope that organizations like La Via Campesina will continue to challenge the WTO and that landless peasants' movements will be able to turn the tide of agro-industrial land grabs.

Yet, whatever the course of these food wars, we expect that tasty, convenient, cheap, shelf-stable, industrially prepared instant noodles will remain significant. As a protean food designed for quotidian consumption, instant noodles have already shown a remarkable capacity to ease themselves into diverse lives. Not only do they provide endless enticement for Japanese consumers and mark the trajectory of life for middle-class Americans; they also become a taste of freedom for prisoners, a facilitator of the often underpaid working day for both office staff and heavy users, and a catalyst of newly configured consumer efficacy for Papua New Guineans. Indeed, especially for those many worldwide hanging on under difficult circumstances, instant noodles have an important role in satiating hunger and in sustaining lives. Accordingly, we find it difficult to imagine the increasingly urbanized food future without this humble form of salty, MSG-enhanced, oily, and sometimes sugary capitalist provisioning. Instant noodles will definitely not save the world, but they will continue to help a wide range of people deal with the often harsh exigencies of their lives. Our conclusion, although offered with reluctance, must be that this is for the better, not for the worse.

Notes

1. Under the heading "Expanding Market," WINA provides the following consumption statistics for 2010, as measured in hundred million portions: China/Hong Kong: 423.0; Indonesia: 144.0; Japan: 52.9; Vietnam: 48.2; United States: 39.6; Republic of Korea: 34.1; India: 29.4; Thailand: 27.1; Philippines: 27.0; Brazil: 20.0; Russia: 19.0; Nigeria: 16.7; Malaysia: 12.2; Mexico: 8.3; Taiwan: 7.8; Gulf Cooperation Council countries: 7.6; Nepal: 7.3; Ukraine: 5.4; Cambodia: 3.3; Poland/Hungary/Czech Republic: 3.1; United Kingdom: 2.6; Myanmar: 2.4; Canada: 2.1; Germany: 1.8; Australia: 1.6; Singapore: 1.2; Fiji and Outskirt Islands: 0.9; South Africa: 0.9; Bangladesh: 0.6; New Zealand: 0.4; France: 0.4; Norway/Finland/Sweden/Denmark: 0.3; Costa Rica: 0.2; Netherlands: 0.2; Peru: 0.2; Belgium: 0.1; Others: 2.0. See World Instant Noodle Association 2011.

2. Thai Eyes 2010.

3. Lal 2010.

4. See Errington, Fujikura, and Gewertz 2012.

5. Japan Today 2011.

6. D. Kushner 2009.

7. Cate 2008: 17.

8. Bobby B. 2010.

9. National Public Radio 2009c.

10. Ton Tan Tin 2012.

11. Sheridan 2008.

12. This was an admittedly nonscientific poll of two thousand residents of the Tokyo area conducted by the Fuji Research Institute, a think tank attached to the Fuji Bank. Asked to rate the best invention of the twentieth century, respondents ranked instant noodles first. See Chorlton 2000.

13. Virtual Japan 2008.

14. The cover of this book portrays it as a "20-something's real world survival guide" and promises "straight talk on jobs, money, balance, life and more" (Aretakis 2006).

15. Shale 2003.

16. Mintz 1985.

17. See Foster 2008; Miller 1998; Watson 1997; and Caldwell 2008. Many scholars have also written about globally traversing, though not globally permeating, foods. Often taking the form of "commodity biographies," their works readily link with capitalist consumption studies. One of the most powerful is by food activist Deborah Barndt (2002). Her *Tangled Routes: Women, Work, and Globalization on the Tomato Trail* is about the unequal relations between workers in Mexico and consumers in the United States and Canada established by genetically engineered tomatoes. Others have considered the connections created by the global flows of maize husks, bluefin tuna, French green beans, papayas, and broccoli. On maize husks, see Long and Villareal 2000; on bluefin tuna, T. Bestor 2004; on French green beans, Freidberg 2004; on papayas, Cook 2004; on broccoli, Fischer and Benson 2006. A major goal of these food-focused discussions is to provoke disquietude about injustice or ill health (both personal and environmental) so that readers, as eaters, might change their food choices or protest in other ways. As the anthropologist Sarah Franklin puts it, "We consume not only as purchasers but as eaters: this is about breakfast, lunch and dinner. The politics comes to us on a plate" (2001: 5). In fact, the politics of breakfast, lunch, and dinner can be quite broad and are often located in contradictions between the interests of the state, corporations, and citizens.

18. For instance, Karen Tranberg Hansen (2003) has focused on used clothing, which appears in its global circulation not only in Euro-American thrift shops, but also in developing countries, such as Zambia. In Zambia, this clothing may be either accepted as is or tailored and combined into ensembles designed for dramatic effect. Comparably, Daniel Miller and Sophie Woodward (2011) show in their edited collection that denim, in its global spread, has been both transforming and transformed. Once considered a quintessentially American product, denim now unites the world as a universal uniform, yet one that allows wearers to configure it to their particular tastes and bodies.

19. Economist 2009.

20. On culinary imperialism, see Whitney 1999. On religious insensitivity, see Ethics Newsline 2001. On "supersizing," see Schlosser 2002. On environmental depletion, see Aiyer 2007. On labor intimidation, see Foster 2008: 197–202. Concerning environmental depletion of water, the chairman and CEO of Coca-Cola, Muhtar Kent, recently pledged "a world where all people have access to safe water. . . . In essence, this is our brand promise, and if a good brand is a promise, then a great brand is a promise kept" (quoted in Kuhn and Tarver 2011: 41).

21. In this regard, instant noodles might be compared to globally ubiquitous blue jeans, which Miller describes as a "humble" product (2010: 420).

22. As Paul Graham, who coined the term, explains: "Ramen profitable means a startup makes just enough to pay the founders' living expenses. This is

a different form of profitability than startups have traditionally aimed for. Traditional profitability means a big bet is finally paying off, whereas the main importance of ramen profitability is that it buys you time" (2009). Graham recommends that those waiting for the big bet to pay off might do better subsisting on rice and beans than on ramen.

23. Mintz 1979. Often consumed daily, these inexpensive hunger killers are easy to like and widely popular across cultures, though sugar and instant noodles may be especially important for poor people in cash-dependent urban and peri-urban circumstances.

24. Bourdieu 1977: 72.

25. The quotes are from Friedman 1995: 78; see also Foster 2008: 1–31; and the articles in Featherstone, Lash, and Robertson 1995.

26. Tsing 2004: 6.

27. J. K. Gibson-Graham are two people who share one name. See Gibson-Graham 2006: 137.

28. The term *fetish* was first applied to religious items, like voodoo dolls or saints' relics, that are believed by many to have intrinsic value (as potent objects) apart from the gods who are (supposed to be) the real source of value. Karl Marx applied the term to commodities to counteract the market-based view of them as inherently desirable goods that have value apart from the labor that brought them into being. Marx argued that to regard commodities as having inherent value (again, to fetishize them) is to overlook the life circumstances of those who make them—to overlook the fact that they are created within contexts of enduring inequality. These are contexts in which, for example, factory owners buy labor, and factory workers—through various types of coercion (if only that most must sell their labor to the owners)—have their labor appropriated as "surplus value." See, especially, Marx's "labor theory of value" (1906).

29. We take this phrase from the title of Mintz's book, *Tasting Food, Tasting Freedom* (1996).

30. To repeat, on McDonald's in Asia, see Watson 1997. On global denim, see Miller and Woodward 2011.

CHAPTER 1. THE TASTE OF SOMETHING GOOD

1. It is not entirely clear where "real" ramen originated, although many think it is from China. We are engaged not in telling its history, but in discussing its post-Ando transformation and worldwide spread. On its history, see Solt 2009; and B. Kushner 2012.

2. Fukutomi 2010. These ramen shops have been common throughout Japan since the early twentieth century and are still popular. Some of them have achieved the status of "grade-B gourmet," with their chefs becoming celebrities.

3. M. Ando 2002: 49–50.

4. M. Ando 2002: 51–52.

5. As we shall see, blending and producing flavors requires specialized knowledge and production techniques. Flavor sachets can easily be outsourced to companies offering economies of scale and experience. One Chinese company, for example, produces eight thousand metric tons of sachets annually,

delivering sachets modestly customized for particular markets. See Henan Pinzheng Food Co., Ltd, n.d.

6. The specific variety of hard wheat selected may depend on market prices and on the degree of noodle firmness desired.

7. One of the differences between noodles and pasta is that pasta is shaped through extrusion, a process in which the dough is forced through small holes in a metal cap at the end of a tube.

8. M. Ando 2002: 57.

9. Steiner 1973. The notion that umami is a fifth primary taste became much more widely accepted once an umami receptor (T1r1+3) was identified. See Zhao et al. 2003.

10. MacBeth and Lawry 1997: 2.

11. Science Daily 2007.

12. Blench and MacDonald 2000: 496.

13. M. Ando 2002: 54.

14. Blench and MacDonald 2000: 496.

15. Perrins 2003: 176.

16. On chicken production, see Stull and Broadway 2004: 36–51; and Striffler 2005.

17. As Lévi-Strauss (1966) would point out, boiling a chicken contrasts importantly with roasting one: while boiling is a sedate and everyday activity, roasting is dramatic and extravagant—what with fat dripping, spitting, and flaring, leaving exteriors charred and interiors raw. Thus, a boiled chicken soup is more appropriately served to a domestic group and a roasted chicken to guests. However, under contemporary circumstances, in which industrial production has greatly reduced the cost of chicken and supermarkets and fast-food outlets cater to the needs of time-short consumers, roasted chicken has become a commonplace meal in the domestic context.

18. Hydrolysis is the breaking (*lysis*) of chemical bonds (in the case of proteins, the peptide bond) through the introduction of water (*hydro*). The process can be catalyzed by acids or by the enzymes of yeast and bacteria. See Aaslyng et al. 1998.

19. In fact, both the chicken- and beef-flavored varieties of PNG-made Maggi noodles list virtually identical ingredients.

20. Henan Pinzheng Food Co., Ltd, n.d.

21. Fabrizio, Potineni, and Gray state that sugar is often used as a "flavor enhancer and taste masker," depending on the "flavor profile and form used" (2010: 143). Sugar is not only inherently flavorful but also useful in obscuring unpleasant tastes.

22. The flavor sachet accompanying the "chicken flavor" instant noodles sold under the Maggi brand in Papua New Guinea lists the following ingredients: maltodextrin (a sweetener, which is added to provide the same "smooth mouth feel" as do fats), Antioxidant 320 (butylated hydroxyanisole, which is added to keep fats from oxidizing and becoming rancid), Color 100 (curcumin, an extract of cumin, which is added to make food yellow), Color 150c (caramel, which is added to make food various shades of brown), Flavor Enhancer 635 (sodium 5'-ribonucleotides, which is a mixture of two other enhancers added to

augment the properties of MSG), onion powder, herbs, spices, celery, soy, and wheat.

23. According to the neuropsychologist Jean-Paul Baird, "This is likely an interaction with obesity as some South American and other . . . [peoples] have been documented to have much higher urinary sodium levels or sodium consumption per person [than in the United States], but have lower CHD [coronary heart disease]" (e-mail communication to Deborah Gewertz, May 13, 2012).

24. The United Kingdom provides an RDA for sodium of 1,500 milligrams. Japan recommends 3,500 milligrams, with the argument that anything lower would be unrealistic given the importance of miso and soy sauce, both high in sodium, to the Japanese diet; moreover, the claim is sometimes made that miso contains potassium and magnesium, which help discharge sodium from the body.

25. Estimates, at least concerning the United States, vary. According to the National Salt Reduction Initiative, "Americans consume roughly twice the recommended limit of salt each day" (Katz and Williams 2010: 25).

26. Linda Bartoshuk, e-mail to Deborah Gewertz, March 14, 2012. There is some debate as to whether the craving for salt is innate. Schulkin (1991) argues that it is. Kroeber (1941) takes the minority position that it is learned.

27. See Wilkins and Richter 1940.

28. Among those most sensitive are the Inuit, whose high-protein diet of seal produces excess urea that must be flushed by drinking a considerable amount of fresh water daily. But much of this water comes from freshwater ice sources, such as icebergs and ice blocks, which are subject to contamination by seawater. Under these circumstances, Inuits have adaptively developed a sensitivity to the taste of salt to ensure that the water they drink does not result in an intake of excess salt and cause cardiovascular diseases. See Hladik 1997 and 2007.

29. McGee 2004: 640.

30. Kurlansky 2002: 18–19, 38.

31. See Wilson and Grim 2000: 48; and McGee 2004: 639–640.

32. Many of these techniques, including mining, were developed during the nineteenth century. See Kurlansky 2002: 303–332.

33. All quotes above are from Tarver 2010: 45.

34. Katz and Williams 2010: 25.

35. Tarver 2010: 46.

36. Several studies have suggested that MSG be used therapeutically to enhance the appeal of food for the elderly so that they eat more of the right things. See Bellisle 1998; and Schiffman 1998.

37. John Crump, interview with Deborah Gewertz and Fred Errington, July 28, 2008.

38. Ikeda, quoted in Sand 2005: 38. Concern with the deficiencies of "traditional" Japanese diets was recurrent in twentieth-century Japan, as we shall see.

39. This fermentation produces amino acids through the same process of hydrolysis mentioned in note 18.

40. Bachmanov 2010: 56.

41. Nature Neuroscience 2000.

42. Beauchamp 2009: 725S.

43. Beauchamp 2009: 725S.

44. See Bartoshuk 2008: 375.

45. In addition, there seem to be taste synergies when high-protein and low-protein umami-rich foods are prepared together, such as when beef or chicken is cooked with vegetables containing free glutamates. See Kurihara 2009: 720S. Moreover, these synergies may be accentuated by the breakdown of proteins in both meat and vegetables resulting in the release of free glutamates, as may be the case in "slow cooking."

46. Rolls 2009: 807S.

47. McCabe and Rolls 2007: 1855.

48. Rolls 2009: 810S.

49. Remo 2011. In another study, a team of sensory experts at Warsaw University tested six soups—mushroom, chicken, red beet, cream of vegetable, asparagus, and pea—as well as one side dish of mashed potatoes for increased palatability when MSG along with another flavor enhancer (disodium 5'-ribonucleotide) were added. Palatability of the mushroom and chicken soups rose markedly, far more than for the other soups. Palatability of mashed potatoes did not change (European Sensory Network 2007).

50. Citriglia 2006; Kasabian and Kasabian 2005.

51. Hoernlein 2011.

52. Schaumburg et al. 1969: 826.

53. The anthropologist Lidia Marte discovered that MSG and refined sugar were having a deleterious effect on her health. This, as she engagingly discusses, forced her to develop coping strategies so that she could continue her research among Dominicans, whose cuisine is high in both substances. See Marte 2010. On the general population's response, see Beyreuther et al. 2007.

54. Hoernlein 2011.

55. Sand 2005.

56. Savoury Systems 2008: 6.

57. McGee 2004: 342.

58. "The generally accepted formula [is] . . . counting 9 calories per gram of fat, 4 for carbs, and 4 for protein" (Wilson 2003).

59. Baik (2010: 271) explains that instant noodles would absorb even more oil if they were not made from high-protein wheat. Thus, the selection of hard wheat as the source of flour contributes both to noodle texture, as mentioned, and conserves the expensive oil used in processing.

60. Leonard, Snodgrass, and Robertson 2010: 4.

61. Leonard 2002: 67.

62. Humans have an expanded small intestine and reduced colon, both of which are appropriate to the digestion of "nutritionally dense, energetically concentrated foods" (Milton 1987: 101).

63. Gewertz and Errington 2010; Wrangham 2010.

64. Mattes 2011.

65. However, Jean-Paul Baird informed us that "the proposal of specific fat taste that is independent of tactile and odor detections that go along with fat in the mouth is more contentious than the idea that there is a specific umami taste" (e-mail communication to Deborah Gewertz, May 13, 2012).

66. McGee 2004: 799.

67. List and Jackson 2007.

68. Concerning the palm oil supply, see Carter et al. 2007. Concerning the soybean oil supply, see Spectrum Commodities n.d.

69. For the cardiovascular effects of edible oils, see Bester et al. 2010: 343. For a comparison between palm and olive oil, see Choudhury, Tan, and Truswell 1995, whose study is cited in a joint publication by the Malaysian Palm Oil Council and the Malaysian Palm Oil Board (2007: 40). See also Sen, Rink, and Khanna 2010.

70. Teng et al. 2010. This is also the conclusion of a panel of experts whose advice to the food industry is summarized in Hayes 2010.

71. Alice Lichtenstein, senior scientist and director, Cardiovascular Nutrition Laboratory, Tufts University, phone interview, May 23, 2011.

72. Kabagambe et al. 2005.

73. Vega-Lopez et al. 2006: 54–55.

74. Reddy 2004; Uusitalo et al. 1996.

75. San Francisco Chronicle 2010. Each of these oils has its agro-industrial advocates. However, the primary source of funding for studies on the relative health effects of these oils comes from the palm oil industry.

76. As of 2012, about 93 percent of the soybeans grown in the United States were genetically changed to enable the use of Monsanto's Roundup herbicide (which kills the weeds around the GM soybeans, but not the Roundup Ready beans themselves). See United Stated Department of Agriculture 2012.

77. This is the case even given the advice by an "expert panel" of seven research scientists to the food industry that, "when possible, the selection of oils or fats to replace *trans*-fatty acids should favor polyunsaturated or monounsaturated fatty acids" (Hayes 2010: 286S).

78. McGee 2004: 645.

79. Temussi 2009: 296.

80. Scott 2005: 457.

81. Mintz 1985: 109.

82. USDA 2002.

83. Glycemic Index Foundation 2011.

84. Mattes 2005.

CHAPTER 2. JAPANESE INSTANT NOODLES IN THE MARKET AND ON THE MIND

1. Yamamoto 2010. The anthropologist Niko Besnier tells us that this title "involves something akin to a pun, because the syllable *men* is the word for 'noodle,' but here *en* also serves as the first syllable of the borrowing *ensaikuropedia*" (e-mail communication to Deborah Gewertz, June 28, 2012).

2. Ton Tan Tin 2012.

3. Noburo Ishigawa, e-mail communication to Deborah Gewertz, September 8, 2010.

4. Kinsella 2000: 128.

5. Condry 2013: 187.

6. Kinsella 2000: 129. Condry elaborates: "Images of the otaku in Japan tend to oscillate between negative portrayals focusing on anti-social behavior

and potentially dangerous habits on the one hand, and, on the other, positive portrayals of future-oriented post-industrial sensibilities that contribute to the global strength of Japanese products in popular culture" (2013: 188).

7. Gibson 2001: 3. See also Lamarre 2004 for a fascinating discussion of the reciprocal relationship between *otaku* culture and corporate markets.

8. Yamamoto 2010: 4.

9. Allison 2009a: 106. See also Kinsella 2000; Iwabuchi 2002; Allison 2009b; Yano 2009.

10. Kelly 2002: 238.

11. Kelly 2002: 234.

12. Gordon 2003: 257.

13. Kelly 1990: 220. See also Lee 2000 for an analysis of how these shifts in family structure and dynamics were reflected in popular animated television programs.

14. On the changing structure of homes and families in Japan, see the articles in Ronald and Alexy 2011.

15. On rice cookers, see Ashkenazi and Jacob 2000: 117. On social change including education and health care, see Gordon 2003: 243–267. On the reworking of the past, see Ivy 1995 and Kelly 1986.

16. In fact, mainstream ideology was never fully realized. Wage differentials remained wide, with many people able to attain only temporary work (Brinton 2010). Educational opportunities remained divergent, with many distinctions on the pre-elementary and postsecondary levels (Slater 2010). Family life remained complex, with women responsible for caring for children, husbands, and elderly relatives, but with only some able to fulfill these obligations (Shirahase 2010; Ezawa 2010). And nonbiomedical healing alternatives remained popular, with many people dubious about modern therapies and values (Kelly 2002). For a comprehensive analysis of the debates among (mostly) Japanese sociologists and political scientists concerning the existence and operation of class relations in postwar Japan, see Hashimoto 2003.

17. The Ajinomoto Museum is one of many corporate museums in Japan. See Lehman and Byrom 2007.

18. For a fascinating analysis of the popularization of MSG as product and the growth of Ajinomoto as a company, see Sand 2005.

19. The anthropologist Marilyn Ivy writes: "Electric appliances fueled the consumer revolution of the 1960s. . . . [They] became the objects of desire, the signs of middle-class inclusion, the unparalleled commodity fetishes for the Japanese in the 1950s and 1960s" (1993: 249).

20. The company was innovative in its advertising. Concerning MSG, two ads especially struck us. One had a picture of a battleship and the following caption (in translation): "Just as a battleship is necessary to the Emperor's battles, so too is Ajinomoto necessary to cooking." Another, a picture of Charlie Chaplin, had the caption (in translation): "Just as he is king of comedy, so too is Ajinomoto the king of seasonings."

21. Field notes taken by Deborah Gewertz, September 4, 2010. When prompted by Japanese instant noodle interests to "let us know what you remember about instant noodles," many Japanese male respondents between

the ages of sixty and sixty-nine echoed Adachi with statements (in translation) like these: "I was amazed when I had instant noodles for the first time"; "I could not believe such food existed when I first had it"; and "I cannot forget the taste of the first instant noodles I had when I was in junior high school" (Japan Instant Noodle Industry Business Association 2007).

22. M. Ando 2002: 75. We wonder what Ando would have thought about a later chairman of Ajinomoto when his company—along with the U.S. company Archer Daniels Midland; another Japanese company, Kyowa Hakko Kogyo; and the Korean companies Sewon America Inc. and Cheil Jedang Ltd.—were convicted of price fixing the amino acid lysine, a vital animal feed supplement.

23. Solt's observation (2009: 132) might be linked to the effort by the Ajinomoto Company to offset, at least symbolically, the extent of the change in which it participated. The company released twenty volumes entitled *The Japanese TASTE—Traditional Foods,* which the Foundation's Guide explains is "all there is to know about the roots of traditional Japanese foods, the process through which they were created, and the ways in which they are made"—available on video and DVD. The release could also be seen as consistent with the company's decision to encode its foundation headquarters with traditional gardens, teahouses, and calligraphy. On the homogenization of food preferences in Japan, see Cwiertka's excellent chapter on the role of home economics education in "reforming home meals" (2006: 87–114).

24. Ando, quoted in Solt 2009: 135, from a Nissin corporate history.

25. Niko Besnier points out a possible irony, asking whether Ando transformed "the oppressive regime of defeat and occupation into the tool with which Japan conquered the palates of the world" (e-mail communication to Deborah Gewertz, June 28, 2012).

26. Solt 2009: 157; Solt 2010: 192.

27. Concerning the postwar promotion of Western-style diets, see Jussaume, Shuji, and Yoshimitsu 2000: 217. However, Japanese anxieties about small stature go back (at least) to the mid-nineteenth century, with three solutions suggested. The first was to adopt a Western-style diet (Steel 2003; Higashiyotsuyanagi 2010). The second was to implement a eugenics program (Robertson 2001). And the third was to transform lifestyles, especially seating arrangements, as it was believed that sitting on the floor with folded legs stunted the straight growth of Japanese people (Ohta and Murohoshi 1989: 249).

28. Association of Instant Food Producers 2011.

29. Solt 2009: 168.

30. If a spouse of a Japanese taxpayer earns less than ¥1,030,000 (US$13,453.76), the taxpayer can make a "spousal deduction" from his or her income. In effect, this encourages many married women to work part time, since earning a larger salary might result in decreasing the overall household income.

31. White 2001: 64.

32. Concerning the Minamata scandal: From 1932 to 1968, the Chisso Corporation dumped an estimated twenty-seven tons of mercury compounds into Minamata Bay. Thousands of people who depended on fish from the bay developed symptoms of methyl mercury poisoning, now known as "Minamata Disease." See Ui 1992; Imamura, Ide, and Yasunaga 2007: 224–225.

33. Shoji and Sugai 1992.

34. There may have been economic incentives as well. Shoji and Sugai explain: "From 1949 to 1950, while the USA was experiencing an economic depression, the surplus milk produced in that country was exported to Japan, placing pressure on the domestic market and increasing the number of people who became dependent on milk as part of their daily food intake" (1992).

35. Shoji and Sugai (1992) conclude that it was actually the introduction of antibiotics that reduced infant mortality.

36. In 1920, 10 percent of infants were fed on commercially prepared formula. By 1970 the percentage had risen to 70 percent (Shoji and Sugai 1992).

37. Shoji and Sugai 1992.

38. Shoji and Sugai 1992.

39. Jussaume, Shuji, and Yoshimitsu 2000: 218. To be more specific, the 1957 Food Safety Law required that the government publish a list of the additives appropriately included in food and provide detailed rules for the proper production and testing of these additives. This law also demanded that food producers have a trained and certified "food safety manager" who would ensure that all the food safety regulations were followed in the production process.

40. More recently, South Korean noodle maker Nongshim Co., Ltd., claimed that its Shin Ramyun brand was "close to a perfect food," but trade officials fined the company 155 million won (US$143,670) for "exaggerating the nutritional value of a new brand of instant noodles" (Kang 2011).

41. Solt 2009: 159.

42. We are indebted to William Kelly for suggesting this point (e-mail communication to Deborah Gewertz, April 19, 2012).

43. As far as we know, instant noodles have been subject to recall within Japan only twice. In October 2008, Nissin recalled its Cup Noodle because of insecticide contamination. One person was reported ill from eating the noodles. In response to this incident, Nissin redesigned the cup to make it less porous, less vulnerable to cross-contamination from the likes of insect spray, which might share space on convenience store shelves. In this instance, Nissin was generally regarded as having responded appropriately: it took immediate and well-publicized steps to rectify the error, protect the public, and defend its brand. At almost the same time, there was an instant-noodle recall for a similar reason by a lesser-known producer, Myojo Foods Co. of Tokyo. See Japan Today 2008.

44. Information about the museum was kindly provided to Tatsuro Fujikura by Shin'ichi Taniguchi, vice-chief of the secretariat of the Ando Foundation.

45. Allison 2009b.

46. Condry provides a fascinating analysis of shifts in dominant visions of Japanese masculinity that correspond to these socioeconomic changes. Quoting the anthropologists James Robertson and Nobue Suzuki, who state that "the middle-class, heterosexual, married salaryman [has been] considered as responsible for and representative of 'Japan'" (2003: 1), Condry elaborates concerning *otaku,* whom he says represent the polar opposite image of manhood compared to the "gregarious, socializing, breadwinner salaryman. If the salaryman is measured by his productivity, then the loner otaku, with his comic book

collections, expensive figurines, and encyclopedic knowledge of trivia, can be viewed as a puzzle of rampant, asocial consumerism" (2013: 187).

47. Shirahase demonstrates that "both men and women have shown a striking tendency to marry later and later in life. In the 45 years from 1960 to 2005 the average age at first marriage has risen by roughly five years for men and six years for women" (2010: 62). See also Kelly and White 2006: 63–65. Kelly (2002: 254) presents data collected by the prime minister's office during 1997 about why women were choosing to remain single. Two-thirds of women reported that they delayed marriage to preserve the economic resources they gained through employment. Over half said that they delayed marriage to continue to enjoy the freedom of independent living (this also reflected a desire to control personal disposable income since most remained living with their parents). He also cites another 1997 government survey in which the first two reasons women gave for remaining single were failure to meet an appropriate spouse and unwillingness to give up their freedom. Concerning single women, as Kelsky makes clear, some behaved so outrageously as to eroticize and sleep with white men (2001: 133–201).

48. White 2001: 71.

49. K. Ando 2009.

50. Nissin competes not only with Japanese producers of instant noodles but also with importers of instant noodles from all over the world.

51. According to Robert Foster, the Coca-Cola Company also introduces a plethora of products into Japan each year: "As many as 200 different products might be available at any given time, some for a single 'season' only" (e-mail communication to Deborah Gewertz, July 16, 2012).

52. Although the Japanese government, in its "Basic Act on Food Education" bill passed in 2005, said that it wanted to encourage Japanese food and a rice-based diet, McDonald's Japan has declared that is going to promote *shoku-iku* by providing hamburger-making classes in schools.

53. For the sake of accuracy, we should mention that a revisionist history of this innovation is provided in *Project X*. This book credits the hardworking salarymen at Nissin, often working against Ando's directions, for the innovation of Cup Noodle. See Katoh 2006.

54. Their names and genders (m or f) are: Tamapi (m), Genki-kun (m), Tenteke-kun (m), Iketeru-kun (m), Chikinstein (m), Chobita (m), Nanbo-kun (m), Takapi (f), Hime-chan (f), Momopi (f), Piyo (f), and Piko (f) (Piyo and Piko are twins). *Tamapi,* derived from *tamago,* means "egg." *Genki* means "vigorous, cheerful, and healthy." *Tenteke,* ideophonic for the sound of a drum used in humorous *rakugo* theater, means that this character is funny. *Iketeru* means "cool." *Chikinstein,* a combination of *chicken* and *Einstein,* means that this character is smart. *Chobita,* derived from *chobitto,* a very small amount, means this character is shy and retiring. *Nanbo,* meaning "how much?" in the dialect of Osaka, means that this character is stingy and greedy. *Takapi* means "proud and conceited," although this character actually yearns for friendship. *Hime* means "princess." *Momopi* means "peach" or "pink," conveying girlishness. And both *Piyo* and *Piko* are onomatopoetic for chirping chicks.

55. Saatchi and Saatchi 2011.

56. Yano 2009.

57. Koki Ando describes what was involved in the development of this product: the developers recognized that the egg dropped on the noodles would probably be straight from the refrigerator and, therefore, would cool the noodles so that they would not cook properly unless the depression for the egg was quite shallow (2009: 178).

58. Price point matters, especially in deciding whether to buy a bowl of noodles that simulates real ramen tastes. One female graduate student told us that "for lunch, if I want a bowl that promises Kyoto-tasting noodles, it's a matter of money. The instant bowl costs about ¥250 [about US$2.75], while a bowl of real ramen costs ¥600 about [US$6.60]. So I would buy the instant." Others to whom we spoke believed that the real thing was worth the extra cost, at least once in a while.

59. K. Ando 2009: 116.

60. Ivy 1993: 254.

61. K. Ando 2009: 199.

62. K. Ando 2009: 160.

63. Some of the surveys were completed in English; others were translated by Tatsuro.

64. Of course, such a woman would not wish the rebukes of what White calls "the role patrol," who would call her "a 'tenuki okusan,' a 'no-hands housewife' . . . . [This would be] the mother who doesn't prepare a home-made lunch but buys one for her child at the kombini [convenience store]; the wife who leaves her husband to buy instant noodles for himself. . . ; the woman who is not available to make tea for an elderly parent at home" (2001: 72–74).

65. K. Ando 2009: 167.

66. Notcot 2008.

67. Yamamoto 2010: 4.

68. Gibson 2001: 3.

69. Another Japanese venture that also reclassifies the everyday into something special is the Sakura Takenaka, a Tokyo restaurant that serves only instant noodles, offering some two hundred varieties. See McNicol 2009: 22.

CHAPTER 3. INSTANT NOODLES IN AMERICA

1. All of the citations from this meeting come from field notes taken by Deborah Gewertz on September 15, 2010. They are close paraphrases of Tatsuro Fujikura's translations from the four Nissin executives present.

2. Maruchan is a privately held subsidiary of the major Japanese food company Toyo Suisan.

3. Maruchan's advent into the U.S. market is conveyed in the Japanese film *The Excellent Company* (Toki 2006). This rather racist, sexist, antiunionist, and jingoist noodle narrative may or may not have been approved by Toyo Suisan, the Japanese company that owns the Maruchan brand; however, it is clear that the filmmakers had access to a Maruchan plant, as the Maruchan name is on the cup-type noodles that are shown passing through an assembly line. In the film, the thinly disguised founder of Toyo Suisan, Kazuo Mori (who

is well known in Japan for having survived the infamous 1939 battle between Japanese and Soviet forces near the Soviet-Manchurian border in which perhaps 95 percent of Japanese soldiers died), grows his thriving enterprise from its postwar origins as a small tuna-transporting operation. In one scene, he states that food is more important than material things while releasing small fish into the harbor where his company began so as to give back to nature; in another, he wears a samurai outfit while fencing. Eventually, the company (known as Sansun in the film) expands, bringing instant noodles into the United States (where Toyo Suisan now operates two instant noodle plants). The company must overcome a range of problems, including the unreliability of Hispanic workers; the nefariousness of a female employee who, in retaliation for having been denied a promotion, falsely accuses an executive of sexual harassment; and the machinations of corrupt union organizers. Eventually, everyone accepts the excellence of the Japanese corporate management style that treats all employees as family members.

4. Pubic relations official, interview with Deborah Gewertz and Frederick Errington, July 23, 2009.

5. McKee 2009.

6. Interview with Deborah Gewertz, Fred Errington, and Tatsuro Fujikura, September 15, 2010. Prisons ordinarily involve longer-term incarceration than do jails.

7. Solomon 2008.

8. Solomon 2008.

9. Aretakis 2006.

10. National Public Radio 2009b: 1.

11. National Public Radio 2009c: 1.

12. National Public Radio 2009d.

13. Leonardi 1989: 340.

14. In fact, recipes to enhance instant noodles are frequently published on American websites.

One such site is "Ramen Hacks: 30+ Easy Ways to Upgrade Your Instant Noodles," by the blogger J. Kenji Lopez-Alt. He describes himself and his project this way: "As a half-Japanese kid in the '80s, I grew up eating instant ramen at least once a week, and it still holds a special place in my gut. The real stuff is great, but sometimes only the add-hot-water pack will do. That said, my tastes have changed and expanded considerably over the years, and sometimes that little flavoring packet just isn't enough. As such, I've spent a lot of time devising ways to upgrade my ramen in cheap, easy ways. Ghetto gourmet, if you will" (2011a). Among the recipes he offers is

> Aloha, Ramen!: I don't know if anyone in Hawaii would go anywhere near this, but I think it's pretty awesome—super salty slices of pan-fried spam, sweet pineapple chunks (you can use fresh or canned), a perfectly fried sunny-side up egg (fried in the same pan as the spam, of course), and a generous squirt of Japanese-style barbecue sauce. You can find this in most Asian grocers (look for the bottle with the bulldog on it), or you can make a quick version at home by mixing 2 tablespoons of worcestershire sauce, a tablespoon of soy sauce, and a half cup of ketchup together. E'ai ka-kou! [Hawaiian for 'let us eat']. (2011b)

15. National Public Radio 2009a; National Public Radio 2009b.

16. National Public Radio 2009a: 1.

17. National Public Radio 2009b: 1.

18. Transcripts of all of these reminiscences can be found at National Public Radio 2009c.

19. National Public Radio advertises a "driveway moment" as the experience of listeners who find a story so compelling that they need to remain in their cars even after arriving home in order to hear the end of it.

20. The Amherst College website describes its food offerings thus: "At Amherst College we want your dining experience to be enjoyable, healthy and with plenty of variety. We have 6 sections available daily: hot entrees, grill, pizza, the lighter side, deli, soup and salad bar for your preference. Our entrees, salads, vegetables, pastries, and desserts consisting of less than 25% of calories from fat will contain the heart healthy symbol" (Amherst College 2012).

21. The interviews took place between October and December 2009.

22. We refer here to Bourdieu's (1984) discussion of social class, specifically how the powerful define aesthetic differences such as taste.

23. We take the term "imagined community" from Benedict Anderson's oft-cited book by the same name (1983). Anderson argues that the development of the nation-state requires that citizens imagine themselves, through such vehicles as print journalism, to be linked by bonds of community. For a sharply contrasting view, one that replaces Anderson's emphasis on memory and identity in the creation of modern nation-states with an emphasis on will and power, see Kelly and Kaplan 2001.

24. In this sense, these stories from middle-of-the-road listeners are very different from perhaps the most famous food-focused remembrances in literature, those provided by Marcel Proust in *Remembrance of Things Past* ([1927] 1989). Although there are debates about the meaning and significance of Proust's famous madeleine, there is general agreement that the recollection and contemplation of a particular sensory taste are central to his creation of a more general sensibility of distinctive taste.

25. We refer here to an assortment of photographs that would appear in the photo albums of the family of (bourgeois) man. Indeed, the experiences conveyed are like those evoked by Edward Steichen's "Family of Man" photographic exhibition at New York's Museum of Modern Art in 1955. The pictures included in this exhibit were generally of family groups and social gatherings and were intended to convey a universalizing view of humanity. As Susan Sontag describes it:

> The "Family of Man" exhibit [was] organized in 1955 by Edward Steichen. . . . Five hundred and three photographs by two hundred and seventy-three photographers from sixty-eight countries were supposed to converge—to prove that humanity is "one" and that human beings for all their flaws and villainies, are attractive creatures. The people in the photographs were of all races, ages, classes, physical types. . . . Steichen's choice of photographs assumes a human condition or a human nature shared by everybody. . . . [In so doing,] "The Family of Man" denies the determining weight of history—of genuine and historically embedded differences, injustices and conflicts. (1977: 32–33)

26. Chalfen 1982.

27. It is unlikely that either an American home movie or a family album would depict a family member's corpse; this fact would have disappointed Deborah and Fred's friends in Papua New Guinea whose photographic collections often contain pictures taken in the morgues of dead kinsmen. They would often use these pictures to determine the nature and source of the death-dealing sorcery and thus the appropriate response.

28. The anthropologist Edmund Leach describes nuclear families as "isolated." He continues: "The family looks inward upon itself; there is an intensification of emotional stress between husband and wife, and parents and children. The strain is greater than most of us can bear. Far from being the basis of the good society, the family, with its narrow privacy and tawdry secrets, is the source of all our discontents" (1968: 44). Somewhat similarly, another close observer of human affairs, Sherlock Holmes, remarked darkly to John Watson concerning the countryside as seen from a train: "You look at these scattered houses, and you are impressed by their beauty. I look at them, and the only thought which comes to me is a feeling of their isolation and of the impunity with which crime may be committed there" (Doyle 1930: 323).

29. In 2009, according to statistics from the Bureau of Justice, 2,096,300 men and 201,200 women were incarcerated in the United States: of these, 693,800 men and 92,100 women were white; 841,000 men and 64,800 women were black; and 442,000 men and 32,300 women were Hispanic. Others incarcerated were Native Americans, Native Alaskans, Asians, Native Hawaiians, and other Pacific Islanders. See West 2009.

30. Goffman describes a total institution as a "forcing house" for changing people (1961: 62).

31. Bosworth and Thomas 2004.

32. Two of these companies are Aramark and Sodexo Marriott. Aramark Correctional Services describes itself as preparing "over 1,000,000 meals a day for state and municipal facilities, partnering with our clients to meet the unique challenges of the corrections environment" at over six hundred correctional facilities throughout North America (Aramark n.d.a.). For critiques of prison labor practices, see Elk and Sloan 2011; Jacobs 2000; and Corporate Watch UK 2004.

33. Elk and Sloan 2011.

34. Aramark n.d.b.

35. We are indebted here to Sidney Mintz's analysis of food as providing Caribbean slaves with a taste of freedom (1996: 33–49).

36. NPR 2009c.

37. Spreads are also known as "breaks," "slams," and "blow-ups."

38. Cali Prisoner 2007.

39. Marlene 2009.

40. Jesse Friedman 2005.

41. For the article, see Stiles 2010b. For the statistics, see Stiles 2010a.

42. Cate 2008: 19.

43. Cate 2008: 20.

44. Stiles 2010b.

45. Cate 2008: 24.

46. Yappie 2007.

47. Angie 2006.

48. Dickerson 2005.

49. Ito-Petersen 2001: 1.

50. This is according to Maruchan's export company, Maxia (n.d.).

51. Tanaka, Furukawa, and Okubo 2010.

52. Nissin's California-based office generously made available as an e-mail attachment on July 21, 2011, part of this survey, from which we have taken this material. The survey, dated February 23, 2011, was conducted by the Alliance Consulting Group and commissioned by Nissin Foods.

53. Nissin Foods is attempting to gain market share by cultivating customers previously uninterested in instant noodles. Still likely price conscious, these potential customers might be convinced to buy bowl-type noodles costing around US$1. In fact, according to one industry analyst, Nissin is doing quite well in this segment, controlling about 60 percent. However, the segment presently constitutes only about 3 percent of the entire instant noodle market in the United States. See Euromonitor International 2010.

54. Sophia Kraemer-Dahlin writes that she found most subjects amenable to talking during their lunch breaks or while doing something mindless, like walking or waiting for the bus. She continues: "My method, therefore, was to approach people who looked bored and explain something about the book and potential interest of . . . [processed] food, careful to distinguish the project from market research. Whenever possible, I extended the interview into conversation, to encourage storytelling. I typically approached people in English and switched to Spanish if the subject's English was poor. When approaching groups speaking Spanish, I usually began in Spanish." In addition, she "tried to preserve the subjects' voices in [her] note taking" (e-mail communication to Deborah Gewertz, September 6, 2011).

55. Sophia Kraemer-Dahlin, e-mail communication to Deborah Gewertz, October 17, 2011.

CHAPTER 4. INSTANT NOODLES IN PAPUA NEW GUINEA

1. López Morales, quoted in Dickerson 2005.

2. Dickerson 2005.

3. Nestlé n.d.

4. Jack 2011.

5. Jack 2011.

6. Jack 2011.

7. Barbara Piperata, e-mail communication to Fred Errington, November 23, 2011.

8. Jack 2011.

9. Roosevelt 1932. See Elyachar 2012 for a discussion of the history in political discourse of the "forgotten man," as well as for the economy considered as a pyramid.

10. Prahalad 2006: xvi.

11. Prahalad 2006. Dr. Patrick Webb (of the Friedman School of Nutrition Science and Policy, Tufts University) cautioned that those truly at the bottom of the pyramid, often dependent on humanitarian aid, including relief feeding, are not direct participants in the market at all (interview with Deborah Gewertz and Fred Errington, August 23, 2010).

12. Aspen Institute 2007: 1.

13. London, quoted in Aspen Institute 2007: 4.

14. Prahalad 2006: 16.

15. W.W. Rostow (1962) postulates that traditional society, when confronted with the preconditions for take-off (often involving coercion to free traditionalists from "superstition"), will begin a drive to maturity and eventually achieve what he considers to be liberating and democratic high mass consumption.

16. Prahalad 2006: 20.

17. Maslow (1943) places "human needs" on five levels—from the base level of physiological needs to that of self-actualization. Furthermore, he argues that physiological needs must be met before humans will work toward higher needs. Among others selling to the BOP, the Moladi Company, which specializes in supplying inexpensive housing, uses Maslow's "hierarchy of needs" to advertise its products (Moladi 2009).

18. For analyses of commerce and communication among the BOP, see Elyachar 2009; Ilahaine and Sherry 2009; Mauer 2009; and Tacchi 2009.

19. See, among others, Jenkins 2005; Kamani 2007; Landrum 2007; Warmholz 2007; and Thomas 2009.

20. Thomas 2009.

21. This is discussed and quoted in Cross and Street 2009.

22. Prahalad envisions BOP-focused products as providing commercial and social good. The Nestlé Corporation would argue that supplying instant noodles—as inexpensive, filling and, it would add, nutritious—is doing social good. Certainly, Nestlé urges consumers to supplement instant noodles with vegetables, greens, and protein. Correspondingly, relatively healthful recipes in Tok Pisin appear on Maggi's instant noodle packages.

23. This was corroborated by World Investment News 2003.

24. This quotation and those in the next paragraph come from an interview with Larry Ori conducted by Deborah Gewertz and Fred Errington on June 23, 2009.

25. For this project, see Gewertz and Errington 2010.

26. See Errington and Gewertz 2004.

27. A variety of small-scale vendors also cater to those on the move. Cooked foods, frequently available on the street or at outdoor markets, include sausages, dough balls, bits of sheep bellies (lamb flaps), and fish pieces.

28. Coca-Cola has engaged in a similar initiative in Papua New Guinea to increase sales and reward initiative. Pushcart-mounted coolers, painted with Coke designs, were made available to entrepreneurs who would wheel them to busy places, such as outdoor markets. However, unlike the pots of soup, the ice-packed cans of Coke needed little monitoring.

29. Given Nestlé's anxieties about a recent cholera outbreak in Papua New Guinea, the company's Sydney office has decided, for the time being, to suspend use of these carts.

30. We have no independent statistics to verify these figures.

31. Wanzefri Wanzahari, interview with Deborah Gewertz and Fred Errington, July 2, 2009. Some of the competition in Papua New Guinea comes from large Indonesian-Chinese or Malaysian-Chinese retail firms, such as Papindo Trading and RH Hypermarkets, which source most of their products from Asia. Papindo, for instance, does not carry Maggi instant noodles in its stores but rather assorted imports, including its own heavily promoted Tiger instant noodles. The apparent exclusion of PNG-made items in these stores has aroused contention. See, for example, Animation Online 2010.

32. In his analysis of Coca-Cola's operations in Papua New Guinea, Robert Foster (2008) makes a similar point concerning the increasingly central role that corporations are expected to have in development; see also Errington and Gewertz's discussion (2004) of the importance ascribed to Ramu Sugar Limited in advancing Papua New Guinea's nationalist project. Indeed, as described by Julia Elyachar, the model Prahalad was refining at the time of his death—that multinational corporations replace their past-looking "best practices" with forward-looking "next practices"—would mean that the state would become even less responsible for meeting BOP needs for goods and services (2012).

33. Nestlé Oceania 2008. Nestlé's product line in Papua New Guinea has long included its Milo malted drink (pictured in figure 17). Milo, which is relatively expensive, can be purchased only occasionally by most Papua New Guineans. As such, it contrasts with Maggi instant noodles. Consequently, Nestlé expected to penetrate and transform the PNG market with Maggi, not Milo.

34. Robert Foster (2008) documents the marketing strategies that Coca-Cola adopted to cope with Papua New Guinea's cultural diversity. Most of these strategies emphasized limited variations on a few themes—that is, "global systems of common difference," to use Richard Wilk's phrase (1995).

35. Marx 1906.

36. James Carrier makes a comparable argument that "seeing individuals as autonomous fetishises them" by removing them from sociocultural contexts (2010: 674).

37. These efficiencies require what the sociologist Anthony Giddens (1990) calls "time-space distantiation" and the geographer David Harvey (1990) calls "time-space compression." See also Inda and Rosaldo 2008: 7–10.

38. Interview conducted on March 17, 2011.

39. To tap consumer preferences in Papua New Guinea's two broadly contrasting ethnographic areas, Deborah and Fred commissioned two PNG researchers to conduct structured interviews in the coastal town of Madang and two researchers to administer these interviews in the highland town of Goroka. These interviews took place during July and August 2009. In addition, to learn about instant noodle preferences in a rural area that still had a subsistence base, they commissioned a former research assistant to conduct interviews in the village of Bumbu, which adjoins Ramu Agricultural Industries. They did not intend these interviews to constitute a random sample. Rather, they sought a broad

overview of the role instant noodles have in the lives of variously located Papua New Guineans. Most of the interviews in Madang and Goroka were with strangers the researchers met while circulating through the towns. Most of the interviews in Bumbu were with friends and family members. In Madang, the researchers interviewed thirty-seven males and forty-three females, ranging in age from ten to sixty-five. In Goroka, they interviewed fifty-five males and twenty-nine females, ranging in age from five to fifty-five. In Bumbu, the researcher interviewed ten males and fifteen females, ranging in age from sixteen to sixty. In total, they conducted 189 interviews with 102 males and 87 females.

40. Lévi-Strauss 1963: 89.

41. Comparably, according to Barbara Piperata, women in the Amazon save the flavor packet to season beans (e-mail communication to Fred Errington, November 23, 2011).

42. Wanzahari, Nestlé's PNG brand manager, said (as we indicated in our introduction) that "noodle sandwiches" are popular among students in PNG's capital. They purchase a cup of noodles from one of the Maggi carts, drink the liquid, and then place the remaining noodles within a split-open scone. Wanzahari welcomed such ingenuity. Anything Papua New Guineans came up with was just fine with him.

43. On evangelical Christianity, see Robbins 2004.

44. See Gewertz and Errington 2010.

CHAPTER 5. MAKING (AND UNMAKING?) A BIG FOOD WORLD

1. Phillips 2006: 46.

2. Momofuku Ando, quoted in K. Ando 2009: 198.

3. K. Ando 2009: 198. Concerning the issues the food industry will face in the future, Ando believes that "as food culture becomes increasingly global and more homogeneous, particularly in cities, the target areas will shift from particular countries or cities to the 30 largest cities around the world . . . . There are more than 30 mega-cities with populations of more than seven million around the world. It is possible to develop a strategy to introduce new food culture to those who live there" (2009: 194).

4. Nissin Food Holdings 2010.

5. International Food Network n.d.

6. John Crump, interview with Deborah Gewertz and Fred Errington, July 28, 2008.

7. Nick Henson and Peter Salmon, interviews with Deborah Gewertz and Fred Errington, June 6 and June 17, 2010.

8. To offset the loss of potency over time, manufacturers usually add more of a vitamin than is indicated on the label. However, since the product may be consumed as soon as it hits the market and consumers may need to be protected from taking too much of a vitamin, the amount added in excess is also regulated.

9. Deborah Maxwell, interview with Deborah Gewertz and Fred Errington, December 2, 2010.

10. Warren Belasco, a professor of American Studies, writes, in an article about the persistence in the United States of the idea that we will all someday be

sustained on meals-in-a-pill, that supplements in the form of vitamin pills (and presumably in vitamin-enriched drinks) "actually *increase* overall food consumption. Once people feel they have taken care of their nutritional needs by popping the right pills, they may then feel free to treat 'real' food as a hedonistic and social experience that extends way beyond mere sustenance—somewhat the way that 'low fat' and 'sugarfree' foods seem to expand, not reduce, waistlines" (2000: 263).

11. Jeremy Whitsitt, Patrick Dunne, Tom Yang, and Alan Wright, interviews with Deborah Gewertz and Fred Errington, August 3, 2010.

12. These Natick food scientists, like many of their colleagues in industry and academia, attend professional meetings at which they present their latest research findings. Fred heard them do this at the 2010 annual meeting of the IFT. During the first symposium, "Novel Processes and Food Safety for Military and Space Feeding," three papers were given: "Strategies for Mitigation of Foodborne Illness in Military Feeding," "Feeding the Astronauts during Long Duration Missions," and "Emerging Food Processing Technologies for Dual Use for Military Combat Rations and Civilian Marketplace." During the second symposium, "Combat Ration Science," another three were given: "Overview of Combat Ration Science," "Overview of Sensory and Consumer Sciences for Ration Development," and "Research Program Overview: Performance Optimizing Nutrition."

13. MREs, sometimes used in relief feeding, have also been dubbed "meals rejected by Ethiopians."

14. MRE Info 2011.

15. Deborah and Fred were told by Whitsitt that he had recently received an overture from the television program *Top Chef,* where chefs are presented with an array of ingredients to transform into meals. Constrained by both these ingredients and time, they compete with other chefs to create the most appealing dishes. During 2009, one episode of the show concentrated on creating welcome-home meals for members of the military. This time, producers proposed to Whitsitt that chefs create MREs that were tastier than the existing ones. Whitsitt was bemused because the program organizer knew nothing about the physical conditions that MREs must be designed to withstand.

16. Department of Defense 2010: 8.

17. Department of Defense 2010: 39.

18. Most of the Natick scientists go on at least one field study, which may include rummaging in dumpsters on army bases to see what components of MREs are thrown away.

19. According to a recent document, the Natick center has fifty-six cooperative agreements with industry and eight with academia. See Darsh and Evangelos n.d.

20. The Department of Defense describes current MRE packaging as a multi-laminate: "This material has four layers—polyester, nylon, foil, and polyolefin—that work together to produce extremely high barrier properties to protect the food against microbial, chemical and physical deterioration under extreme environments. Ongoing research is looking at using the material that will remove

the foil [in so doing, microwaving becomes feasible] and reduce the weight of the packaging" (2010: 12).

21. A comparison we find instructive is with car tires, which are normally inflated to (merely) thirty to thirty-five pounds per square inch.

22. The spores have a tough inner membrane. Although no one is sure, PATS may disrupt this membrane and trigger germination, rendering the cell vulnerable to lower levels of heat than would otherwise be the case.

23. Concerning their tastiness, "Whatever" e-mailed Yahoo! Answers with the following question (with punctuation slightly altered):

> After Hurricane Gustav swept through town, our friendly government benefactors were here handing out MREs. I ate 2 or 3 of them while waiting for electricity and for stores to restock. I was actually pleasantly surprised at how good they were—especially the raisins. I have to be pretty hungry to be willing to eat raisins, but when I tasted these, they were great (and not just because I was hungry). They were more plump and juicier than normal raisins. The package said that they were "osmotic," which is apparently a different method for drying, rather than the sun-dried raisins that are supposed to be so great. So, my question is, do stores sell osmotic raisins? Are there certain brands that are osmotic? Where can I get them (other than in MREs)? (Whatever 2008)

24. Concerning local populations affected by warfare, the Department of Defense provides a scaled-down version of MREs as humanitarian aid to civilians affected by disaster. Called Humanitarian Daily Rations, they contain no animal products or by-products that might offend people of different religions. Designed to provide "a full day's sustenance to a moderately malnourished individual," they deliver about 2,200 calories and come in fifteen menus (Department of Defense 2010: 52). Here is one: lentil stew, herb rice, two packages of MRE™ crackers, peanut butter, strawberry jam, fruit pastry, shortbread, and an accessory pack containing red pepper, salt, sugar, a spoon, matches, a napkin, and an alcohol-free towelette.

25. Pollan 2008: 8.

26. Pollan 2008: 1–9.

27. Pollan 2009.

28. Pollan has this co-optation in mind when he writes that "capitalism is marvelously adaptive, able to turn the problems it creates into new business opportunities" (2008: 135).

29. Sloan 2009a: 31–32.

30. These quotes come from a summary of the session included in *Food Technology*. See Sloan 2009b.

31. Bruhn 2009: 29, 30, 35.

32. Brody 2009: 79.

33. Clydesdale, quoted in Davis, Clemens, and Dubost 2008: 20.

34. Clydesdale 2009: 136. It might be countered that frozen or canned foods have to travel long distances from producers to consumers as well. However, those in the food industry would likely respond that, because frozen and canned foods are compact and relatively stable, they can be transported more efficiently and cheaply than if they were fresh and more perishable.

35. Maureen Dowd, in her *New York Times* column, reports that Waters "is well aware of the criticism leveled at her in blogs for condescension and food snobbery. In a post on Friday called 'Alice in Wonderland,' National Review stirred the pot against her: 'The truth is, organic food is an expensive luxury item, something bought by those who have resources.'" (Dowd 2009).

36. Clydesdale 2009: 136. Of course, these are market-based solutions, concerned with efficient distribution of food to those who can actively participate in the market—those who are able to buy.

37. Floros, Newsome, and Fisher 2010. In addition to the three major authors, seventeen food scientists from academia and industry contributed to this report.

38. Floros, Newsome, and Fisher 2010: 13.

39. The report explains, in ways that acknowledge widespread criticism of the green revolution, that "the vastly improved varieties resulting from improved plant-breeding techniques require much larger inputs of fertilizer and water. Poor farmers often cannot afford the fertilizer, and adequate water supplies are becoming an increasing problem in many areas. Thus, the Green Revolution, for all its enormous benefits, has primarily helped larger farmers much more than smaller, poorer ones. In addition, pesticide applications in the developing world are too often inappropriate or excessive—in some cases because the farmer is unable to read the label—and there is no structure (e.g., a regulatory agency such as the Environmental Protection Agency) to regulate their use" (Floros, Newsome, and Fisher 2010: 13).

40. Floros, Newsome, and Fisher 2010: 1.

41. Thus, in an article directed not at Pollan but at Eric Schlosser (another major critic of the food system), *Food Technology*'s senior editor, Donald Pszczola, writes: "The author of *Fast Food Nation* . . . believes that 'the current food system is broken' and that 'everyone needs organic food.' It would be interesting to explain to me how it would be possible to feed the world population using only organic farming methods . . . . [F]ood processing makes possible the feeding of seven billion people. As the population continues to grow, perhaps even double, it will be necessary for advancements in food processing to keep up" (2011: 78–79).

42. In *The Ritual Process* (1969), Victor Turner distinguishes *societas* from *communitas*. The former is the state of everyday affairs, filled with social hierarchies and practical exigencies. The latter is the state of extraordinary affairs, filled with social leveling and the possibility of life transformed. In effect, from the food industry perspective, Pollan would seem to promise the latter; Clydesdale, the former.

43. Floros, Newsome, and Fisher 2010: 2–3.

44. Floros, Newsome, and Fisher 2010: 8. Of course, these palatable, calorie-dense foods are likely to be high in fats, salt, sugar, and, perhaps, MSG.

45. Nestle 2007: 375.

46. Floros, Newsome, and Fisher 2010: 18. In this sense, a personal preference for nutrient-rich Big Shotz (and the willpower to avoid too many gummy candies—or marshmallowy muffins and chocolate bars) might be seen as a strategic exercise of survival skills.

CONCLUSION

1. Nissin Foods Holdings 2010.
2. Institute of Food Technologists 2009.
3. Kuhn 2011: 44.
4. Tempointeractive 2011.
5. What's On Xiamen 2010.
6. What's On Xiamen 2010.
7. What's on Xiamen 2010.
8. Nestlé Malaysia n.d.
9. Bickel et al. 2000: 6 cites the USDA for this definition of food security.
10. World Instant Noodles Association 2008.
11. World Instant Noodles Association 2008.
12. World Instant Noodles Association 2010.
13. Nissin Foods Holdings 2010.
14. Pollan 2011.
15. Pollan 2011. Pollan specifically recommends that the U.S. government "underwrite farmers' transition to organic and other kinds of sustainable agriculture; support the renaissance in local meat production by making it easier to build and run small slaughterhouses; use crop subsidies to reward farmers for diversifying their fields and growing real food rather than 'commodity crops' like corn and soy; enforce federal antitrust laws to break up the big meatpackers and seed companies."
16. Nestle 2007: 376–386.
17. Centers for Disease Control and Prevention 2011.
18. Hyman 2010. Hyman elaborates: "The poorest areas of the country are also the sickest and have the highest rates of obesity, diabetes, and premature death. These people are dying younger, and life expectancy is plummeting in the poorest states. These states also happen to be the fattest. For example, Mississippi—the poorest state in the union—had poverty rates over 20 percent, obesity rates over 33 percent, and extremely high childhood obesity rates."
19. Pollan 2011.
20. Gardner and Halwell 2000: 7.
21. Cohen cites statistics collected by the United Nations that suggest that, while the population of more developed nations (specifically in North America, Europe, Japan, Australia, and New Zealand) will decline by 3 percent, the population of less developed nations (specifically in Africa, Latin America, the Caribbean, Asia [excluding Japan], Melanesia, Micronesia, and Polynesia) will grow by 59 percent. See Cohen 2002: 88, which is based upon 1998 U.S. census data. Concerning the commonly accepted projection of nine billion people by 2050, see Food and Agriculture Organization 2009.
22. Cohen 2002: 86–87. Although the "Report of the UN Expert Group Meeting on Population Distribution, Urbanization, Internal Migration and Development" agrees that it will be an urban world, the report clears up several misconceptions: "Most of the urban population growth is accounted for by the population in small cities (under 500,000), rather than that in large and mega-cities. Indeed, most of the large cities are growing at a relatively slow pace now, and are likely to grow even more slowly in the future" (United Nations 2008: 3–4).

23. According to a speech given in 2005 by World Bank President Paul Wolfowitz, "Since 1980, China accounted for 75 percent of poverty reduction in the developing world" (Finfacts Ireland 2005).

24. Food and Agriculture Organization 2009: 6.

25. Godfray et al. 2010: 817.

26. The importance to food security of reducing U.S. subsidies that promote the use of grains for producing ethanol is agreed upon by those with very different political perspectives. See, for example, Collier 2008 and Patel 2011. Concerning ethanol production from sources other than grains, there is considerable interest in developing biofuels from such cellulosic sources as the stover from corn harvesting—the leftover leaves, husks, and cobs. See, for instance, Webber 2012 and Prokop 2012. Concerning a shift away from feedlot feeding, the environmentalist Jonathan Foley writes that "even small shifts in diet, say, from grain-fed beef to poultry, pork, or pasture-fed beef, can pay off handsomely" (2011: 65).

27. On both precision agriculture and reduced tillage, see Foley 2011.

28. Jackson 2010: 151–172.

29. Chappell 2007.

30. Smil 2001: 180, 132. Smil states that without use of "nitrogen fertilizers we would be able to feed only about 2.4 billion people, or just 40% of today's total" (2001: 160). Interestingly, the environmentalist Wes Jackson, although somewhat misinterpreting Smil's appraisal as indicating that "40 percent of humanity would not be here," accepts Smil's conclusion of the centrality of nitrogen fertilizer in contemporary life with this wry proviso: "This is certainly a true enough statement given the reality of our cattle, pig, and chicken welfare programs" (2010: 79–80).

31. On eating less, etc., see Foley 2011. On unrealistic sell-by dates, see Godfray et al. 2010: 816.

32. Gustavsson et al. 2011.

33. See Food and Agriculture Organization 2009: 17; Godfray et al. 2010: 813.

34. Nelson et al. 2009: appendix, 13.

35. On drip irrigation, see Foley 2011. On selecting for drought tolerance, see Godfray et al. 2010: 815.

36. Brown and Jacobson 2005.

37. Carter et al. 2007. Michael Sheridan's 2008 video traces these practices from rain forest to packages of instant noodles. There are currently limited industry efforts by such organizations as the Roundtable on Sustainable Palm Oil to ensure that environmental and sustainability concerns are addressed. See Roundtable of Sustainable Palm Oil 2009.

38. Godfray et al. 2010: 814.

39. Food and Agriculture Organization 2009: 22.

40. Gates Foundation 2011.

41. Collier 2008: 68.

42. Collier 2008: 76. Collier also believes that the world at large would benefit if, "in return for Europe's lifting its self-damaging ban on GM products, the United States should lift its self-damaging subsidies supporting domestic biofuel" (2008: 68).

43. Beachy, quoted in Borrell 2011: 83. Concerning the controversy over genetically modified organisms (GMOs), see Antoniou, Robinson, and Fagan 2012. Their comprehensive, book-length report, *GMO Myths & Truths,* presents a list of thirty serious concerns about the effects of GMOs on human and animal health. Among them are uncertainties about the consequences both of the consumption of genetically modified Roundup Ready crops (such as soybeans, corn, and alfalfa) as well as the massive use of the herbicide Roundup, designed to kill competitors of these crops.

44. Nelson et al. 2009: viii. This study, undertaken by the International Food Research Institute and projected to 2050, examined yields of major crops (rice, wheat, maize, soybeans, and groundnuts) under two higher-temperature scenarios, one wetter and one dryer. According to either and taking into account the possible boost to photosynthesis provided by increased carbon dioxide levels, additional demands on agricultural productivity will be likely if widespread malnutrition, especially among children, is to be averted. For more concerning the effects of weird weather on agricultural productivity, see Karl, Melilo, and Peterson 2009: 71–78.

45. Godfray et al. 2010: 813.

46. Food and Agriculture Organization 2009: 26.

47. Messer 2009.

48. Brown and Jacobson 2005: 21.

49. Filer 2011.

50. CPNSJOB.COM 2012.

51. Food and Agriculture Organization 2009: 3.

52. As an example of this consolidation, the historical sociologist Philip McMichael shows that, "in Latin America, firms, including Ahold, Carrefour, and Wal-Mart, comprise 70–80 percent of the top five supermarket chains" (2005: 284).

53. This mode of capitalist provisioning has been called the "life sciences integrated paradigm." It emerges from the "productionist paradigm," with the addition of smart agricultural techniques, including GM modifications and the others described above. See Lang and Heasman 2004.

54. Clemens 2011: 11.

55. See Boyer 2010.

56. As the economist Amartya Sen (1983) has famously pointed out, those who starve during famines are the poor. The problem is not one of food availability per se—there is usually enough food within a region to feed everyone. Rather, the problem is one of food access. Those who starve will be the poor, who lack "entitlements" to food. Indeed, some in the same region may get rich (and fat) because of their superior access to food.

57. Common Dreams.org 2012.

58. This is accomplished by placing these subsidies in what is called a "green box" and, in so doing, giving them a go-ahead into the indefinite future.

59. Fitday n.d.

60. Field 2011.

61. Garrett 2011.

62. Penelope Schoeffel, e-mail communication to Deborah Gewertz, December 10, 2011.

63. Via Campesina 2011.

64. Desmarais 2008: 139.

65. This corresponds to what Lang and Heasman term "the ecologically integrated paradigm" (2004).

66. These agro-ecological technologies include "organic matter accumulation, nutrient cycling, soil biological activity, natural control mechanisms (disease suppression, biocontrol of insects and weeds), resource conservation and regeneration (to include soil, water and germ plasm), general enhancement of agrobiodiversity and synergisms between components" (Lang and Heasman 2004: 27–28).

67. Via Campesina 2008.

68. Windfuhr and Jonsén 2005: xii.

69. Peter Singer and Jim Mason (2006) point out that it is morally weak to argue in favor of supporting those you know simply because you know them over supporting those you do not know, especially since those you do not know in the developing world may well be in fairly desperate circumstances. Comparably, the anthropologists Dorothy Holland and Diana Gomez (2011), who studied local growers in North Carolina, found that these growers were neither well informed nor especially concerned about the circumstances of farm workers in distant fields.

70. Smit, Nasr, and Ratta 2001: 7.

71. Smit, Nasr, and Ratta 2001: 4.

72. Bryld 2003: 79; see also Smit, Nasr, and Ratta 2001: 4.

73. Smit, Nasr, and Ratta 2001: 4.

74. Food and Agriculture Organization 2010: 4.

75. Thaman 1995: 209. See also Thaman, Elevitch, and Kennedy 2006.

76. Post Courier 2004.

77. As Smit, Nasr, and Ratta put it: "The majority of the total economy in many cities is informal or non-monetary, and urban agriculture is commonly among the larger, if not the largest element in the informal economy" (2001: 2).

78. See Brown and Jameton 2000; Bryld 2003.

79. Food and Agriculture Organization 2010: 5.

80. Brown and Jameton suggest that urban agriculture has a range of benefits beyond the production of food: it may employ youth, provide a means of relaxation and stress release, and make neighborhoods "greener" and more pleasant (2000). Battaglia argues that among Trobriand Islanders living away from home in Port Moresby, urban gardening is an example of cultural nostalgia provocative of "bliss" (1995: 80).

81. Mintz 2006: 3–11.

82. Lang and Heasman 2004: 183.

References

Aaslyng, Margit, Magni Martens, Leif Poll, Per Nielson, Hanne Flyge, and Lone Larsen
 1998 Chemical and Sensory Characterization of Hydrolyzed Vegetable Protein, a Savory Flavoring. *Journal of Agricultural Food Chemistry* 46:481–489.

Aiyer, Ananthakrishnan
 2007 The Allure of the Transnational: On Some Aspects of the Political Economy of Water in India. *Cultural Anthropology* 22:640–658.

Allison, Anne
 2009a The Cool Brand, Affective Activism and Japanese Youth. *Theory, Culture & Society* 26:89–111.
 2009b Precarious Sociality: Social Life—and Death—for Youth in Post-Corporate Japan. www.scribd.com/doc/24296146/Precarious-Sociality, accessed August 11, 2012.

Amherst College
 2012 Food Facts. www.amherst.edu/campuslife/dining/food_facts, accessed August 14, 2012.

Anderson, Benedict
 1983 *Imagined Communities: Reflections on the Origin and Spread of Nationalism*. London: Verso.

Ando, Koki
 2009 *Mission: Destroy Cup Noodle!* Tokyo: Nissin Foods Holdings Co., Ltd.

Ando, Momofuku
 2002 *The Story of the Invention of Instant Ramen*. Osaka: Nissin Food Products Co., Ltd.

Angie

 2006 Response to "Prison Surprise." Official Ramen Homepage. www
  .mattfischer.com/ramen/?p = 460&cpage = 1#comments, accessed February 28, 2012.

Animation Online

 2010 Papindo is a Good Company. www.network54.com/Forum/186328
  /thread/1293323317/last-1339929017/Papindo+is+a+good+company,
  accessed August 14, 2012.

Antoniou, Michael, Claire Robinson, and John Fagan

 2012 GMO Myths and Truths: An Evidence-Based Examination of the
  Claims Made for the Safety and Efficacy of Genetically Modified Crops.
  London: Earth Open Source. http://earthopensource.org/index.php
  /reports/58, accessed August 23, 2012.

Aramark

 n.d.a. Correctional Institutions. www.aramark.com/Industries/Correctional
  Institutions/, accessed August 14, 2012.

 n.d.b. Commisary Solutions. www.aramarkcorrections.com/Products_
  Services/Commissary_Solutions/, accessed August 14, 2012.

Aretakis, Nicholas

 2006 *No More Ramen: The 20-Something's Real World Survival Guide.*
  Scottsdale, AZ: Next Stage Press.

Ashkenazi, Michael, and Jean Jacob

 2000 *The Essence of Japanese Cuisine: An Essay on Food and Culture.*
  Philadelphia: University of Pennsylvania Press.

Aspen Institute

 2007 A Closer Look at Business Education: Bottom of the Pyramid. http://
  caseplace.org/pdfs/BOP.pdf, accessed November 25, 2012.

Association of Instant Food Producers

 2011 Sokusekimen seisan suryo no suii, March 2011 [Changes in the consumption of instant noodles]. www.instantramen.or.jp/data/data04
  .html, accessed June 20, 2011.

Bachmanov, Alexander

 2010 Umami: Fifth Taste? Flavor Enhancer. *Perfumer and Flavorist* 25:52–57.

Baik, Byung-Kee

 2010 Effects of Flour Protein and Starch on Noodle Quality. In *Asian Noodles: Science, Technology, and Processing,* edited by Gary Hou,
  261–284. Hoboken, NJ: John Wiley.

Barndt, Deborah

 2002 *Tangled Routes: Women, Work and Globalization on the Tomato
  Trail.* Lanham, PA: Rowman and Littlefield.

Bartoshuk, Linda

 2008 Taste. In *Sensation and Perception,* edited by Jeremy Wolfe, Keith
  Kluender, Dennis Levi, and Linda Bartoshuk, 360–383. Sunderland,
  MA: Sinauer Associates.

Battaglia, Debbora

 1995 On Practical Nostalgia: Self-Prospecting among Urban Trobrianders.
  In *Rhetorics of Self-Making,* edited by Debbora Battaglia, 77–96.
  Berkeley: University of California Press.

Beauchamp, Gary
    2009   Sensory and Receptor Responses to Umami. *American Journal of Clinical Nutrition* 90:723S-727S.

Belasco, Warren
    2000   Future Notes: The Meal-in-a-Pill. *Food and Foodways* 8:253–271.

Bellisle, France
    1998   Nutritional Effects of Umami in the Human Diet. *Food Review International* 14:309–319.

Bester, D., A.J. Esterhuyse, E.J. Truter, and J. van Rooyen
    2010   Cardiovascular Effects of Edible Oils. *Nutrition Research Reviews* 23:334–348.

Bestor, Theodore
    2004   *Tsukiji: The Fish Market at the Center of the World.* Berkeley: University of California Press.

Beyreuther, K., H.K. Biesalski, J.D. Fernstrom, P. Grimm, W.P. Hammes, U. Heinemann, O. Kempski, P. Stehle, H. Steinhart, and R. Walker
    2007   Consensus Meeting. *European Journal of Clinical Nutrition* 61:304–313.

Bickel, Gary, Mark Nord, Cristofer Price, William Hamilton, and John Cook
    2000   Measuring Food Security in the United States. Alexandria VA: USDA. www.fns.usda.gov/fsec/files/fsguide.pdf, accessed December 4, 2011.

Blench, Roger, and Kevin MacDonald
    2000   Chickens. In *The Cambridge World History of Food,* edited by Kenneth Kiple and Kriemhild Orneals, 496–499. Cambridge: Cambridge University Press.

Bobby B.
    2010   Comment on "Prison Surprise." The Official Ramen Homepage. www.mattfischer.com/ramen/?p = 460, accessed February 27, 2012.

Borrell, Brendan
    2011   Food Fight. *Scientific American* 304:80–83.

Bosworth, Mary, and Jim Thomas
    2004   Food. In *The Encyclopedia of Prisons and Correctional Facilities.* www.referenceworld.com/sage/Prisons/index_C32377C39B534A3D-95BC5B0E19974260.htm, accessed August 14, 2012.

Bourdieu, Pierre
    1977   *Outline of a Theory of Practice.* Cambridge: Cambridge University Press.
    1984   *Distinction: A Social Critique of Judgment and Taste.* Cambridge, MA: Harvard University Press.

Boyer, Jefferson
    2010   Food Security, Food Sovereignty, and Local Challenges for Transnational Agrarian Movements: The Honduras Case. *Journal of Peasant Studies* 37:319–351.

Brinton, Mary
    2010   Social Class and Economic Life Chances in Post-Industrial Japan: The "Lost Generation." In *Social Class in Contemporary Japan:*

Structures, Sorting, and Strategies, edited by Hiroshi Ishida and David Slater, 114–133. London: Routledge.

Brody, Aaron
    2009   Our World Hungers for Packaging. *Food Technology* 63 (2): 78–80.

Brown, Ellie, and Michael Jacobson
    2005   *Cruel Oil: How Palm Oil Harms Health, Rainforest, and Wildlife.* Washington, DC: Center for Science and the Public Interest.

Brown, Kate, and Andrew Jameton
    2000   Public Health Implications of Urban Agriculture. *Journal of Public Health Policy* 21:20–39.

Bruhn, Christine
    2009   Understanding 'Green' Consumers. *Food Technology* 65 (7): 28–35.

Bryld, Erik
    2003   Potentials, Problems, and Policy Implications for Urban Agriculture in Developing Countries. *Agriculture and Human Values* 20:79–86.

Caldwell, Melissa
    2008   Domesticating the French Fry: McDonald's and Globalism in Moscow. In *The Anthropology of Globalization,* edited by Jonathan Inda and Renato Rosaldo, 237–253. Oxford: Blackwell.

Cali Prisoner
    2007   Response to "Prison Surprise." Official Ramen Homepage. www .mattfischer.com/ramen/?p = 460&cpage = 1#comments, accessed February 28, 2012.

Carrier, James
    2010   Protecting the Environment the Natural Way. *Antipode* 42:668–685.

Carter, Claire, Willa Finley, James Fry, David Jackson, and Lynn Willis
    2007   Palm Oil Markets and Future Supply. *European Journal of Lipid Science Technology* 109:307–314.

Cate, Sandra
    2008   Baking Bread with a Spread in a San Francisco County Jail. *Gastronomica* 8:17–24.

Centers for Disease Control and Prevention
    2011   U.S. Obesity Trends. www.cdc.gov/obesity/data/trends.html, accessed March 1, 2012.

Chalfen, Richard
    1982   Home Movies as Cultural Documents. In *Film/Culture: Explorations of Cinema in Its Social Context,* edited by Sari Thomas, 126–138. Metuchen, NJ: Scarecrow Press.

Chappell, Jahi
    2007   Shattering Myths: Can Sustainable Agriculture Feed the World? *Food First Backgrounder, Institute for Food and Development Policy* 14: pages unknown.

Chorlton, Jan
    2000   Japanese Name Instant Noodles Best Invention. ABC News. http:// abcnews.go.com/International/story?id=81946&page=1, accessed November 25, 2012.

Choudhury, Naswrin, Liling Tan, and Steward Truswell
  1995   Comparison of Palmolein and Olive Oil. *American Journal of Clinical Nutrition.* 61:1043–1051.
Citriglia, Matthew
  2006   Umami: Taste Receptor, Tactile Sensation and Flavor Intensifier. Winegeeks. www.winegeeks.com/articles/115, accessed August 3, 2011.
Clemens, Roger
  2011   Striving to Meet Society's Food Needs. *Food Technology* 65 (10): 11.
Clydesdale, Fergus
  2009   Equal Partner for a Healthy Future. *Food Technology,* 63 (8): 136.
Cohen, Joel
  2002   World Population in 2050: Assessing the Projections. www.bos.frb .org/economic/conf/conf46/conf46d1.pdf, accessed November 11, 2011.
Collier, Paul
  2008   The Politics of Hunger. *Foreign Affairs* 87:67–79.
Common Dreams
  2012   Gates Foundation Pours $10 Million into Genetically Modified Crops. www.commondreams.org/headline/2012/07/15, accessed September 3, 2012.
Condry, Ian
  2013   *The Soul of Anime.* Durham, NC: Duke University Press.
Cook, Ian
  2004   Follow the Thing: Papaya. *Antipode* 36:642–664.
Corporate Watch UK
  2004   Sodexho: A Corporate Profile. www.corporatewatch.org.uk/?lid=834, accessed November 25, 2012.
CPNSJOB.COM
  2012   Lowongan Kerja Bewani Oil Palm Plantations. www.cpnsjob.com /lowongan-kerja-bewani-oil-palm-plantations.html, accessed March 2, 2012.
Cross, Jamie, and Alice Street
  2009   Anthropology at the Bottom of the Pyramid. *Anthropology Today* 25:4–9.
Cwiertka, Katarzyna
  2006   *Modern Japanese Cuisine.* London: Reaktion Books.
Darsh, Gerald, and Kathy Evangelos
  n.d.   Natick Soldier Center and DoD Combat Feeding. www.dodneregional .org/matchmakers/conferences/docs/me/Natick_Soldier_Cente_DoD_ Combat_Feeding.pdf, accessed February 17, 2012.
Davis, Sarah, Roger Clemens, and Joy Dubost
  2008   Clemens, Slavin Appointed to 2010 Dietary Guidelines Panel. *Food Technology* 62 (12): 20.
Department of Defense
  2010   Operational Rations of the Department of Defense. Natick: AMSRD-NSC-CF.

Desmarais, Annette
  2008   The Power of Peasants: Reflections on the Meanings of La Via Campesina. *Journal of Rural Studies* 24:138–149.
Dickerson, Marla
  2005   Steeped in a New Tradition. *Los Angeles Times.* articles.latimes.com/2005/oct/21/business/fi-ramennation21, accessed March 2, 2012.
Dowd, Maureen
  2009   The Aura of Arugulance. *New York Times.* www.nytimes.com/2009/04/19/opinion/19dowd.html, accessed February 29, 2012.
Doyle, A. Conan
  1930   *The Complete Sherlock Holmes.* New York: Doubleday.
Economist
  2009   An Alternative Big Mac Index. www.economist.com/node/14288808?story_id = E1_TQNRRRDR, accessed August 1, 2011.
Elk, Mike, and Bob Sloan
  2011   The Hidden History of ALEC and Prison Labor. *The Nation.* www.thenation.com/article/161978/alec-exposed, accessed August 14, 2012.
Elyachar, Julia
  2009   Women's Sociality, Infrastructure, and the Making of Payments Space in Cairo. Paper presented at the "Bottom of the Pyramid in Practice" conference, Irvine, CA, June 1–2.
  2012   Next Practices: Knowledge, Infrastructure, and Public Goods at the Bottom of the Pyramid. *Public Culture* 24:109–129.
Errington, Frederick, Tatsuro Fujikura, and Deborah Gewertz
  2012   Instant Noodles as an Anti-Friction Device: Making the BOP with PPP in PNG. *American Anthropologist* 114:19–31.
Errington, Frederick, and Deborah Gewertz
  2004   *Yali's Question: Sugar, Culture, and History.* Chicago: University of Chicago Press.
Ethics Newsline
  2001   McDonald's Scalded by Controversy over Beef-Laced French Fries. www.globalethics.org/newsline/2001/05/29/mcdonalds-scalded-by-controversy-over-beef-laced-french-fries/, accessed August 1, 2011.
Euromonitor International
  2010   Packaged Food: Noodles in the U.S. www.euromonitor.com/noodles-in-the-us/report, accessed November 25, 2012.
European Sensory Network
  2007   Complex Interplay. www.esn-network.com/umami_hedonic_effectso.html, accessed May 3, 2011.
Ezawa, Aya
  2010   Motherhood and Class: Gender, Class, and Reproductive Practices Among Japanese Single Mothers. In *Social Class in Contemporary Japan: Structures, Sorting, and Strategies,* edited by Hiroshi Ishida and David Slater, 197–220. London: Routledge.
Fabrizio, Kerry, Rajesh Potineni, and Kim Gray
  2010   Instant Noodle Seasonings. In *Asian Noodles: Science, Technology, and Processing,* edited by Gary Hou, 141–154. Hoboken, NJ: Wiley.

Featherstone, Mike, Scott Lash, and Roland Robertson, eds.
1995 *Global Modernities*. London: Sage.

Field, Michael
2011 Samoa Rewarded for Turkey Tail Turnaround. Stuff. www.stuff
.co.nz/business/world/6062457/Samoa-rewarded-for-turkey-tail-
turnaround, accessed March 1, 2012.

Filer, Colin
2011 The New Land Grab in Papua New Guinea. Paper presented at the
"Global Land Grabbing" conference, University of Sussex, April 6–8.
http://actnowpng.org/sites/default/files/The%20new%20land%
20grab%20in%20Papua%20New%20Guinea%20Colin%20Filer
.pdf, accessed March 1, 2011.

Finfacts Ireland
2005 China Responsible for 75% of Poverty Reduction in the Developing
World Since 1980. www.finfacts.ie/irelandbusinessnews/publish
/article_10003611.shtml, accessed March 1, 2012.

Fischer, Edward, and Peter Benson
2006 *Broccoli and Desire: Global Connections and Maya Struggles in Postwar Guatemala*. Stanford, CA: Stanford University Press.

Fitday
n.d. Nutrition Information For: Turkey, Tail, Cooked. www.fitday.com
/webfit/nutrition/All_Foods/Poultry/Turkey_tail.html, accessed November 25, 2012.

Floros, John, Rosetta Newsome, and William Fisher
2010 Feeding the World Today and Tomorrow: The Importance of Food
Science and Technology. *IFT Scientific Review*. onlinelibrary.wiley.
com/doi/10.1111/j.1541–4337.2010.00127.x/pdf, accessed November 25, 2012.

Foley, Jonathan
2011 Can We Feed the World and Sustain the Planet? *Scientific American*
305:60–65.

Food and Agriculture Organization
2009 How to Feed the World in 2050. www.fao.org/fileadmin/templates
/wsfs/docs/expert_paper/How_to_Feed_the_World_in_2050.pdf,
accessed March 1, 2012.
2010 Growing Greener Cities. www.fao.org/ag/agp/greenercities/pdf/GGC-
en.pdf, accessed December 28, 2011.

Foster, Robert
2008 *Coca-Globalization*. New York: Palgrave Macmillan.

Franklin, Sarah
2001 Sheepwatching. *Anthropology Today* 17:3–10.

Freidberg, Susanne
2004 *French Beans and Food Scares: Culture and Commerce in an Anxious
Age*. Oxford: Oxford University Press.

Friedman, Jesse
2005 Prison Cooking. www.freejesse.net/book/prison_cooking_essay.htm,
accessed July 23, 2011.

Friedman, Jonathan

  1995   Global System, Globalization and the Parameters of Modernities. In *Global Modernities,* edited by Mike Featherstone, Scott Lash, and Roland Robertson, 29–90. London: Sage.

Fukutomi, Satomi

  2010   Rāmen Connoisseurs. In *Japanese Foodways, Past and Present,* edited by Eric Rath and Stephanie Rassman, 257–274. Urbana: University of Illinois Press.

Gardner, Gary, and Brian Halwell

  2000   *Underfed and Overfed: The Global Epidemic of Malnutrition.* Washington, DC: Worldwatch Institute.

Garrett, Jemima

  2011   Samoa Wins Approval to Join WTO. Radio Australia. www.radioaustralia.net.au/international/radio/onairhighlights/samoa-wins-aproval-to-join-wto, accessed September 23, 2012.

Gates Foundation

  2011   Agriculture Development. www.gatesfoundation.org/agricultural development/Documents/agricultural-development-strategy-over view.pdf, accessed March 1, 2012.

Gewertz, Deborah, and Frederick Errington

  2010   *Cheap Meat: Flap Food Nations in the Pacific Islands.* Berkeley: University of California Press.

Gibson, William

  2001   Modern Boys and Mobile Girls. *The Guardian.* April 1. www.guardian.co.uk/books/2001/apr/01/sciencefictionfantasyandhorror.features, accessed February 28, 2012.

Gibson-Graham, J. K.

  2006   *The End of Capitalism (As We Knew It).* Minneapolis: University of Minnesota Press.

Giddens, Anthony

  1990   *The Consequences of Modernity.* Stanford, CA: Stanford University Press.

Glycemic Index Foundation

  2011   GI Foods Advanced Search. www.glycemicindex.com/, accessed February 27, 2012.

Godfray, H. Charles, John Beddington, Ian Crute, Lawrence Haddad, David Lawrence, James Muir, Jules Pretty, Sherman Robinson, Sandy Thomas, and Camilla Toulmin

  2010   Food Security: The Challenge of Feeding 9 Billion People. *Science* 327:812–818.

Goffman, Erving

  1961   *Asylums: Essays on the Social Situation of Mental Patients and Other Inmates.* Garden City, NY: Anchor Books.

Gordon, Andrew

  2003   *A Modern History of Japan.* Oxford: Oxford University Press.

Graham, Paul

  2009   Ramen Profitable. www.paulgraham.com/ramenprofitable.html, accessed February 27, 2012.

Gustavsson, Jenny, Christel Cederberg, Ulf Sonesson, Robert van Otterdijk, and Alexandre Meybeck
    2011   *Global Food Losses and Food Waste.* Rome: Food and Agriculture Organization.

Hansen, Karen Tranberg
    2003   Fashioning Zambian Moments. *Journal of Material Culture* 8:301–309.

Harvey, David
    1990   Between Space and Time: Reflections on the Geographical Imagination. *Annals of the Association of American Geographers* 80:418–434.

Hashimoto, Kenji
    2003   *Class Structure in Contemporary Japan.* Melbourne: Trans Pacific Press.

Hayes, K. C.
    2010   Fatty Acid Expert Roundtable. *Journal of the American College of Nutrition* 29:285S-288S.

Henan Pinzheng Food Co., Ltd
    n.d.   Instant Noodles Seasoning Powder And Sauce Sachets. http://pinzhengfood.en.busytrade.com/selling_leads/info/1852234/Instant-Noodles-Seasoning-Powder-And-Sauce-Sachets.html, accessed May 2, 2011.

Higashiyotsuyanagi, Shoko
    2010   The History of Domestic Cookbooks in Modern Japan. In *Japanese Foodways, Past and Present,* edited by Eric Rath and Stephanie Rassman, 129–144. Urbana: University of Illinois Press.

Hladik, Claude
    1997   Primate Models for Taste and Food Preferences. In *Food Preferences and Taste,* edited by Helen Macbeth, 15–26. New York: Berghahn Books.
    2007   Salt as a "Non-Food." In *Consuming the Inedible,* edited by Jeremy MacClancy, Jeya Henry, and Helen Macbeth, 121–130. New York: Berghahn Books.

Hoernlein, Carol
    2011   What Exactly is MSG? www.msgtruth.org/whatisit.htm, accessed February 27, 2012.

Holland, Dorothy, and Diana Gomez
    2011   Gibson-Graham and the Work of Social Movements. Paper presented at the 2011 meeting of the American Anthropological Association, Montreal, November 17.

Hyman, Mark
    2010   The Link Between Poverty, Obesity and Diabetes. Huffington Post. www.huffingtonpost.com/dr-mark-hyman/not-having-enough-food-ca_b_721344.html, accessed March 1, 2012.

Ilahaine, Hsain, and John Sherry
    2009   Moving the Bottom of the Pyramid Upward. Paper presented at the "Bottom of the Pyramid in Practice" conference, Irvine, June 1–2.

Imamura, Tomoaki, Hiroo Ide, and Hideo Yasunaga
    2007   History of Public Health Crises in Japan. *Journal of Public Health Policy* 28:221–237.

Inda, Jonathan, and Renato Rosaldo
    2008   Tracking Global Flows. In *The Anthropology of Globalization,* edited by Jonathan Inda and Renato Rosaldo, 3–46. Oxford: Blackwell.
Institute of Food Technologists
    2009   Winners Announced for Institute of Food Technologists Student Competition. www.ift.org/newsroom/news-releases/2009/june/25 /winners-student-competition.aspx, accessed May 4, 2012.
International Food Network
    n.d.   Welcome to the International Food Network. www.intlfoodnetwork .com/index.php?option = com_content&view = frontpage&Itemid = 1, accessed August 24, 2011.
Ito-Petersen, Yoko
    2001   Japan's Maruchan a Big Hit among Hispanics. www.allbusiness.com /specialty-businesses/minority-owned-businesses/912359-1.html, accessed February 28, 2012.
Ivy, Marilyn
    1993   Formations of Mass Culture. In *Postwar Japan as History,* edited by Andrew Gordon, 239–258. Berkeley: University of California Press.
    1995   *Discourses of the Vanishing: Modernity, Phantasm, Japan.* Chicago: University of Chicago Press.
Iwabuchi, Koichi
    2002   *Recentering Globalization: Popular Culture and Japanese Transnationalism.* Durham, NC: Duke University Press.
Jack, Andrew
    2011   Brazil's Unwanted Growth. *Financial Times.* www.ft.com/cms /s/2/6e0319c2–5fee-11e0-a718–00144feab49a.html#axzz2DLtz9Vpn, accessed November 26, 2012.
Jackson, Wes
    2010   *Consulting the Genius of the Planet.* Berkeley: Counterpoint.
Jacobs, Ron
    2000   The New Slave Ships. www.uvm.edu/sparc/nwom/sodexho/ron.html, accessed September 23, 2012.
Japan Instant Noodle Industry Business Association
    2007   Instant Ramen's Home Page. www.instantramen.or.jp/about /retire/02.html, accessed May 25, 2012.
Japan Today
    2008   Nissin Recalls 500,000 Cups of Noodles After Insecticide contamination. www.japantoday.com/category/business/view/nissin-recalls-500000- cups-of-noodles, accessed July 11, 2011.
    2011   Nissin Donates 1 Million Packs of Noodles for Quake Victims. www. japantoday.com/category/business/view/nissin-donates-1-million- noodles-packs-for-quake, accessed March 28, 2011.
Jenkins, Rhys
    2005   Globalization, Corporate Social Responsibility and Poverty. *International Affairs* 81:525–540.
Jussaume, Raymond, Hisano Shuji, and Taniguchi Yoshimitsu
    2000   Food Safety in Modern Japan. *Japanstudien* 12:211–228.

Kabagambe, Edmond, Ana Baylin, Alberto Ascherio, and Hannia Campos
2005 The Type of Oil Used for Cooking Is Associated with the Risk of Nonfatal Acute Myocardial Infarction in Costa Rica. *Journal of Nutrition* 135:2674–2679.

Kamani, Ansel
2007 The Mirage of Marketing at the Bottom of the Pyramid. *California Management Review* 49:90–111.

Kang, Seongbin
2011 Korean Noodle Maker in Hot Water Over Advertising. *Reuters.* www.reuters.com/article/2011/06/27/us-korea-noodles-idUSTRE75Q1DO 20110627, accessed February 28, 2012.

Karl, Thomas, Jerry Melilo, and Thomas Peterson
2009 *Global Climate Change Impacts in the United States.* Cambridge: Cambridge University Press.

Kasabian, Anna, and David Kasabian
2005 *The Fifth Taste: Cooking with Umami.* Denver: Universe.

Katoh, Tatashi
2006 *Project X Challengers Cup Noodle.* Gardena, CA: Digital Manga Publishing.

Katz, Barbara, and LuAnn Williams
2010 Salt Reduction Gains Momentum. *Food Technology* 64 (5): 25–32.

Kelly, John, and Martha Kaplan
2001 *Represented Communities.* Chicago: University of Chicago Press.

Kelly, William
1986 Rationalization and Nostalgia: Cultural Dynamics of New Middle-Class Japan. *American Ethnologist* 13:603–618.
1990 Showa: The Japan of Hirohito. *Daedalus* 119:209–227.
2002 At the Limits of New Middle-Class Japan: Beyond "Mainstream Consciousness." In *Social Contracts Under Stress,* edited by Olivier Zunz, Leonard Schoppa, and Nobukiro Hiwatari, 232–254. New York: Russell Sage Foundation.

Kelly, William, and Merry White
2006 Students, Slackers, Singles, Seniors, and Strangers: Transforming a Family-Nation. In *Beyond Japan,* edited by Peter Katzenstein and Takashi Shiraishi, 63–82. Ithaca, NY: Cornell University Press.

Kelsky, Karen
2001 *Women on the Verge: Japanese Women, Western Dreams.* Durham, NC: Duke University Press.

Kinsella, Sharon
2000 *Adult Manga: Culture and Power in Contemporary Japan.* Honolulu: University of Hawaii Press.

Kroeber, Alfred
1941 Cultural Element Distribution: XV. Salt, Dogs, Tobacco. *Anthropological Records* 6:1–20.

Kuhn, Mary
2011 At the Forefront of Food Science. *Food Technology* 65 (8): 26–47.

Kuhn, Mary, and Toni Tarver
  2011   On a Green Growth Track. *Food Technology* 65 (7): 35–43.
Kurihara, Kenzo
  2009   Glutamate. *American Journal of Clinical Nutrition*. 90:719S-722S.
Kurlansky, Mark
  2002   *Salt*. New York: Walker.
Kushner, Barak
  2012   *Slurp! A Social and Culinary History of Ramen—Japan's Favorite Soup*. Leiden: Brill.
Kushner, David
  2009   Drug Sub-Culture. *The New York Times*. www.nytimes.com/2009/04/26 /magazine/26drugs-t.html, accessed February 27, 2012.
Lal, C.K.
  2010   The Coming Anarchy. *Republica Opinion*. www.myrepublica.com /portal/index.php?action = news_details&news_id = 18714, accessed February 27, 2012.
Lamarre, Thomas
  2004   An Introduction to the Otaku. *EnterText* 4:151–187.
Landrum, Nancy
  2007   Advancing the "Base of the Pyramid" Debate. *Strategic Management Review* 1:1–12.
Lang, Tim, and Michael Heasman
  2004   *Food Wars: The Global Battle for Mouths, Minds and Markets*. London: Earthscan.
Leach, Edmund
  1968   *Runaway World*. London: BBC Books.
Lee, William
  2000   From *Sazae-san* to *Crayon Shin-chan*. In *Japan Pop!* edited by Timothy Craig, 186–203. Armonk, NY: M.E. Sharpe.
Lehman, Kim, and John Byrom
  2007   Corporate Museums in Japan: Institutionalizing a Culture of Industry and Technology. Paper presented at the Ninth International Conference on Arts and Cultural Management, Valencia, July 8–11.
Leonard, William
  2002   Dietary Change Was a Driving Force in Human Evolution. *Scientific American* 288:63–71.
Leonard, William, J. Josh Snodgrass, and Marcia Robertson
  2010   Evolutionary Perspectives on Fat Ingestion and Metabolism in Humans. In *Fat Detection*, edited by Jean-Pierre Montmayeur and Johannes le Coutre, 3–18. Boca Raton, FL: CRC Press.
Leonardi, Susan
  1989   Recipes for Reading. *PMLA* 104:340–347.
Lévi-Strauss, Claude
  1963   *Totemism*. New York: Beacon.
  1966   The Culinary Triangle. *Partisan Review* 3:586–595.
List, Gary, and Michael Jackson
  2007   Giants of the Past: The Battle Over Hydrogenation (1903–1920). *Inform* 18:403–405.

Long, Norman, and Magdalena Villareal
  2000 Small Product, Big Issues. *Development and Change* 29:725–750.
Lopez-Alt, J. Kenji
  2011a Ramen Hacks: 30+ Easy Ways to Upgrade Your Ramen. Serious Eats. www.seriouseats.com/2011/03/ramen-hacks-30-easy-ways-to-upgrade-your-instant-noodles-japanese-what-to-do-with-ramen.html, accessed February 28, 2012.
  2011b Aloha Ramen. Serious Eats. www.seriouseats.com/2011/03/ramen-hacks-30-easy-ways-to-upgrade-your-instant-noodles-japanese-what-to-do-with-ramen-slideshow.html#show-147417, accessed October 20, 2011.
Macbeth, Helen, and Sue Lawry
  1997 Food Preferences and Taste. In *Food Preferences and Taste,* edited by Helen Macbeth, 1–13. New York: Berghahn Books.
Malaysian Palm Oil Council and Malaysian Palm Oil Board
  2007 *Fact Sheets: Malaysian Palm Oil.* Selangor: Malaysian Palm Oil Council and Malaysian Palm Oil Board.
Marlene
  2009 Response to "Prison Surprise." Official Ramen Homepage. www.mattfischer.com/ramen/?p = 460&cpage = 1#comments, accessed October 21, 2011.
Marte, Lidia
  2010 MSG and Sugar. In *Adventures in Eating,* edited by Helen Haines and Clare Sammells, 145–163. Boulder: University of Colorodo Press.
Marx, Karl
  1906 *Capital.* New York: Modern Library.
Maslow, Abraham
  1943 A Theory of Human Motivation. *Psychological Review* 50:370–396.
Mattes, Richard
  2005 Soup and Satiety. *Physiology and Behavior.* 83:739–747.
  2011 Accumulating Evidence Supports a Taste Component for Free Fatty Acids in Humans. *Physiology and Behavior* 104:624–631.
Mauer, Bill
  2009 Whose Non-Interoperability? Paper presented at the "Bottom of the Pyramid in Practice" conference, Irvine, CA, June 1–2.
Maxia
  n.d. Maxia EMC: Your Export Partner for Latin America and Europe. http://maxiaemc.net/about-us--contact.html, accessed November 26, 2012.
McCabe, Clara, and Edmund Rolls
  2007 Umami. *European Journal of Neuroscience* 25:1855–1864.
McGee, Harold
  2004 *On Food and Cooking.* New York: Scribner.
McKee, David
  2009 Globalization of Instant Noodles. World Grain. www.world-grain.com/News/Archive/Globalization%20of%20instant%20noodles.aspx, accessed September 5, 2012.

McMichael, Philip
  2005   Global Development and the Corporate Food Regime. In *New Directions in the Sociology of Global Development,* edited by Frederick Buttle and Philip McMichael, 265–299. Amsterdam: Elsevier.
McNicol, Tony
  2009   A Food to Feed Billions. *Wingspan* March: 20–23.
Messer, Ellen
  2009   Rising Food Prices, Social Mobilizations, and Violence: Conceptual Issues in Understanding and Responding to the Connections Linking Hunger and Conflict. *NAPA Bulletin* 32:12–22.
Miller, Daniel
  1998   Coca-Cola: A Black Sweet Drink from Trinidad. In *Material Cultures,* edited by Daniel Miller, 169–187. Chicago: University of Chicago Press.
  2010   Anthropology in Blue Jeans. *American Ethnologist* 37:415–428.
Miller, Daniel, and Sophie Woodward
  2011   *Global Denim.* Oxford: Berg.
Milton, Katherine
  1987   Primate Diets and Gut Morphology. In *Food and Evolution,* edited by Marvin Harris and Eric Ross, 93–116. Philadelphia: Temple University Press.
Mintz, Sidney
  1979   Time, Sugar, and Sweetness. *Marxist Perspectives* 2:56–73.
  1985   *Sweetness and Power.* New York: Viking Penguin.
  1996   *Tasting Food, Tasting Freedom.* Boston: Beacon.
  2006   Food at Moderate Speeds. In *Fast Food/Slow Food,* edited by Richard Wilk, 1–11. Lanham, PA: Altimira Press.
Moladi
  2009   Bottom of the Pyramid/Bottom of the Pyramid Housing/Maslow. http://moladi.com/bottom_of_the_pyramid.htm, accessed October 27, 2010.
MRE Info
  2011   MRE Menus XXXI (2011). www.mreinfo.com/us/mre/menus-xxxi-2011.html, accessed May 14, 2012.
National Public Radio
  2009a   Chef Chang's Momofuko: A Romance with Ramen. www.npr.org/templates/story/story.php?storyId=114289124, accessed November 26, 2012.
  2009b   David Chang's Ramen: Not Your Average Noodle. www.npr.org/templates/story/story.php?storyId=120012206, accessed November 26, 2012.
  2009c   Ramen Noodles Serve Up a Bowl of Nostalgia. www.npr.org/templates/story/story.php?storyId=120360464, accessed November 26, 2012.
  2009d   Demographics: Who Is the NPR Audience? www.wqub.org/media/NPR%20Profile%20stats%202009/NPR%20demographics.pdf, accessed October 20, 2011.

Nature Neuroscience
2000 Umami Taste Receptor Identified. www.nature.com/neuro/press_release/nn0200.html, accessed February 27, 2012.

Nelson, Gerald, Mark Rosegrant, Jawoo Koo, Richard Robertson, Timothy Sulser, Tingju Zhu, Claudia Ringler, et al.
2009 *Climate Change: Impact on Agriculture and Costs of Adaptation.* Washington, DC: International Food Policy Research Institute.

Nestle, Marion
2007 *Food Politics: How the Food Industry Influences Nutrition and Health.* Berkeley: University of California Press.

Nestlé
n.d. Popularly Positioned Products. www.nestle.com/CSV/CreatingShared-ValueCaseStudies/AllCaseStudies/Pages/PPP-Popularly-Positioned-Products.aspx, accessed February 29, 2012.

Nestlé Malaysia
n.d. Maggi Tastylite. www.maggi.com.my/en/happenings/newproducts/tastylite.htm, accessed November 26, 2012.

Nestlé Oceania
2008 Creating Shared Value Report. www.nestle.com.au/AboutUs/CreatingSharedValue/Documents/CSV_Full_Report_2008.pdf, accessed November 26, 2012.

Nissin Food Products
2011 Chikirar Island and Friends. www.chikinramen.jp/ehon/, accessed July 11, 2011.

Nissin Foods Holdings
2010 To Our Shareholders. www.nissinfoods-holdings.co.jp/english/inv/pdf/ar10_04.pdf, accessed November 21, 2012.

Notcot
2008 Nissin Cup Noodle Ads. www.notcot.com/archives/2008/01/nissin-ads.php, accessed July 11, 2011.

Ohta, Shigeru, and Ryugo Murohoshi
1989 Meiji 20–30nendai no rikugunkankeizasshi ni miru taiiku kiji [Articles on health education found in army-related journals during Meiji 20s and 30s (1887–1906)]. *Tokyogakugeidaigaku Kiyou dai5 bumon* 41:247–254.

Patel, Raj
2011 Can the World Feed 10 Billion People? *Foreign Policy.* www.foreignpolicy.com/articles/2011/05/04/can_the_world_feed_10_billion_people, accessed November 12, 2011.

Perrins, Christopher
2003 *Firefly Encyclopedia of Birds.* Buffalo, NY: Firefly Books.

Phillips, Lynne
2006 Food and Globalization. *Annual Review of Anthropology* 35:37–57.

Pollan, Michael
2006 *The Omnivore's Dilemma.* New York: Penguin Press.
2008 *In Defense of Food: An Eater's Manifesto.* New York: Penguin Press.

2009   Big Food vs. Big Insurance. *New York Times.* www.nytimes.com/2009 /09/10/opinion/10pollan.html?pagewanted = all, accessed February 29, 2012.

2011   Michael Pollan Answers Readers' Questions. *New York Times Magazine.* www.nytimes.com/interactive/2011/10/02/magazine/29mag-food-issue.html?ref = magazine#/pollan, accessed March 1, 2012.

Post Courier

2004   Making Ends Meet Through Gardening. *Rural Industry Weekly.* www.postcourier.com.pg/20040226/rural02.htm, accessed March 1, 2012.

Prahalad, C. K.

2006   *The Fortune at the Bottom of the Pyramid.* Upper Saddle River, NJ: Wharton School Publishing.

Prokop, Marcella

2012   On the Road with Cellulosic Ethanol. *Vital* Summer: 28–31.

Proust, Marcel

(1927) 1989   *Remembrance of Things Past.* New York: Vintage.

Pszczola, Donald

2011   Are We Moving Backwards? *Food Technology* 65 (7): 78–79.

Reddy, Srinith

2004   Cardiovascular Disease in Non-Western Countries. *New England Journal of Medicine* 350:2438–2440.

Remo, Thomas

2011   Umami—The Fifth Dimension of Taste. *Cooking for Profit.* www. cookingforprofit.com/feature_umami.html, accessed February 27, 2012.

Robbins, Joel

2004   The Globalization of Pentecostal and Charismatic Christianity. *Annual Review of Anthropology* 33:117–143.

Robertson, James, and Nobue Suzuki

2003   *Men and Masculinities in Contemporary Japan: Dislocating the Salaryman Doxa.* London: Routledge.

Robertson, Jennifer

2001   Japan's First Cyborg? Miss Nippon, Eugenics and Wartime Technologies of Beauty, Body and Blood. *Body & Society* 7:1–34.

Rolls, Edmund

2009   Functional Neuroimaging of Umami Taste. *American Journal of Clinical Nutrition* 90:804S-813S.

Ronald, Richard, and Allison Alexy, eds.

2011   *Home and Family in Japan: Continuity and Transformation.* London: Routledge.

Roosevelt, Franklin Delano

1932   The Forgotten Man. http://newdeal.feri.org/speeches/1932c.htm, accessed November 11, 2010.

Rostow, Walt Whitman

1962   *The Process of Economic Growth.* New York: Norton.

Roundtable on Sustainable Palm Oil
    2009   Promoting the Growth and Use of Sustainable Palm Oil. www.rspo
            .org/, accessed December 27, 2011.
Saatchi and Saatchi
    2011   The Future Beyond Brands: Lovemarks. www.lovemarks.com/index
            .php?pageID = 20020, accessed February 25, 2012.
Sand, Jordan
    2005   A Short History of MSG. *Gastronomica* Fall: 38–49.
San Francisco Chronicle
    2010   Global Vegetable Oils Market to Reach 169 Million Metric Tons by
            2015, According to a New Report by Global Industry Analysts, Inc.
            www.sfgate.com/business/article/Global-Vegetable-Oils-Market-to-
            Reach-169-Million-2458952.php, accessed November 26, 2012.
Savoury Systems
    2008   Organic Flavors that Nature hand Always Intended. *Food Technol-
            ogy* 62 (8): 6.
Schaumburg, Herbert, R. Byck, R. Gerstl, and J. H. Mashman
    1969   Monosodium L-Glutamate. *Science* 163:826–828.
Schiffman, Susan
    1998   Sensory Enhancement of Foods for the Elderly with Monosodium
            Glutamate and Flavors. *Food Review International* 14:321–333.
Schlosser, Eric
    2002   *Fast Food Nation: The Dark Side of the All-American Meal.* New
            York: Perennial.
Schulkin, Jay
    1991   *Sodium Hunger.* Cambridge: Cambridge University Press.
Science Daily
    2007   Your Gut Has Taste Receptors. www.sciencedaily.com/releases/2007/08
            /070820175426.htm, accessed November 26, 2012.
Scott, Kristin
    2005   Taste Recognition: Food for Thought. *Neuron* 48:455–464.
Sen, Amartya
    1983   *Poverty and Famine: An Essay on Entitlement and Deprivation.*
            Oxford: Oxford University Press.
Sen, Chandan, Cameron Rink, and Savita Khanna
    2010   Palm Oil-Derived Natural Vitamin E α-Tocotrienol in Brain Health
            and Disease. *Journal of the American College of Nutrition* 29:314S–323S.
Shale, Arlene
    2003   Nepal: A Mount Everest of Noodles. http://ecs.com.np/feature_detail
            .php?f_id = 311, accessed February 27, 2012.
Sheridan, Michael
    2008   Instant Noodles. http://vimeo.com/11383604, accessed January 23,
            2010.
Shirahase, Sawako
    2010   Marriage as an Association of Social Classes in Low Fertility Rate
            Society: Towards a New Theory of Social Stratification. In *Social Class*

in Contemporary Japan: Structures, Sorting, and Strategies, edited by Hiroshi Ishida and David Slater, 57–83. London: Routledge.

Shoji, Kichiro, and Masuro Sugai
 1992 The Arsenic Milk Poisoning Incident. In *Industrial Pollution in Japan,* edited by Jun Ui. Tokyo: United Nations Press. http://archive.unu.edu /unupress/unupbooks/uu35ie/uu35ie00.htm, accessed July 11, 2011.

Singer, Peter, and Jim Mason
 2006 *The Way We Eat: Why Our Food Choices Matter.* Emmaus, PA: Rodale.

Slater, David
 2010 The "New Working Class" of Urban Japan: Socialization and Contradiction from Middle School to the Labor Market. In *Social Class in Contemporary Japan: Structures, Sorting, and Strategies,* edited by Hiroshi Ishida and David Slater, 137–169. London: Routledge.

Sloan, Elizabeth
 2009a Top 10 Food Trends. *Food Technology* 63 (4): 22–44.
 2009b The New Value Equation. *Food Technology* 63 (8): 52–58.

Smil, Vaclav
 2001 *Enriching the Earth.* Cambridge: MIT Press.

Smit, Jac, Joe Nasr, and Annu Ratta
 2001 Who Are the Urban Farmers? In *Urban Agriculture: Food, Jobs and Sustainable Cities,* edited by Jack Smit, Joe Nasr, and Annu Ratta. http://jacsmit.com/book/Chap03.pdf, accessed December 28, 2011.

Solomon, Christopher
 2008 When Times Are Tight There's Ramen. http://ramen-noodles.livejournal. com/104989.html, accessed November 26, 2012.

Solt, George
 2009 Taking Ramen Seriously: Food, Labor and Everyday Life in Modern Japan. PhD diss., University of California, San Diego.
 2010 Ramen and U.S. Occupation Policy. In *Japanese Foodways, Past and Present,* edited by Eric Rath and Stephanie Rassman, 188–200. Urbana: University of Illinois Press.

Sontag, Susan
 1977 *On Photography.* New York: Farrar, Straus, and Giroux.

Spectrum Commodities
 n.d. Soybean Oil. www.spectrumcommodities.com/education/commodity /bo.html, accessed December 27, 2011.

Steel, William
 2003 *Alternative Narratives in Modern Japanese History.* New York: Routledge.

Steiner, Jacob
 1973 The Gustofacial Response: Observation on Normal and Anencephalic Newborn Infants. *Symposium on Oral Sensation and Perception* 4:254–278.

Stiles, Matt
 2010a What Texas Inmates Buy. *Texas Tribune.* www.texastribune.org /library/data/texas-prison-commissary-sales/, accessed October 21, 2011.

2010b Texas Prisoners Spend $95 Million at Commissaries. *Texas Tribune.* www.texastribune.org/texas-dept-criminal-justice/texas-department-of-criminal-justice/texas-prisoners-spent-95-million-at-commissaries/, accessed October 21, 2011.

Striffler, Steve
2005 *Chicken.* New Haven, CT: Yale University Press.

Stull, Donald, and Michael Broadway
2004 *Slaughterhouse Blues.* Belmont, CA: Wadsworth Books.

Tacchi, Jo
2009 E-shopping through Drive-by WiFi. Paper presented at the "Bottom of the Pyramid in Practice" conference, Irvine, CA, June 1–2.

Tanaka, Katsunori, Naoki Furukawa, and Yoshi Okubo
2010 *Japan: Consumer Products.* New York: Goldman Sachs.

Tarver, Toni
2010 Desalting the Food Grid Food. *Food Technology* 64 (8): 45–50.

Tempointeractive
2011 Brawijaya University Wins International Food Technology Competition. www.tempo.co.id/hg/nasional/2011/06/22/brk,20110622-342560,uk .html accessed November 26, 2012.

Temussi, Piero
2009 Sweet, Bitter and Umami Receptors: A Complex Relationship. *Trends in Biochemical Sciences* 34:296–302.

Teng, Kim-Tiu, Phooi-Tee Voon, Hwee-Ming Cheng, and Kalanithi Nesaretnam
2010 Effects of Partially Hydrogenated, Semi-Saturated, and High Oleate Vegetable Oils on Inflammatory Markers and Lipids. *Lipids* 45:385–392.

Thai Eyes
2010 Mama Instant Noodle Soup Thailand. www.thai-eyes.com/thaifood /mama-instant-noodle-soup-thailand/, accessed February 27, 2012.

Thaman, R.R.
1995 Urban Food Gardening in the Pacific Islands: A Basis for Food Security in Rapidly Urbanising Small-Island States. *Habitat International* 19:209–224.

Thaman, R.R., C.C. Elevitch, and J. Kennedy
2006 Urban and Homegarden Agroforestry in the Pacific Islands: Current Status and Future Prospects. In *Tropical Homegardens: A Time-Tested Example of Sustainable Agroforestry,* edited by B.M. Kumar and P.K.R. Nair, 25–41. New York: Springer.

Thomas, Paul
2009 The Bottom of the Pyramid. Institute for Money, Technology, and Financial Inclusion. www.imtfi.uci.edu/imtfi_bopppts, accessed February 29, 2012.

Toki, Moyuru
2006 *The Excellent Company.* Tokyo: Toei Company.

Ton Tan Tin
2012 Ramen Noodle Diary. www.youtube.com/user/tontantin, accessed November 26, 2012.

Tsing, Anna
  2004   *Friction.* Princeton, NJ: Princeton University Press.
Turner, Victor
  1969   *The Ritual Process.* Chicago: Aldine.
Ui, Jun
  1992   Minamata Disease. In *Industrial Pollution in Japan,* edited by Jun Ui. Tokyo: United Nations Press. http://archive.unu.edu/unupress/unup books/uu35ie/uu35ie00.htm, accessed July 11, 2011.
United Nations
  2008   Report of the UN Expert Group Meeting on Population Distribution, Urbanization, Internal Migration and Development. www.un.org /esa/population/meetings/EGM_PopDist/EGM_PopDist_Report.pdf, accessed November 13, 2011.
United States Department of Agriculture
  2002   Agricultural Fact Book: 2001–2002. www.usda.gov/factbook /chapter2.pdf, accessed August 2, 2011.
  2012   Adoption of Genetically Engineered Crops in the U.S. www.ers.usda .gov/data-products/adoption-of-genetically-engineered-crops-in-the-us.aspx, accessed November 26, 2012.
Uusitalo, Ulla, E. J. Feskens, J. Tuomilehto, G. Dowse, U. Haw, D. Fareed, F. Hemraj, H. Gareeboo, K. G. Alberti, and P. Zimmet
  1996   Fall in Cholesterol in Total Cholesterol Concentration Over Five Years in Association with Changes in Fatty Acid Composition of Cooking Oil in Mauritius: Cross Sectional Survey. *British Medical Journal* 313:1044–1046. www.bmj.com/content/313/7064/1044?ijkey = 6c7adb45834ef4f e7914ce8f4955a6eec385b05e&keytype2 = tf_ipsecsha&linkType = ABST&journalCode = bmj&resid = 313/7064/1044, accessed December 17, 2011.
Vega-Lopez, Sonia, Lynne Ausman, Susan Jalbert, Arja Erkkilä, and Alice Lichtenstein
  2006   Palm, and Partially Hydrogenated Soybean Oils Adversely Alter Lipoprotein Profiles Compared with Soybean and Canola Oils in Moderately Hyperlipidemic Subjects. *American Journal of Nutrition* 2006:54–62.
Via Campesina, La
  2008   Via Campesina's Solidarity with Cuba. http://viacampesina.org/en /index.php/our-conferences-mainmenu-28/5-maputo-2008-main-menu-68/motions-adopted-at-the-vth-conference-mainmenu-69/615-via-campesinas-solidarity-with-cuba, accessed November 26, 2012.
  2011   The International Peasants Voice http://viacampesina.org/en/index .php/organisation-mainmenu-44, accessed November 26, 2012.
Virtual Japan
  2008   Ramen. http://virtualjapan.com/wiki/Ramen, accessed April 21, 2012.
Warmholz, Jean-Louis
  2007   Poverty Reduction for Profit? Working Paper No. 160, Queen Elizabeth House, Oxford University: 1–27.

Watson, James
  1997 McDonald's in Hong Kong. In *Golden Arches East,* edited by James Watson, 77–109. Stanford, CA: Stanford University Press.
Webber, Michael
  2012 More Food, Less Energy. *Scientific American* January: 74–77.
West, Heather
  2009 Prison Inmates at Midyear 2009: Statistical Tables. http://bjs.ojp .usdoj.gov/content/pub/pdf/pim09st.pdf, accessed November 26, 2012.
Whatever
  2008 Where Can I Buy Osmotic Raisins? http://answers.yahoo.com/question /index?qid=20080908194629AACrYge, accessed November 26, 2012.
What's On Xiamen
  2010 Japanese Instant Noodle King Koki Ando to Improve Father's Invention. www.whatsonxiamen.com/wine_msg.php?titleid=1160. html, accessed November 26, 2012.
White, Merry
  2001 Ladies Who Lunch. In *Asian Food,* edited by Katarzyna Cwiertka and Boudewijn Walraven, 63–75. Honolulu: University of Hawaii Press.
Whitney, Craig
  1999 Protesters Just Say No to "McDo"; Jospin Glad. *New York Times.* www.nytimes.com/1999/09/15/world/protesters-just-say-no-to-mcdo-jospin-glad.html?ref = josebove, accessed August 1, 2011.
Wilk, Richard
  1995 Learning to Be Local in Belize. In *Worlds Apart,* edited by Daniel Miller, 110–133. London: Routledge.
Wilkins, L., and C.P. Richter
  1940 A Great Craving for Salt by a Child with Cortico-Adrenal Insufficiency. *Journal of the American Medical Association* 114 (10): 866–868.
Wilson, Jerry
  2003 The Hidden Carbs in Food. http://wilstar.com/lowcarb/hiddencarbs. htm, accessed May 19, 2011.
Wilson, Thomas, and Clarence Grim
  2000 Sodium and Hypertension. In *The Cambridge World History of Food,* edited by Kenneth Kiple and Kriemhild Orneals, 848–856. Cambridge: Cambridge University Press.
Windfuhr, Michael, and Jennie Jonsén
  2005 *Food Sovereignty: Towards Democracy in Localized Food Systems.* Warwickshire, UK: ITDG Publishing.
World Instant Noodles Association
  2008 Osaka Declaration: The Sixth World Instant Noodles Summit. http:// instantnoodles.org/summits/osaka/declaration.html, accessed February 27, 2012.
  2010 Kuala Lumpur Declaration: The Seventh World Instant Noodles Summit. http://instantnoodles.org/summits/kuala_lumpur/declaration. html, accessed March 1, 2012.
  2011 Expanding Market. http://instantnoodles.org/noodles/expanding-market.html, accessed February 17, 2012.

World Investment News
  2003   Interview with Mr. Eric Gan. www.winne.com/fiji/to12interview
         .html, accessed on January 17, 2010.
Wrangham, Richard
  2010   *Catching Fire.* New York: Basic Books.
Yamamoto, Toshio
  2010   Sokusekimensaikuropedia 1: Kappumen -2000nenhen [Instant noo-
         dle encyclopedia 1: Cup-men up to 2000]. Tokyo: Shakaihyoronsha.
Yano, Christine
  2009   Wink on Pink: Interpreting Japanese Cute as It Grabs the Global
         Headlines. *Journal of Asian Studies* 68:681–688.
Yappie
  2007   Tulan   Restaurant.   Citysearch.   http://sanfrancisco.citysearch.com
         /profile/868236/san_francisco_ca/tulan_restaurant.html#seenIn, accessed
         October 21, 2011.
Zhao, Grace, Yifeng Zhang, Mark Hoon, Jayaram Chandrashekar, Isolde
    Erlenbach, Nicholas Ryba, and Charles Zucker
  2003   The Receptors for Mammalian Sweet and Umami Taste. *Cell* 115:
         255–266.

Index